The Theatre of Marie Jones:
Telling stories from the ground up

The Theatre of Marie Jones:
Telling stories from the ground up

Edited by Eugene McNulty and Tom Maguire

Carysfort Press

A Carysfort Press Book in association with Peter Lang
The Theatre of Marie Jones: Telling Stories from the Ground Up
Edited by Eugene McNulty and Tom Maguire

First published in Ireland in 2015 as a original by Carysfort Press
58 Woodfield
Scholarstown Road
Dublin 16, Ireland
ISBN 978-1-78874-799-8
©2015 Copyright remains with the authors

Typeset by Carysfort Press
Cover design by eprint limited

This book is published with the financial assistance of
The Arts Council (An Chomhairle Ealaíon) Dublin, Ireland

Caution: All rights reserved. No part of this book may be or utilized in any form or by any electronic, mechanical, or other means, now known or hereafter invented including photocopying and recording, or in any information storage or retrieval system without permission in writing from the publishers.

Contents

Acknowledgements   ix

1 | Introduction   1
   Eugene McNulty and Tom Maguire

2 | Interview: David Grant   23

3 | Marie Jones and Charabanc:
   Popular Theatre in / for Northern Ireland   25
   Eugene McNulty

4 | Finding her legs: *Lay Up Your Ends*
   and Marie Jones's international success.   51
   Charlotte J. Headrick

5 | Interview: Brenda Winter   65

6 | Purchasing Power:
   Material Culture and the Function of America
   in Marie Jones's post Charabanc plays   73
   Deirdre O'Leary

7 | An Alternative Peace Process:
   Violence and Reconciliation in Marie Jones's Plays.   91
   Wei H. Kao

8 | Marie Jones and the DubbelJoint Theatre Company:
   Performance, Practice, and Controversy   107
   Fiona Coffey

9 | Interview: Tim Loane   123

10 | 'I am a Protestant Man, I'm an Irish Man' : Politics, Identity, and *A Night in November* in Performance   127
Eleanor Owicki

11 | Masculinity and the Performance of Gendered Identities in the plays of Marie Jones.   141
Catherine Rees

12 | Interview: Paula McFetridge   155

13 | 'Popular Feminisms' and the Radical Within: Menopausal Women's Desire for Visibility in Marie Jones's *Women on the Verge of HRT*   163
Shonagh Hill

14 | Women's Suffrage and the Politics of Militancy in *The Milliner and The Weaver*   181
Dawn Fowler

Playography   195
Bibliography   197
Notes on Contributors   207
Index   211

Acknowledgements

The editors would like to acknowledge the support of Eamonn Jordan at Carysfort Press, for his unceasing support, good humour and patience. The work of our peer reviewers has been indispensable and is much appreciated. As editors we are grateful, too, for the support we have received from our own institutions, University of Ulster and St Patrick's College (Dublin City University).

Much of the research presented here would not have been produced without the assistance of the staff of the Linenhall Library, Belfast in navigating the Theatre Archive in person. We are grateful, too, to the practitioners who gave up their time to be interviewed by us: David Grant, Tim Loane, Paula McFetridge and Brenda Winter. Our contributors have been patient, responsive, efficient and generous in their dealings with us and we would like to thank them also.

Carysfort Press would like to thank the Arts Council and Carmel Naughton for their subventive support for the company, and for this publication, in 2014.

1 | Introduction

Eugene McNulty and Tom Maguire

As a playwright whose work has been mounted in community venues, in schools, in subsidized theatres and commercially across the island, in London's West End and on Broadway, Marie Jones is one of the most versatile and successful writers in Ireland. Not only has she sustained an enviable record of new writing credits, but her work has both been remounted and transferred following initial productions in ways that few of her Irish contemporaries can match. Her theatre awards include a 1999 Irish Times/ESB Award for Best New Production and Laurence Olivier Award for Best New Comedy in 2001, for *Stones in His Pockets*; and a John Hewitt Award for outstanding contribution to culture, tradition and the arts in Northern Ireland. She has received honorary doctorates from both of Northern Ireland's universities and in 2002 was presented with an OBE. Moreover, the period of her emergence and flourishing as a writer coincided with an unprecedented growth in the appetite for live theatre and in companies responding to that appetite on the island. Her role in changing this landscape for theatre is unmatched. Her success is all the more remarkable given that that same period marked some of the darkest days of the Troubles; that as a co-founder of Charabanc she was claiming a right to work as a woman and an artist in a climate where so many had found these to be mutually exclusive; that her plays are so disparate in form and context of production; and that her work does not shy away from addressing difficult topics.

Today theatre in Northern Ireland is characterized by the artistic talent, leadership and energy of the women who direct many of its production companies (including Zoe Seaton at Big Telly, Paula McFetridge at Kabosh, Emma Jordan at Prime Cut and Lisa May at

Bruiser) and lead local venues (such as Anne McReynolds at the MAC, Jill Holmes at The Marketplace in Armagh, and Pauline Ross at the Derry Playhouse). Women writing for the theatre (and being produced) include: Lucy Caldwell, Maria Connolly, Stacey Gregg, Leesa Harker, Rosemary Jenkinson, Jennifer Johnston, Fionnuala Kennedy, Nicola McCartney, Bernie McGill, Lisa McGee, Morna Regan, and Abbie Spallen, alongside Jones and Brenda Winter. However, as Eugene McNulty discusses in Chapter Three and David Grant outlines in his interview, when Jones co-founded Charabanc with Carol Scanlon, Brenda Winter, Eleanor Methven and Maureen McAuley in 1983, not only were there few opportunities for women to work in the theatre at all, there were even fewer opportunities for them to take control of the means of production, the power exercised by Mary McNally at the Lyric remaining the exception. Thus, while Christina Reid's *Tea in a China Cup* was to be produced at the Lyric in November 1983 and Anne Devlin would premiere *Ourselves Alone* at Liverpool's Playhouse Studio two years later, theatre written, produced and performed by women was a novelty in Northern Ireland for much of the 1980s. As with many other playwrights writing from a subaltern position, Jones has, however, always refused to be labelled according to any single identity label that might separate her (and her work) as of a secondary order. Nonetheless, the audacity of the founders of Charabanc to make such a radical intervention in the cultural life of their society cannot be overestimated.

Through her work with Charabanc and subsequently, Marie Jones has continued to make significant interventions through a diverse range of works, working methods and contexts of production. The scope of the content she has engaged with is charted later in this Introduction and throughout this collection. At its most trenchant, hers has been a vital voice articulating the politics of the personal and the everyday. She has made public the challenges of women's work in holding together a family in the face of economic hardship, patriarchal power structures, or ill-health. She has charted the impact of ageing on female identity. She has challenged the sectarianism of the monolithic identity blocs in Northern Ireland through her plays and the choice of venues to tour. She has challenged structures of representation within which the lives of ordinary people are marginalized and their agency constrained. She has opened up new audiences to theatre, including through writing work for young audiences; the staging of her work in community settings, including in prisons; and has embraced the challenges of place in site-specific performances. There are few innovations in (Northern) Irish theatre in which she has not had a hand.

Despite these distinctive and remarkable aspects of her oeuvre, in scholarly terms, her work is largely neglected, particularly in contrast to the attention lavished on a relatively small band of her Irish contemporaries. As Wei H. Kao notes in his essay in this volume, only a small number of her plays have been published, without, as yet, a select anthology. As Shonagh Hill's essay picks up, critical treatments have been few and far between, often isolated essays or as part of works dealing with groups of works or writers. This volume of essays seeks both to remedy that critical gap and to explore the work seriously in its theatrical context and *as theatre*. The essays here trace both her own development as a writer and the contribution that she has made to what has become a vibrant theatrical culture in Northern Ireland, charting too the ways in which she has contributed to the theatre across the island and internationally.

Biography

Marie Jones was born in 1951 and brought up in East Belfast: her affiliation to her native city and her roots remain undiminished by her successes. In 2013, for example, she joined one of her three sons, Matthew McElhinney, for an 11-night run of *Crimea Square*, a multi-authored community play directed by Jo Egan, telling the history of the Shankill Road. She was in part acknowledging her debt to her native city as a source of inspiration and expressing a profound commitment to the culture in which she remains immersed. As a child, her engagement with the theatre was limited to annual trips to the Grand Opera House for the pantomime at Christmas. Even as she progressed to secondary school, at Orangefield Girls, there were few opportunities for her to be exposed to making or attending the theatre. This does not mean that she had not a clear sense of the power of the performative. In an interview with Lyn Gardner for *The Guardian*, she recalled how the women of her family sharing stories had a significant impact on her understanding of storytelling and performance (The Bard of Belfast). As she revealed when receiving the honorary degree of Doctor of Letters from the University of Ulster in 2006, she left formal education at the age of fifteen and, disposing of her school books, vowed never to return.

This did not mean she was without ambition or determination. She had become taken with the work of James Young, then running the Group Theatre in Belfast's city centre. Young had established himself as a firm favourite of Ulster audiences on radio and in live theatre, where he starred in plays and sketch shows. As manager and director at the Group, he had an unrivalled success in a string of successful shows. Jones wrote to Young and asked him for a chance to act. Young's response was unexpectedly positive and she was cast in *Little Boxes*, working for the next six months. When that came to an end, however, she had to take up a series of semi-skilled office jobs. She maintained her interest in theatre, however, and in 1976 joined the Young Lyric Players, the only bridge at that time between the amateur and professional theatre. This provided her with an opportunity to develop her skills as an actor, to engage with a widened repertoire of dramatic works, and to meet other people who, like her, were passionate about making theatre. Of course, the difficulties in making the step to making a living as an actress were enormous, and as Eugene McNulty shows in the next chapter, it was as a response to the frustration at this that Charabanc was created.

Although the public persona of Marie Jones is of the vivacious and successful playwright and actor, always busy and hardly pausing for breath in her conversation, it should not be forgotten that she has also many personal dimensions to her life that have come to condition her work. Before establishing Charabanc, she was already sharing a house off the Ravenhill Road with Eleanor Methven that had become a hub for an emergent cultural scene, as David Grant notes in his interview. When she later married Ian McElhinney, this house would become their family home. However, in pursuing her original dreams for a career in the theatre, Jones felt compelled to leave her first husband and then seven-year old son (Gardner, The Bard of Belfast). She understands personally the nature of the choices facing her characters. McElhinney has been a stalwart and active supporter of all that she has done subsequently. Already established as a successful actor, he would be the producer for the first production of *Lay Up Your Ends* – Charabanc's first play, inspired by the 1911 Mill strikes in Belfast (discussed in detail in the following two chapters). As a writer and director, he would also bring to the production of Jones's plays the ability to push her to refine her work, both on the page and in the rehearsal room, particularly after she broke with Pam Brighton and DubbelJoint. As Paula McFetridge discusses in her interview, McElhinney has brought also a commercial acumen to the production of her work, helping negotiate the transfers and co-productions that have allowed it to be exported beyond Northern Ireland in ways that no others have managed consistently. McFetridge also points out the extent to which her children and wider family have remained central to Marie Jones's identity. It is all too easy to forget that playwrights also live domestic lives too that the demands of bringing up a family may be as critical in determining what is written as social crises and grand themes.

Characterizing Jones's Work

Three fundamental aspects inform all Marie Jones's works: an openness to collaboration with others in the process; the origins in and engagement with the same popular culture that she enjoys today; and an unerring sense of what works on stage. There is no small irony in remarking on Jones's openness to collaboration given that one of the things for which she is widely known is the legal case brought by Pam Brighton over her contribution to the creation of *Stones in His Pockets* as director of the original production. Brighton maintained that she should jointly benefit from its success because of her contribution during rehearsals. A British court found against her claim in 2004. Yet from the very first days of working together on *Lay Up Your Ends* (1983), Brighton was the director of many of Charabanc's productions, including Jones's first solo credited play, *The Hamster Wheel*, going on to found DubbelJoint with Jones and Mark Lambert in 1991, where she again directed the premieres of a number of Jones's works at the West Belfast Festival. Brighton had also a considerable track record as a producer of radio drama for the BBC in Belfast, and nurtured a range of writers and performers, including Jones, through her work there, as the interview with Paula McFetridge attests.

McFetridge points too to the ways in which Jones's openness in the rehearsal room has characterized all her writing. She is a writer whose experience as an actor, particularly in her Charabanc days, has allowed her to trust others to reshape and hone her writing; this may have been even as the production was touring, as can be seen in the next chapter. Undoubtedly her writing has been enhanced too where remounts of the production have necessitated or allowed further refinements of the script. Thus, plays like *Christmas Eve Can Kill You*, *Weddins, Weeins and Wakes*, *The Blind Fiddler*, *A Night in November* and *Stones in His Pockets* have benefitted from the opportunity to rework and rewrite material. Jones has been helped in this by working repeatedly with the same actors, including Tim Loane, Conleth Hill and, most especially, Dan Gordon. Her loyalty to such people comes largely from an affinity with their understanding of the popular, rooted in shared or similar working-class cultures, and their willingness to reciprocate her trust in them. Actors too have provided the provocation or inspiration for her to write. *Fly Me to The Moon* in 2012 was the response to a conversation with two local actors, Tara Lynne O'Neill and Katie Tumelty, lamenting the dearth of significant roles for women in local theatre: after listening and talking, Jones engaged the same impulse that had inspired the founding of Charabanc.

Those who have ever read a script produced by Marie Jones testify to the ways in which it seems to resist the conventions of the page. As both Tim Loane and Paula McFetridge recall, actors new to her manner of presenting words on a page struggle at the first read-through to come to terms with the parts written for them. As David Grant remarks in his interview, this is largely a matter of Jones's ear for the nuances of oral culture, something she shares with her original mentor James Young (Moore, Stap Fightin). She writes phonetically and her command of Belfast vernacular allows her to trace sonically the impulses and actions of her characters. She has a strong sense of the rhythms of speech and how these can be used to create and resolve conflicts. She understands too that oral cultures are embodied and that words need to be made to live by the actors. Stage directions are sparse; the expectation is that the rehearsal room is where the work of staging is done.

Given the foundational importance of her experience with Charabanc in her career as a writer, we have allowed a complete chapter to chart Jones's time with the company, providing a critical context in which the other essays may be read (McNulty, Marie Jones and Charabanc). In the rest of this Introduction we provide a commentary on her time after Charabanc to identify the key stages in her development as playwright, beginning with her work for Replay Productions.

Jones and Replay: Extending the Audience

In the latter years of her involvement with Charabanc Marie Jones had begun to widen the range of her writing activities to include devising plays specifically for younger audiences. Her one-time Charabanc colleague, Brenda Winter, was at this same time developing stronger interests in the field of drama in educational contexts. In 1988 Winter established Replay, a company whose goal was to bring high-quality drama into educational spaces (initially primary, secondary, and special educational needs schools, but developing later to include a broader conception of learning spaces such as museums etc.). Such aims, of course, in many ways echoed those that lay at the heart of the original Charabanc project. Indeed Winter makes an explicit link between the two (see interview with Brenda Winter in this volume): 'I'd originally conceived Replay as a kind of Charabanc for schools. In other words, it was to be a group that privileged the language of this place, the culture and history of this place – and brought that work into the schools.' It was thus natural that Winter would look to Jones to come up with work that could fulfil this ideal. In the years ahead Jones would not only write Replay's first production *Under Napoleon's Nose* (1988) but would go on to write five further plays for the company.

Irrespective of the context, Jones's success as a playwright has always been based on her ability to read her audiences. Over the years she has proven herself adept at judging the best angle of attack to gain and sustain their interest, and in capturing the manners, idiosyncrasies and speech that an audience will recognize as authentic (and, usually, as a version of themselves). If anything these are attributes that are even more important when dealing with younger audiences, many of whom may be encountering formal theatre for the first time. Winter's sense that Jones would understand Replay's objectives was well judged, and the partnership was a successful one. We can see, for example, Jones's ability to capture the stresses of modern teenage life in the play *Yours Truly* (1993). *Yours Truly* explores the pressures of image and acceptance that regulate so many elements of teen life by exploring the relationships of a group of young girls and their obsessive engagement with the fantasy lives encountered in a fictional teen magazine. Intercutting the reality of the girls' lives with scenes drawn from the fictional world of the magazine, Jones examines the pressures on teenagers to be sexually advanced and active. The earlier piece, *The Cow, the Ship, and the Indian* (1991), similarly reveals Jones's ability to fine tune her language to the needs of that most demanding of all audiences, primary school children. Opening in a small cottage in late nineteenth-century Fermanagh, *The Cow, the Ship, and the Indian* follows the fortunes of the O'Donnel family as they are forced to move to America after being evicted from their land by an avaricious landlord. In America they encounter stories of 'Red Indians' who have likewise been removed from their lands by the forces of colonialism and forced to abandon their language in favour of English (a process that the O'Donnels are struggling to come to terms with themselves). While perhaps heavy-handed – and indeed one could argue that its over-determined ideological positioning is somewhat unsettling given the educational context in which it was to be performed – the play undoubtedly captures Jones's linguistic and performative flexibility, and her innate understanding of the needs and capabilities of younger audiences. As Brenda Winter, thinking about Jones's success with younger audiences, recalls: 'You know we went into some tough schools, but we never had an unruly audience' (see interview in this volume).

Jones, DubbelJoint, and after

The period immediately after leaving Charabanc was a busy one for Jones. In 1991 Jones, Pam Brighton and Mark Lambert, founded DubbelJoint. The name – a compound of Dub(lin) Bel(fast) Joint – reflected the new company's ambition to produce work that was relevant to the whole island and to tour this work accordingly. As Imelda Foley has suggested: 'Given the joint efforts by the two Arts Councils to liaise on practical programmes, the founding ideology was timely and appropriate' (48). In a change from the position adopted by Charabanc, however, DubbelJoint very much grounded itself in the cultural milieu of nationalist West Belfast. As Fiona Coffey's essay shows, this would itself become a source of controversy since, from the outset, DubbelJoint would be closely associated with the West Belfast Festival (later to become Féile an Phobail) and the company's new works premiered at the festival. The first of these new works was *Hang All the Harpers* (1991), a piece jointly written by Jones and Shane Connaughton, which explores the ways in which certain musical forms have been appropriated (or rejected) by different political communities. The play charts the role of the harp in Irish history and attempts to trace the pressures such cultural production came under in the course of Ireland's various political phases. *Hang All the Harpers* takes its audiences from the seventeenth-century edict of Elizabeth I (from which the play takes its title) through the Belfast Harp Convention in the 1790s, Thomas Moore in the nineteenth century, and up to contemporary Northern Ireland. In its concern for the intersection of music and political identity it picked up on some of the thematic concerns that Jones had begun to explore in Charabanc's *The Blind Fiddler of Glenaduach* (discussed more fully in McNulty's and Kao's essays).

Echoes of Charabanc's seductive blend of the comedic with the political can be seen too in DubbelJoint's next production in 1992, *Christmas Eve Can Kill You*. Although Jones was credited as the sole writer, as both Paula McFetridge and Tim Loane testify in their interviews, both the original production and each of its subsequent restagings, benefitted from the work with the directors and actors in the rehearsal room, and the opportunity for Jones to rewrite material. Set largely in a taxi driven by the indefatigable Mackers, the audience views the machinations of manic last minute Christmas preparations by way of the stories told by the assortment of fares picked up along the way. Reviewer Karen Fricker summarizes it thus: 'the husband stuck in the pub on the way home from picking up the turkey, the family of women tearing each other up on their way to a do, and Macker's buddy, who is masquerading as Santa and peddling contraband vodka from his sack'.

The group's next project would take Jones in an interesting new direction as a writer for the stage. Her version of Gogol's *The Government Inspector* was first produced at the West Belfast Festival / Féile an Phobail on 1 August 1993. A Programme Note for these first performances also reveals the newly directed politicality of DubbelJoint in comparison to Charabanc:

> When DubbelJoint decided to do a version of Gogol's wonderful comedy, it seemed a surprisingly simple matter to substitute late 19th century Ireland for early Russia and British governance for Tsarist rule. To replace a group of provincial Russians with their craven desire to mimic Moscow with their counterpoints in Ulster and their conviction that a British accent could speak no wrong.

In this regard *The Government Inspector* would set the scene for DubbelJoint's next, more controversial, venture. Marie Jones's *A Night in November* was first performed on 8 August 1994 at the Belfast Institute of Further and Higher Education campus on the Whiterock Road. It was directed by Pam Brighton, with a set designed by Robert Ballagh, and was performed, in what was widely regarded as an acting tour-de-force, by Dan Gordon. Of all Marie Jones's work, *A Night in November* is undoubtedly the most divisive, and the one to which most critical opprobrium has been directed. As Tom Maguire has elsewhere written, for a writer who was 'raised within the staunchly loyalist working class of East Belfast', *A Night in November* could well be read as 'a public repudiation of the politics of her background' (*Making Theatre* 139). Others have detected in the work an empowering directness and a searching out of a positive alterity, with Ophelia Byrne, for example, perceiving the piece as 'epitomizing a moment of possibility and hope in the long history of the Troubles'. The play's contemporary political import was reinforced by the fact that it was on tour when the IRA's 1994 ceasefire was announced.

The play takes its title from the night in November 1993 when the Republic of Ireland and Northern Ireland soccer teams met for a competitive match in Belfast's Windsor Park. The outcome would decide if the Republic qualified for the following year's World Cup in the USA. As it turned out the result was a draw, which was enough to secure the Republic's passage to the tournament finals in America. But the match is less remembered for its result than it is for the violently hostile atmosphere that greeted the Republic's players and fans in Windsor Park. The play tells the story of one Northern Irish supporter, Kenneth, and his reaction to the hatred that he witnesses that evening as he stands on the terraces. Kenneth is a middle-class Protestant civil-servant, a dole clerk, who has largely lived an unreflective life, has kept his head down and played along with the low-level sectarianism that had become such an ingrained part of Northern Ireland. It is this element of the play that is perhaps the most interestingly nuanced; while 'the Troubles play' had established working-class sectarianism as a major trope by that time, *A Night in November*, at least in part, attempted to open up 'a more elusive phenomenon, the genteel discrimination of the Belfast middle classes' (Johnston 199). Kenneth's controversial transformation is triggered by two key events. The first is his fateful trip to the infamous Windsor Park match with his father-in-law Ernie Thompson, a die-hard bigot. Even before the match begins Kenneth reports the hostile chants coming from the Northern Irish supporters. While unpleasant, there is really nothing new in this for Kenneth; but as the atmosphere turns even more rancid he begins to look and listen in a different way. Kenneth is left stunned as the chants turn to the recent real life events of Greysteel, when loyalist gunmen opened fire into a pub at Halloween, shouting 'Trick or Treat' as they fired indiscriminately into the crowded Rising Sun bar. Ernie revels in starting the chant of 'Trick or Treat' amongst the Northern Ireland supporters. As he listens and watches, Kenneth undergoes an epiphany, seeing this moment as the logical culmination of the low-level sectarianism that he had engaged in throughout his life. The speed of this transformation – and the fact that the play focuses only on the horrors of Loyalist violence – have been critiqued by those who see the play as profoundly unsubtle and politically problematic. The same kinds of criticism have been brought to bear on Kenneth's second Damascene moment – a rather oddly contrived scene that involves him visiting the West Belfast home of his Catholic colleague Jerry. In this journey into 'otherness', Kenneth becomes a Candide-like figure as he ventures into unknown territories with a curious naivety. The untidy unpredictability of Jerry's home, which Kenneth would once have seen as a sign of Catholic slovenliness, is transformed for Kenneth into a signification of love and a freedom of expression, polar opposites to what Kenneth now sees as the cold ordered world of his house and culture. The scene's essentialist renderings of class and religion are undoubtedly troubling, but theatrically it adds another layer to the story of Kenneth's journey.

This is a journey that will soon take him to America. For, spurred on by his recent experiences, Kenneth decides to sell his golf clubs and use the money to join the legion of Republic of Ireland supporters heading to the World Cup. The pace of Kenneth's transformation is startling but, the stage energy is irresistible and is certainly another example of Jones's ability to grab an audience and take it with her. At Dublin Airport Kenneth realizes that his work suit and tie is hardly the most appropriate garb for a football fan, but the Republic supporters that surround him soon supply him with a more apt t-shirt, in green, white and orange. His change of costume is emblematic of the reconstruction of his identity (Maguire, You're Only Putting It On). The stage set likewise undergoes its own transformation with the platform that serves as football terracing flipping from the red, white and blue of Windsor Park to the green, white and orange that serves as the backdrop for the Republic of Ireland fans' invasion of the World Cup game in New York.

In New York Kenneth rapidly embraces the sense of community constructed by the travelling fans and it is clear that his new allegiance to the Republic of Ireland team goes beyond his new t-shirt. For some this is exactly the problem of course, as the play does seem to suggest that one can alter one's identity as easily and as quickly as one can change one's shirt. For others, the play's transformative movement is successful exactly because of its radical quality, which opens up a space where real alterity is revealed as possible. Certainly the piece ends with a clear and powerful declaration of alterity by Kenneth. As the fans invade New York's streets to celebrate the Republic's victory over Italy in the match news begins to filter through of yet another Northern Irish horror – the murders by loyalist paramilitaries of five Catholics in a pub as they watched the match in Loughinisland. Horrified by the news, Kenneth turns to a friend he has made on the trip, declaring the completion of his repudiation of sectarianism and the completion of his new sense of self: 'tonight I absolve myself ... I am free of them Mick ... I am free of it, I am a free man ... I am a Protestant Man, I'm an Irish Man' (98).

As with the play as a whole, the ending has proven to be critically divisive: Kenneth's seeming disavowal of his cultural and political background has been considered insulting by some; while others have felt that it has not been justified sufficiently in the play's breakneck speed events; while more still have been perturbed by the implicit suggestion that 'Protestant man' and 'Irish man' are somehow normatively mutually exclusive. Despite, or because, of all this, *A Night in November* gave DubbelJoint its first major popular success and established the base for what would become a remarkably fruitful period in its history.

The following year saw the production of two new plays: *Ethel Workman Is Innocent* and *Women on the Verge of HRT*. Of the two it is *Women on the Verge of HRT* that has had the most impact, from its first production in August 1995 at the Belfast Institute of Further and Higher Education campus, on the Whiterock Road. It tells the story of two middle-aged women, Vera and Anna (Jones played the part of Anna in the original production), their struggle with the effects of ageing, and their sense of cultural invisibility. The two women are massive fans of the Irish singer Daniel O'Donnell (a fact that contains within it some knowing jokes about ageing), and the first act takes place in a bedroom of what was at that time O'Donnell's hotel – *The Viking House Hotel* – in Kincasslagh (Co. Donegal). The second, radically different, act, takes place on a nearby beach and invites its audience into a magical realist space that sharply contrasts the straight realism of the earlier scenes. As explored more fully in Hill's nuanced essay for this volume, at the heart of the play stands the issue of middle-aged female sexuality and the ways in which modern culture renders it something troubling, or indeed, something to be disavowed. Vera's husband, Dessie, has left her for a younger woman (they have since had a baby boy together) and the first scenes are dominated by Vera's anger at being left: 'and then that bastard and his wee bride and his wee baby and all the lads clapping him on the back. 'Oh well done there, Dessie. I see the oul weapon is still in good working order. See you haven't run out of ammunition yet.' Christ! It makes me so sick' (7-8). In a clumsy attempt at pragmatism, Anna (who, we will discover, is trapped in a loveless, and sexless, marriage) counsels Vera that she should simply prepare herself for a middle-age free of sex and desire, provoking a virulent rejection by Vera. It is into this discussion that the hotel waiter (Fergal) arrives, and he is clearly intrigued and somewhat intimidated by these two women's openly sexual language. While attracted to Vera, Fergal also seems unsure what to do next. The close confines of the hotel bedroom begin to feel like a trap and reflect the social claustrophobia that the women clearly feel is closing in around them.

The second act's change of location, to the beach, is thus important in lots of different ways. The natural space enables the women – and Fergal, who joins them – to rupture the social boundaries in which they have felt trapped, to explore their agency in a way that is far removed from the over-determined roles that have defined their lives up until this point. In contrast to the restrictive realism of the hotel room, the beach marks a space where past and present can coexist, where the real and the mythic can commune. The act opens, for example, with the sound of the Banshee wailing, a mythic figure whom Vera begins to understand in a new way: 'I am listening to you, Banshee. You are wailing because they wrote you off just because you got old and they couldn't hack it. Maybe she was going through the change' (22). Thus in this liminal space, transformation becomes possible and anything can happen over the course of the night. Fergal appears in the guise of various characters that have helped define the women's story so far, allowing the women to speak in a newly open way to those who have hurt them. Vera and Anna are likewise transformed in this in-between space and the play's shift from realism to anti-illusionist techniques becomes increasingly important. By the end, the two women are able to unleash their newly empowered sense of self in song, proclaiming that neither they nor their passion will lie down and die. What makes *Women on the Verge of HRT* such a success is its ability to articulate a sophisticated cultural critique while capturing the humour through which Vera and Anna maintain their sense of self in a world that attempts to make them quiet. As Luke Clancy puts it in an interview with Jones, this is another example of her ability 'to pick out, focus on and then speak clearly and distinctly to exactly the people to whom she wants to speak' (Speaking for the Powerless).

This was a prolific period for Jones and 1996 saw DubbelJoint premiere two new pieces by her. *Eddie Bottom's Dream* (discussed further by Fiona Coffey) is a not fully successful satire on a German-backed plan to build a new golf-course in Donegal. Controversy is sparked when the locals are ordered to remove a 'fairy thorn' to make way for the new course. The plan brings them into conflict with the fairy people, and the result is a folkloric satire in which wily locals are pitted against capitalist outsiders. The same topic is revisited in Jones's other production of that year, *Stones in His Pockets*, the play for which Jones is still best known. The production history of *Stones in His Pockets* is less straightforward than most of Jones's other works. While it was first produced in 1996, the play with which most people are familiar is a re-worked version that Jones brought back to the stage in 1999. This re-worked version would become a massive popular success for Jones, enjoying a long run on the West End and touring widely across the UK and USA.

Stones in His Pockets tells the story of two film extras (Jake and Charlie) as they work on a Hollywood production in a small Kerry town. A two-hander, the play requires its actors to inhabit not just their main roles but all the characters (thirteen in total) with whom they interact on and off the film set. As Mark Phelan has noted, 'Jake and Charlie function as Stoppardesque Rosencrantzs and Guildensterns', their comic commentary working to bring that which is usually background to the fore and make performative subtexts the explicit matter of the play (Authentic Reproductions 244). In this regard *Stones In His Pockets* may be viewed as Jones's most ambitious work. Her work, as we've seen, has often concerned itself with the meta-performative and the ways in which performance infiltrates all aspects of everyday life; but in *Stones* she turns attention to the nature of Irishness itself, to the ways in which versions of Ireland and the Irish have been produced in /for a system of international commodification. The set on which the actors are working, for example, is for a film called *The Quiet Valley*. The nod to Ford's classic *The Quiet Man* firmly locates the play's action in a meta-territory of cultural signification and globalized reception (a space, of course, in which *Stones In His Pockets* now in its turn plays its part). Jones's most successful work is then, as Phelan eloquently parses it, a '"play-full", postmodern deconstruction of the commodification of Irish culture in the era of the Celtic Tiger' (Authentic Reproductions 235).

This knowing playfulness can be seen at work in those moments when the film's star (Caroline Giovanni) worries about the inauthenticity of her accent (her character is a nineteenth-century Anglo-Irish lady of the local Big House). Giovanni's accent is, of course, terrible, but, crucially, the extras are also aware of the dynamics of cultural reception within which the film is working, in which the accent will be judged less by its fidelity to how real Irish people speak, than by its similarity to representations in other Hollywood films. The point brings us back to the roots of Jones's career with Charabanc. English actresses playing Irish women at the Lyric (as discussed in Chapter Three) here become film stars playing Irish leads so often that the real and the image turn into self-replicating versions of each other. The challenge for Charlie and Jake, as it had been for Charabanc, is how to bring their counter-vision to fruition. The trigger for the two men to move from dreaming to action is the tragedy that haunts the background of the action, and also gives the play its title. Young Sean Harkin is a lost soul trapped in a place that offers little opportunity or employment. Far from the rural idyll that the American film crew sees, the village is in reality withering away due to economic under-development. Its remote beauty is in fact the only thing it has to offer to a modern system of commodification – the Hollywood crew will capture it and leave. Sean has been excluded from the film set (he has developed a drink and drugs problem) and, seeing no way to change his dead-end existence, fills his pockets with stones and walks out into the waters to drown. His friend, Fin, delivers the news at the close of the first act in a moment that powerfully counters the notion of the Irish 'product' that the film crew have set out to capture, and confirms Jake and Charlie in their desire to capture an Irish reality that is beyond the 'Hollywoodification' of which they have found themselves part. The play's final moments are thus intricately layered with meta-performative signification. Jake and Charlie become echoes of the younger Marie Jones as they set out to take control of the narrative and thus their self-representation, determined to make their own film and tell their own stories.

Telling stories from the ground up is Jones's great strength, and in the same year that the re-worked *Stones In His Pockets* became such a success for her she was also working on a piece that returned her to the very definition of community theatre. *The Wedding Community Play* (1999), co-written with Martin Lynch, was an extraordinarily ambitious piece of site-specific theatre. Developed through extended working with community groups from both sides of Belfast's political divide, the piece involved its audience travelling by bus to different locations in East Belfast to witness a bride and groom preparing for a cross-community marriage. Moving from one house to the next involved the audience travelling from a predominantly Protestant area to the Catholic enclave of Short Strand. Thus the audience replicated the sense of boundary crossing explored within the piece itself. This same year also saw Jones make a return to the adventures and tribulations of Vera and Anna. *Women on the Verge Get a Life* (1999) sees the two women, now 50, go on holiday to the Gambia, where they learn some, rather clumsily handled, lessons about men and women. While another box-office hit for Jones, the critical reaction – particularly to the play's handling of race – was decidedly mixed.

Jones 2000 – present

The year 2000 saw Jones work extensively with Tinderbox, one of the most significant new theatre companies to emerge in the North of Ireland in the post-Charabanc period. First off in April, following previews at Enniskillen's Ardhowen Theatre, *Ruby: the life of Ruby Murray* premiered at the Group Theatre, Belfast. The play tells the story of Belfast-born singer Ruby Murray, who achieved massive chart fame in the 1950s and remained something of a cult hero in the city of her birth. At the height of her fame Murray had five singles in the UK Top 20, a feat that has not often been equalled. Jones's treatment of Murray's rather tough life charts not just her rise to fame but her later decline with all of its struggles with drink and the various men who took advantage of her. Murray has remained a much-loved figure in Belfast, and Jones has spoken of the personal nature of the project to bring her life to the stage: 'Her background was not unlike mine and I came to know the world which became her world, the world of showbiz with its high spots and disappointments, the way she reached the top and the later decline' (Johnston 186).

The localism of the story, as John McGrath might put it (*A Good Night Out*), certainly made *Ruby* a success in Belfast but has limited its appeal internationally. In this same year Jones also participated in Tinderbox's *Convictions* project, a collection of site-specific pieces performed at the Crumlin Road Courthouse (Belfast) in October 2000. As the audience moved around the now unused Courthouse (scene of some of Northern Ireland's most famous trials and just across the road from Crumlin Road Gaol), it encountered various scenes being played out for them as if in real time. Over the course of the evening the audience encountered work by seven writers: Marie Jones, Daragh Carville, Damian Gorman, Martin Lynch, Owen McCafferty, Nicola McCartney, and Gary Mitchell. Jones's piece took place in (and was named) 'Court No.2', and involved the audience intruding on a meeting to discuss transforming the courthouse into a 'heritage centre' (an idea that was, and continues to be, under consideration for the building). The set-up allows Jones, and by extension those watching on in the audience, to consider issues around commemoration (official or otherwise) and the role of 'heritage space' in consolidating the North's new post-Troubles realities. Staying far away from any trite presentation of culture as a healing solution for all ills, the piece signals very clearly that those living in the North are a long way from settling on an agreed version of the past.

The years immediately following these Tinderbox collaborations proved to be very difficult for Jones. The next four years would be largely consumed by the court case dealing with the *Stones in His Pockets* copyright issue, and it would be 2004 before Jones would take another work to the stage: the re-written and extended version of *The Blind Fiddler*. In the years ahead, however, Jones would return to her usual high-level of creative output. 2005 saw the first production of *A Very Weird Manor*, a mad-cap comedy about a Belfast man, living as a 'beach bum' in Australia, who inherits an old crumbling manor in the

Irish countryside. The play centres on his decision to bring a 'reality-TV' crew with him as he returns to Ireland to turn the old house into a high-end hotel. This meta-media playfulness returned Jones to territory that had proven so successful in *Stones in His Pockets*, but while *A Very Weird Manor* certainly strives to recapture the performative layering of the earlier piece, it lacks its more subtle analytical frames. The drive to draw on popular entertainment forms is constant within Jones's work and her self-image as a writer who writes for those usually occluded from mainstream theatre. Thus her involvement with two musical projects – *The Chosen Room* (2008, Youth Music Theatre) and *Dancing Shoes: The George Best Story* (2010) – fits perfectly with her trajectory as a writer who has always valued the impact of music in performance. Music would also play a rather less successful part in Jones's next piece, *Rock Doves* (2010), which features the somewhat misjudged idea of a transvestite Tina Turner tribute act whose trials and tribulations function with varying degrees of success as commentaries on the dysfunctional political stasis that had come to dominate Northern Ireland.

Rather more successful is that year's other new Jones play, *The Milliner and the Weaver*. As Dawn Fowler's essay in this volume discusses, this opened the Tricycle Theatre's *Women Power and Politics* season on 4 June 2010. If *A Very Weird Manor* was a misfiring return to the territory of *Stones In His Pockets*, *The Milliner and the Weaver* was a much better judged and executed return to the political and philosophical terrain of *Lay Up Your Ends* (see discussion in following two chapters). Set in a small mill house in East Belfast in 1914, *The Milliner and the Weaver* explores the tensions and subsequent fall-out when those who have found themselves united by the women's suffrage movement find themselves equally divided by the home-rule cause. The short one-act piece marked a real return to form for Jones and the piece was greeted as an eloquent and powerful examination of Ireland's complex gender politics.

Further success came with *Fly Me to the Moon* in 2012, which also marked Jones's debut as a director. Its story centres on two community care workers, Francis and Loretta, who have looked after 84 year old Davy, whose lonely existence has been punctuated by their visits, his Frank Sinatra records, and his modest bets on the horses. The two women are left in a comically handled dilemma when Davy passes away unexpectedly and they have to choose whether or not to cash in his pension and collect his unexpected race winnings (Davy had placed a winning bet on a horse called 'Fly Me to the Moon'). While the play inhabits a comedic space imbued with Jones's well-honed ear for Belfast speech and bawdy humour, it also invites its audience to consider some fundamentally serious issues. It returns to the demands on carers explored in *The Hamster Wheel*, inflected by the relationship between class and healthcare; reveals the isolation of a community's elders; and critiques the economization of fundamental human dignity. In so doing it reminds us of Jones at her best, comedic but not trivial, bawdy but humane, funny but not unserious.

The layout of this book

The essays that follow take up the threads that this summary of Jones's work has begun to identify. They are organized in an approximately chronological order, from Jones's emergence as a writer with Charabanc. Eugene McNulty's essay sets out both the context for the creation of the company and traces some of the features that will become defining characteristics of Jones's work as a writer back to her experiences with the company. He demonstrates how Charabanc's goals aligned with the proposals for a radical popular theatre, articulated by John McGrath in *A Good Night Out*, whereby forms of popular culture guide the development of performance works that engage with the lived experiences of working class audiences.

A similar project is undertaken by Charlotte Headrick in examining how work that is so closely defined by its Northern Irish origins was able to transfer to other contexts. Providing a close account of her own staging of *Lay Up Your Ends* at Oregon State University, Headrick identifies how she overcame some of the potential challenges of the historical Belfast setting for a North American audience. She is able to point to the economics of ownership and publishing as the key factor that has limited further productions of the play, while demonstrating that the development of Jones's status as a writer in North America owes much to a developing business acumen that saw publication going hand-in-hand with productions as they transferred or were remounted.

The sense to which scrutiny of a playwright's oeuvre has to be informed by an engagement with the social and economic conditions of playwriting is taken up in Deirdre O'Leary's essay on Jones's work after Charabanc. O'Leary seeks to interrogate how Jones critiques the relationship between globalization and material cultures, through the recurrent juxtaposition of American culture and capital and the representation of the experiences of everyday Irish life. She suggests that in Jones's works such global forces operate to both reify and liberate senses of identity. Clearly, given Jones's own successes on each side of the Atlantic, such explorations reflect back on her own experiences as a playwright.

Wei H. Kao's essay turns the focus back to Jones's engagement with her primary audience in Northern Ireland. He examines the ways in which her works can be understood as an extended project of peacebuilding. Jones's capacity for comedy enables her to satirize the obstacles that stand in the way to a sustained peace outside the walls of the theatre auditorium. He demonstrates that Jones's consistent treatment of sectarianism is as something that limits the capacity of living for both its proponents and its victims. Any community identity that demands more of those affiliated to it than it offers by way of benefit in return is regarded as entirely suspect, laughable but also inherently violent.

Fiona Coffey's essay focuses in detail on Jones's work with DubbelJoint. She argues that this was a project that clearly sprang from many of the same impulses as Charabanc and within which Jones enjoyed one her most prolific and successful phases as a writer. However, the company's increasingly close identification with the nationalist/Republican community of West Belfast, through the works that it produced apart from Jones's, created a context within which Jones's personal success would only lead to her further estrangement from the company. This estrangement was to reach its zenith in the legal dispute with co-founder Brighton.

Eleanor Owicki provides an opportunity to review the ways in which one of the plays premiered by DubbelJoint could function outside of its original context of production. In this she is picking up on the same question asked by Charlotte Headrick, but her focus is on a comparison between the original staging of *A Night in November* in 1994 with Dan Gordon as Kenneth McAllister and the 2007 production at the Grand Opera House in Belfast with Patrick Kielty. As well as identifying how the context of performance of the later production was haunted by the original, she argues that the achievements of the peace process after the 1998 Good Friday Agreement, can be discerned in the ways in which each production was staged and received.

Catherine Rees turns to a different dimension of Jones's work: its treatment of masculinity. She develops a close comparative study of *A Night in November* and *Stones in his Pockets*, to suggest that they chart versions of masculinity in crisis under the pressures of dominant normative codes. In this, she extends the understanding of Jones's work beyond something focused on women's experience, while at the same time demonstrating how it engages with aspects of popular culture far beyond the milieu in which the plays are set. As in other essays, Rees draws attention to the ways in which Jones's theatrical playfulness allows her to reveal the ways in which social identities are constructed and, therefore, how they might be both deconstructed and reconstructed.

This issue of social identity is picked up too in Shona Hill's essay. With a detailed examination of *Women on the Verge of HRT*, Hill argues that Jones's play provides exactly the kind of visibility of which her middle-aged female characters, Anna and Vera, dream. She demonstrates how the powerful affective dimensions of the play in performance, set in train by its use of popular performance forms, provide particular kinds of pleasures that provoke within the spectator an exploration of the contradictory radical within. Jones's position as a voice of a radical feminism (however unwilling she is to be labelled) is further articulated by Dawn Fowler's essay on a production of *The Milliner and The Weaver* as part of the Tricycle Theatre's *Women Power and Politics* season in June 2010. There is a sense that the play returns Jones to her roots with Charabanc's first production, *Lay Up Your Ends*. It picks up on the challenges facing two women struggling to find a political voice through the suffragette movement in the Belfast of 1914. Fowler demonstrates the ways in which Jones deploys the personal experiences of her characters to illuminate how the impulses of class, national identity and sectarianism threaten the kind of solidarity on which political advancement for women is predicated. Placing Jones's play within the context of the season as a whole allows Fowler to develop a consideration of a wider context of reception that reveals a radical potential that exceeds the capacity of the play in isolation.

Between these essays, we have also included a sequence of interviews with practitioners who have worked with Jones and can therefore bring particular insights to her work that are hidden to those who have only experienced it from the auditorium or on the page. These serve as both key sources and commentaries that are intended to enrich the views from the outside presented within the academic essays. They are important too in giving a sense of Marie Jones as a working playwright. They articulate the conditions under which she has produced some of her best work. Nonetheless, this volume is not a form of hagiography and we have encouraged contributors to identify weaknesses, issues and challenges within specific productions that they discern or that have been pointed out by others. There has been a significant gap sometimes between the critical reception of her plays and that of audiences, themselves expert in their own tastes and values. While these audiences have not always sustained loyalty to Jones, their openness to her best work demonstrates the subtlety of production and reception that marks out the best of popular theatre.

2 | David Grant

Interviewed by Tom Maguire

In this interview with Tom Maguire, David sets out the context in which Marie Jones was involved in setting up Charabanc, explaining how radical a step it was at the time.

TM: Can you give us a brief summary of your experience in theatre here?

DG: I came back from Cambridge to work on the Belfast Festival in 1982. I hadn't really intended to stay but somehow just did. As you can imagine it was a very difficult time for theatre: the year after the hunger strikes ... In a nutshell there was very little going on. The Lyric was an interesting place because Leon Rubin was there at the time with that surge of the Troubles dramas. Students are often astounded when I tell them that in 1980 Field Day was the first ever independent [touring] theatre company to get funding from the Arts Council of Northern Ireland: they are so used to that model of funding for independent theatre companies. And I know there's been quite a lot said about the status of Field Day with all of its heavyweight board members as against Charabanc, but clearly in that climate the very emergence of Charabanc was absolutely astounding.

I would have been very close to Sam McCready – he was a great mentor and I was one of his [Lyric] Drama Studio people in those days. So we were in a little tiny coterie of theatre people. Playzone had just come and gone – a sort of one-off experiment – Andy Hinds and Marie were both involved in that. But really the Drama Studio was a tremendous surge of energy, with so many people like Carole Scanlan, Brenda Winter and myself that came through that. There were a lot of student teachers from Stranmillis [Teacher Training College] with others like myself who came through a general audition. We would drink in the York Hotel and we were vaguely aware of other younger theatre people around.

But I first became aware of Marie as part of Charabanc in 1983 with *Lay Up Your Ends* and its first performance at the Arts [Theatre]. At that stage the Charabanc girls all lived in the house in Ravenhill and that became a bit of a 'social central'. I was just a 'sensitive' director, as I was working half the time at the Festival and doing a show a year at The Crescent [Arts Centre]. There was a great sense of excitement at the time.

I think there were only two initiatives ever funded by economic development money – the ACE Schemes as they called them. One was Charabanc and I think that was interesting. There was a very sympathetic civil servant because, typically, there was a really hard-headed attitude in government in Northern Ireland that the arts were not part of the economy, whereas in the South all these schemes were being used routinely to shore up arts centres. So, one of the most extraordinary things then about Charabanc was that they did get money from that job creation scheme. The only other time I'd heard of it happening was the [Siobhan] O'Casey company. Funding was always going to be an issue and I remember the row when Eleanor Methven discovered that surreptitiously the Arts Council had shifted them onto Cultural Traditions funding without telling them, basically obliging them to be doing work that constantly addressed the sectarian issue. I certainly would have seen all those early plays that were written from a devising process.

TM: You wouldn't have been part of the target audience for that work?

DG: Famously the audience that had queued up out of the steps and onto the street to see *Lay Up Your Ends* with their carpet slippers on, because they were the millies, was the working class women who had been interviewed for the show. I mean that generation that *Lay Up Your Ends* is about, enough of them were still alive and around. So of course there was an intention to have a more popular audience, but actually it was one of the big stories in Belfast at the time. Anyone who was interested in theatre would have gone. There was a tremendous sense of a happening, an event, just as much, I think, as with *Translations* in 1980.

3 | Marie Jones and Charabanc: Popular Theatre in / for Northern Ireland

Eugene McNulty

Introduction

At the end of *Stones In His Pockets* one of the central characters, Jake, asks: 'Why couldn't it be done, don't we have the right to tell our own story, the way we want it?' (54). In the context of the play, the question marks a moment of meta-theatrical signification: indexing the possibility of a counter-story, an alternative view of things. But there's something more than this at work in the ripples that Jake's question provokes: that desire – 'to tell our own story, the way we want it' – is at the centre of Marie Jones's career as a playwright. Jones's life in the theatre (as a writer, actress, and director) has been dominated by the drive to tell stories from the ground up, drawing on materials (language, events) found in the communities that she knows so intimately. In that regard, her work is closely aligned with John McGrath's sense of a 'mode of theatre ... which speaks the language of working-class entertainment and tries to develop that language to make critical, progressive theatre primarily for popular audiences' (100). McGrath's sense of a newly relevant theatre resonates strongly with Jones's engagement with the popular and with community-based theatre praxis. His sense too that 'the theatre is by its nature a political forum, or a politicizing medium, rather than a place to experience a rarefied artistic sensibility in an aesthetic void' (83), speaks quite directly to Jones's self-image as a writer:

> The people I write for are the people who are in my plays. They are really just ordinary people who really are powerless; who really don't have a voice. I've always felt that I have this huge

responsibility, because the background I grew up in, nobody had any power, nobody had any voice. We were shafted, walked over everywhere. But now I have this arena, this power, this space to say: 'This is still me; this is the people I care about; these are the things that matter' (qtd. in Clancy).

Jones's nuanced understanding of the type of theatre she strives to create, and the kind of audiences she wishes to cultivate, is important when locating her work within a critical context. Theatre criticism is often predicated on firmly ingrained binaries of high versus low culture, and this is certainly evident in some of the critical attention that Jones's work has garnered: 'Jones writes the kinds of plays that make theatre critics sneer and ordinary audiences cheer' (*The Guardian*, 11 August 2004). Tellingly, she is only too aware of the ideological subtexts of such critical gradations:

> My plays get accused of being low art all the time ... Even by the arts establishment in my own city. But what's wrong with being popular? I sometimes feel that people want to keep the theatre as some kind of special preserve for people like them, educated, cultured people; they don't like it when a play packs out the theatre with ordinary people having a good time (*The Guardian*, 11 August 2004).

John McGrath's equally unequivocal resistance to such critical boundaries is important as a further reminder to theatre practitioners and critics alike: 'there *are* indeed different kinds of audience, with different theatrical values and expectations, and ... we have to be very careful before consigning one audience and its values to the critical dustbin' (3). Approaching this issue from a slightly different angle, Marie Jones has made the case that: 'It sometimes feels as though people think that if you're funny, you can't possibly be a serious playwright' (*The Guardian*, 11 August 2004). This essay explores Jones's particular brand of popular theatre, with its mix of the comic and the serious, as it was first developed in her work with Charabanc Theatre Company (McGrath's idea of popular theatre is also explored in Shonagh Hill's essay in this volume). It also seeks to establish the contextual terrain for the critical engagement to be found in this collection's subsequent essays. Its starting premise, in this regard, is that it is impossible to fully understand Jones's development as a playwright without first returning to the founding and subsequent success of Charabanc (1983 -1995).

The early 1980s were undoubtedly challenging times for theatre in Northern Ireland. But while the business of theatre may have been problematic, this is not to suggest an absence of the performative.

Indeed, the business of 'everyday life' during the Troubles was deeply imbued with elements of the performative. Negotiating communal, confessional, and political boundaries all necessitated nuanced role playing as everyone in a sense became a 'social actor', displaying certain aspects of identity while masking others. As John P. Harrington & Elizabeth J. Mitchell so succinctly parse it:

> Northern Ireland's charged atmosphere of sectarian division encourages a considerable amount of dramatic political performance within, and about, its borders. Social and dramatic actors, in and out of the theatre, give performances scripted to alter or confirm their particular definition of political reality (1).

In terms of Marie Jones's work, Harrington and Mitchell's sense of the North's complex matrix of identity-performance is aptly suggestive. It points us to the ways in which the North's intricate psycho-geography, social auto-surveillance, and politicized language code-play result in a lived reality wherein identity is not simply performative – it is also, at times, meta-performative. It is in the spaces between – between the real and the imagined, between the truth and the official story, between inner belief and outer mask, between quotidian experience and institutional political discourse – that Jones has usually found the space in which to explore lived reality and its possible alternatives.

The Charabanc project was a key component of Northern Ireland's theatre renaissance at the start of the 1980s. Claudia Harris describes this as 'a golden decade for Northern Irish drama', which had the effect of making 'the North, and Belfast in particular, a centre for dramatic arts similar to early twentieth-century Dublin' (Harris, Introduction *Four Plays* ix). The comparison is telling, suggesting a link between performative energy and moments of political uncertainty. Those connected with Charabanc, confronted by what was now an entrenched conflict, were not alone in their belief that the cultural realm had to respond more forcefully not just to the conditions in the North but to the underlying causes shaping those conditions. While the need was clear for a recalibration in the relationship between cultural production and social engagement, there was less consensus about just what shape such a rearticulation should take. What emerged during this period were two distinct models for a theatre practice that sought relevance and persuasive reach beyond the auditorium. Charabanc embodies one model, a model predicated upon grass-roots activism and communal narrative-making. A second model that emerged during this period was the Field Day Theatre Company, which was established in Derry in

1980 by Brian Friel and Stephen Rea and supported by a Board of Directors of cultural heavyweights such as Seamus Heaney, Tom Paulin and Seamus Deane (see Richtarik, *Lines* 20). These figures, along with the sense that Friel's future plays would get their first outing through the company, provided Field Day with the kind of prominence and momentum that is a rarity to say the least for new theatre companies. Charabanc couldn't have been more different – as Maria R. DiCenzo puts it: 'Charabanc could boast no notable members; instead, it was founded by a group of unknown, unemployed actresses with trade unionists for board members' (176).

It has become routine critical practice to set up Charabanc and Field Day as mutual foils in Northern Irish theatre history; and these were undoubtedly two very different companies – in outlook, resources, methodology and ambition. But alongside these differences there is value in noting just how fully the two shared a very particular moment in the North's cultural and political history. Helen Lojek unpacks these connections usefully:

> Both Field Day and Charabanc ... made clear assumptions about the power of drama and its connection with contemporary reality; both sought audiences beyond the urban middle class; and both offered food for thought to observers interested in the relationship between drama and culture in Ireland (*Playing Politics* 83-84).

Each in their different way was interested in the spaces not usually sounded out by the theatre of the day, and, in turn, in occupying those spaces in a manner that revealed their multivalent potentials. While Field Day may have been concerned with a grand narrative of Ireland's 'fifth province', and Charabanc with methodologies attuned to discovering and telling the untold stories of Northern Ireland's everyday life, there is a sense in which these were different modes of engagement (using quite different methodological angles of attack) with a common problematic: empowering cultural representation in a place consumed by competing narratives resistant to the very idea of shared representational spaces.

The history of Charabanc, in this regard, begins with a sense of frustration, a response to the occlusion and lack of proper opportunity in Northern Ireland's conservative institutional theatre-world. Beyond the auditorium's walls, moreover, these were frustrations bound up with the problems of over-determined gender roles and restrictive class boundaries in a profoundly unequal society. As Marie Jones remembers:

> There were about five of us, who were all Belfast actresses, working in the theatre, not doing very challenging work, because there weren't many challenging roles for women ... I mean even if there were only small parts in the Lyric or whatever, they'd bring over English actresses. And we'd start to think, in that colonial way you found here: 'We're not even good enough to go on the stage' (qtd. in Clancy).

The idea that the Lyric Theatre would pay for English actresses to travel 'across the water' to Belfast was particularly galling for those watching on from the occluded side-lines. While this was attributable at least in part to stringent policing of Equity's closed-shop approach to employment for actors, it was also regarded by many as an example of an inferiorist attitude to the local in deference to the 'metropolitan'. Brenda Winter's summation is clear and unambiguous: 'The employment prospects for actresses living and working in Belfast at this time were truly dire. It was indignation that galvanized the founders of Charabanc into doing something about their disempowered situation' (That's Not Theatre 20). But the issues at work here were about more than gender. There was also a gathering sense that the Belfast theatre-scene provided no real opportunity for Belfast's working-class communities to see themselves, their dilemmas, passions and possibilities, on stage. Such lives, and the social conditions that shaped them, were largely absent from Belfast's stages. Divided by much else, men and women on the Falls and Shankill roads largely shared the same opinion of the city's theatres – these were places with very little to do with them, staging versions of the world far removed from the lived reality of their daily existence.

It is all of this, and more, that informed the decision of five Belfast actresses to found a new company. The five women who came together to form Charabanc Theatre Company were Sarah (Marie) Jones[1], Eleanor Methven, Maureen McAuley, Carol Scanlan (subsequently Moore) and Brenda Winter. While Charabanc would rapidly learn to articulate a sophisticated rationale for its productions and the methodologies out of which they were born, the primary motivator in the company's early days was more directly related to the professional frustrations felt by this group of Belfast actresses. Quite simply, in the absence of quality female roles the actresses felt driven to create work for themselves. If that had been the limit of the company – staging other people's plays as a way of earning a living – it is unlikely that Charabanc would be a name remembered much beyond a small circle of Belfast theatre obsessives. In this regard, Claudia Harris's suggestion, that 'Charabanc's history is a triumphant story of women creating their own work and in the process changing the shape of Irish drama' (Introduction *Four Plays* x), reveals just how much further the founders of Charabanc travelled in their quest to create work for themselves.

In addition to their frustrations over the lack, and quality, of the roles available to them, the five founders of Charabanc also shared a more thoroughgoing dissatisfaction with the nature *per se* of theatre in Belfast at that time. They soon realized that they needed not simply to create employment for themselves, but to create the kind of theatre that spoke to them and the place that was Northern Ireland in 1983. A key issue in this regard was gender inequality – the lack of opportunities for women in theatre was, as they knew only too well, a micro-level reflection of the macro social and political position of women in Ireland either side of the border at that time. Yet, while clearly committed to exploring the various power dynamics at play in this ideological matrix, the Charabanc founders were hesitant about overtly labelling their project in feminist terms. As Eleanor Methven recounts:

> When Charabanc started, it was from a very pragmatic economic base and was completely actor led ... It was not a theoretical base. We really didn't come at it from an academic point of view... We didn't think if it in any feminist terms – it was an unconscious feminism, if you like (qtd. in Harris, Introduction *Four Plays* xxviii).

This hesitancy around terminology may seem slightly odd from a theatre group that would go on to be so clearly committed to tackling the politicality of everyday life. But, as explored more fully in Charlotte J. Headrick's essay in this volume, in place of the possible limitations imposed by debates concerning ideological positions and the specifics of gender politics, the founders of Charabanc were more concerned to inhabit an inclusive performative space. This was to be a space concerned more with the fundamentals of power distribution in Northern Ireland. As Marie Jones put in it 1987: 'We've been fighting for three and a half years to say we're a working-class theatre company. That's all we are. People will not accept that ... We never really say we're a Belfast women's theatre company' (interview in Martin 97). The emphasis was very much on working outside entrenched positions of power and the absence of spaces of representation for working-class communities on both sides of the political divide.

The ideas that drove Charabanc had many lines of influence. The idea of a theatre that was community-based, socially-engaged and, at times, politically oppositional was one that by the early 1980s had had a long history, particularly in Britain and the United States. In Britain a myriad of companies had already emerged, each of which, in their different ways, sought to challenge the political, class, and gender hegemonies of mainstream cultural production. Companies such as Red Ladder, Monstrous Regiment of Women, Joint Stock and, most famously, John McGrath's 7:84, were all established with the aim of rearticulating theatre as communally engaged and, where necessary, as a site of overt political resistance. In place of the traditional theatre hierarchy whereby a text with a single author is brought to life by a well-oiled mechanism of designated roles (producer, director, actors and so on), these companies drew on more collaborative and fluid modes of working. Interviews with real people, workshopping, improvisation, team writing – all of these techniques emerged as ways of reorienting traditional assumptions about the nature and function of theatre in society. As Carol Martin puts it, what we see at work here is a 'growing awareness ... that art, especially performance, could be a forum for invoking powerful and creative forces of cultural, social, and spiritual worlds' (88). In terms of Northern Irish theatre, the founders of Charabanc were amongst the first to 'plant their work in the nexus of community life' (Martin 88).

In this they were aided by the guidance and knowledge of two figures with strong links to the British popular political theatre movements: Martin Lynch and Pam Brighton (each discussed more fully below). In these terms too, the short-lived Belfast community theatre company, Playzone (est. 1978), of which Marie Jones (along with other theatre notables such as Stephen Rea and Andy Hinds) was a member, deserves more recognition as a site of influence than it is usually accorded. Playzone's drive to produce theatre from the real-world experiences of the communities within which it worked provided a working model for the newly formed Charabanc. Martin Lynch's work likewise provided a model from which the Charabanc founders drew inspiration. Indeed Carol Moore describes Martin Lynch as acting as the group's 'mentor' in the early months of its existence (Impulse to Imagination 149). Lynch had started his public life as a political and community activist, but had soon recognized the power of theatre to engage with real-world issues with the kind of efficacy and subtlety largely absent from direct political mechanisms. While he worked initially with the 'Turf Lodge Fellowship Community Theatre' in the late 1970s, by 1981 his first play, *Dockers*, had premiered at the Lyric Theatre, demonstrating how community theatre could be translated into one of the city's main houses. Crucially, Lynch's play was borne out of direct engagement with the city's dock-workers, many of whom he invited to the opening night at the Lyric Theatre. In Brenda Winter's words:

> The effect of this play on those of the Charabanc actresses present for the premiere was dramatic ... If the dockers felt empowered by witnessing their lives enacted on stage, the local actors felt equally validated through hearing their own accent, idiom and cultural identity revitalized on the stage of the Lyric Theatre (That's Not Theatre 23).

Still perhaps a little unsure of their ground, the women initially approached Lynch to write some material for them. Lynch's response took them somewhat by surprise; he would later recall the moment as comic in its obviousness:

> At the first meeting with the actresses I listened as they told me how they wanted me to write a play about the experience of Belfast women! The absurdity of this struck me immediately and I asked them why *they* couldn't sit down and write about their experiences as Belfast women. This produced an instant silence, followed by laughter (Why This Play? 117).

It was a crucial moment in Charabanc's history. The suggestion 'led the company into ways of working that distinguished it from a mainstream of Irish theatre still concerned primarily with the production of dramatic literature by individual playwrights' (Maguire, *Making Theatre* 109). These ways of working, as Claudia Harris has noted, 'would seem foreign to those who privilege the creative model of a single playwright whose vision is then produced by a director and design team' (Introduction *Four Plays* xxvii). While encouraging the five Charabanc founders to engage with the creative process themselves, Lynch nevertheless ended up working closely on what would become the company's first production, *Lay Up Your Ends* (1983). Indeed in the whirlwind of creativity that marked the company's first months of existence it would seem that Lynch took the main writing role for this piece.[2] However it is also clear that Marie Jones was a major contributor to the writing process, and *Lay Up Your Ends* effectively marked her apprenticeship as a playwright. In the years ahead Jones would become the company's writer in residence and she would be 'credited with the scripts which grew from the group's largely self-discovered method of collaboration' (Harris, Introduction *Four Plays* xi).

Lay Up Your Ends

Lay Up Your Ends is important for Jones's development as a playwright not simply because of its subject matter or performance style, but because of the process through which it found its way from idea to stage. Charabanc's founders were convinced of the need to explore dimensions of Northern Irish history and life that had remained resolutely off-stage, and in hitting upon the Belfast mill strike of 1911 they struck very fruitful territory. The shift back in time may at first seem odd for a new theatre company seeking contemporary relevance, but Martin Lynch's memory of the process suggests a politically reflexive need to understand the present as the product of the past: 'we realized that the women of today couldn't be viewed in isolation from the history of our own mothers and grand-mothers. Their experience, in many senses made the Belfast women of today' (Why This Play? 118). The play's title indeed indexes the complexity and sophistication of Charabanc's intentions and ambitions. 'Lay up your ends' was the phrase shouted out in the mills when the linen strands broke on a machine – laying up the ends was the process whereby the strands were reconnected to allow the weaving to begin again. *Lay Up Your Ends* is, then, a play built on the symmetry of title and intent. It is not just the narrative strands of a 1911 event that are pieced together again on stage, but rather the social, cultural, and political connective tissues that link the 'then' of the play with the 'now' of the audience.

At the heart of the 1911 mill strike were issues that struck at the very core of what had brought the five founders of Charabanc together in the first place: the nature of work and its gendered divisions; class as a symptom of power dynamics; the question of representation and the unrepresented. In the play's opening scene we can see how these various texts and subtexts are firmly established, as the mill girls discuss the new working conditions that have been passed down by the owners:

> Lizzie: 'Any person found away from their usual place of work, except for necessary purposes, or talkin' with anyone out of their own alley will be fined 2d for each offence. No singin'. You're not even allowed to stop to fix your hair'.
> [...]
> Florrie: 'All persons in our employ shall serve four weeks' notice before leavin' their employ, but E Bingham and Company shall, and will, dismiss any person without notice being given'.
> Ethna: Does it say anythin' about breathin'? Are we still allowed to breathe? (48)

Thereafter the play charts the women's decision to strike, inspired in part by the rhetoric of union activists such as James Connolly and Jim Larkin, the resistance they met (from their husbands as well as the mill owners), and their eventual return to work, which, while not totally on their own terms, did lead to the establishment of a branch of the Irish Transport and General Workers especially for the Belfast mill women. There was a rather apt symmetry at play in the idea of the Charabanc women challenging their own working conditions by giving voice to a group of historical women who had so radically done the very same thing. *Lay Up Your Ends* was, in Claudia Harris's eloquent terms, a unique industrial protest' (Introduction *Four Plays* xiii).

The performance style of *Lay Up Your Ends* was heavily influenced by the introduction of Pam Brighton to the group. As noted above, it was Brighton, through her work with companies such as Monstrous Regiment, who provided the strongest link between Charabanc and the experimental theatre tradition that had developed in Britain over the previous decade. As a result, Charabanc's work was 'characterised by flexible performance modes, recognizable to anyone familiar with the 1970s British alternative touring theatre' (Maguire, *Making Theatre* 110). In performance this meant costume changes on stage in full view, beer boxes taking the place of industrial machinery, furniture, platforms for political speeches, and breaches in the fourth-wall as actors break character to engage directly with the audience. Thus *Lay Up Your Ends*, and much of Charabanc's work that followed it, was 'quite deliberately anti-illusionist' (Lojek, *Playing Politics* 91). This was 'not cottage drama in which an interior set is lovingly recreated and audiences are encouraged to enter into the fiction that actors have become the characters' (Lojek, 91). One result is that 'audiences are encouraged to remember that actors play roles' and that social constructions, such as over-determined gender and class roles, are likewise largely performative in nature (Lojek, 91). Such performative shifts were not restricted to women playing men; just as importantly the same actresses who played the parts of the mill girls also took on the roles of the mill owners' wives. We can get a sense of the resultant ironies in this exchange when two such wives break off from their rehearsal for a concert in aid of the workhouse – their husbands, as the stage directions sharply inform us, sit on its Board of Guardians – to discuss the striking women:

> **URSULA:** You house them, give them a living, try to get them out of their slum-ridden conditions by providing work for them. Those ... those ... bitches!

[...]
LYDIA: Well I've always thought that if they had some of the finer things in life – take their minds off striking... Some Gilbert and Sullivan, perhaps ... some poetry ... some of the lighter, more romantic poets. I feel ... (95)

Lydia's rather clumsy notion of culture as an improving tool identifies another of the play's targets: the role of hegemonic culture in sustaining the political status quo. For example, when the members of Charabanc were researching the play they noticed that the women's strike had garnered very little attention in the newspapers. The striking women had largely been excluded from the mechanics of representation, a fact that played a major part in the strike's subsequent absence from much official historiography.[3] In a later scene, involving Ursula and her mill-owning husband (Eric Bingham), the play weaves this representational absence into its very fabric:

URSULA: Oh absolutely. I think the unrest is as good as over. You're down to ... what? ... Three hundred die-hards, no strike money, no support in any art or part of the city – and the newspapers handled it really well, didn't they?
ERIC: Hardly a mention. (106)

The moment is a metonym for the play as a whole: historical absence replayed in the context of contemporary presence. The temporal duality was reinforced further by the notes included in the Programme for its first performances. Ian Mc Elhinney, the company's Producer, informed those first audiences that Charabanc's main goal was to explore 'the diversity of our own history in this province'; while Martin Lynch explicitly unpacked the social and political connections between 1911 and 1983:

> Here was a story well worth telling, and bearing in mind the current attacks by the likes of Thatcher and Tebbit on the very principle of organised Trade Unionism, the story would serve as a timely reminder to female (and male) workers of today, just why Trade Unions are vital and how exactly our parents and grandparents suffered and struggled in their time to make life that much more bearable for the working-classes of today.

These programme notes would have done much to shape the play's reception at its opening night at the Belfast Civic Arts Theatre on 15 May 1983. Indeed even before a word was spoken from the stage this was by all accounts a remarkable night for a Belfast theatre in the early eighties. Everyone involved in Charabanc was keen to extend the project's sense of inclusivity to the opening night, and all those who had contributed to the play's genesis were invited to come along. As Claudia

Harris recalls (see also David Grant interview in this volume), the 'lobby was buzzing before the premiere performance of *Lay Up Your Ends*' but what was perhaps most notable was that the:

> theatregoers gathering there in friendly clusters that Sunday night were an unusual mix even for the Arts ... Those who had told their stories of working in the linen mills, who had by their histories made this night possible, many who had never gone to a play at a downtown theatre before, were now rubbing shoulders with the theatre faithful (Harris, Introduction *Four Plays* xi).

As Carol Moore notes, these early performances were 'rough theatre but with dramatic sophistication', and they set the scene for Charabanc's growth and ambition (Impulse to Imagination 150).

Marie Jones, Charabanc's writer in residence:

The methodologies that had proved so successful in the case of *Lay Up Your Ends* set a template for Charabanc's next number of productions. The nature of Marie Jones's role in the company would, however, subtly shift over the course of the remaining decade. While Charabanc's second production, *Oul Delf and False Teeth* in 1984, was still very much the result of a collaborative writing process (the original script credits 'Marie Jones and the Charabanc Theatre Company'), by the time we reach the two plays produced in 1986 (*Gold on the Streets* and *The Girls in the Big Picture*) we are dealing with plays produced by Charabanc but which credit Jones as the major writer. These years effectively marked Jones's evolution from an actor who wrote to a writer who acted.

Work began on *Oul Delf and False Teeth* soon after the first run of *Lay Up Your Ends* came to a close, and it was first performed at Belfast's Civic Arts Theatre on 26 Feb 1984. Once again the group had hit upon a moment in the North's history, the 1949 elections, the ideological contours of which, as well as its subsequent neglect in the official record, fitted well with the company's self-image and objectives. *Oul Delf and False Teeth*, replicating the dynamics of the '49 elections, pits the attempts of those campaigning for the Labour Party, and for a vision of politics concerned with the inequalities of class and the uneven distribution of capital, against the entrenched positions of identity politics (Irish nationalist and Ulster Unionist alike) in the North. Those sitting in the audience were implicitly invited to re-examine this moment of political possibility in 1949 with the consequences of its failure, consequences that were all too obvious in 1984 Northern Ireland. *Oul Delf and False Teeth* picks up on many of the concerns that

Lay Up You Ends raised: both present identity politics as divisive and as built upon the over-writing of other potentially unifying discourses marked by analyses of class and power.

In her journal from this period director Pam Brighton gives a fascinating insight into the collaborative nature of the process out of which *Oul Delf and False Teeth* emerged:

> The discussions are positive with people contributing their particular skills – Brenda is tremendous at historical background; Martin at lining up the politics; Marie with her grasp of Belfast character and language. I try to focus it onto a dramatic structure (Six Characters 144).

This antithesis to the then dominant creative model – dependent on a single authorial voice honed in a process that is intimately private – goes to the heart of the early Charabanc project. Not that it was without its problems, as Brighton would have it: 'Sometimes the working process of Charabanc feels like someone newly delivered of quads – how to deal with it within the confines of normal space?' (Six Characters 146) Brighton's journal also articulates just how carefully Charabanc considered issues of performative style and its impact:

> Initially we'd been thinking of the campaign as a theatrical structure with two vaudeville characters weaving through keeping the audience informed. These were introduced partly through fear of the piece becoming dangerously naturalistic in style (Six Characters 145).

The hesitancy around naturalistic performance reveals a company intent on breaking the hegemony of realism in order to explore more interventionist cultural territory. The play would go on to end, for example, with a Brechtian transition to song as the entire cast took to the stage for a rendition of the politically charged 'Belfast the glory of Tories'.

Oul Delf and False Teeth is set in the world of Belfast's post-war market traders and focuses largely on the women who made a living from trading on their stalls. The banter, humour, and conflicts, of the market stall-holders provide a context, and an interpretative space, for the political tensions that build up as the various parties canvass for votes. One of these women, the Catholic Anna McManus, has married Sam McManus, a Protestant who has returned from service in the war replete with socialist ideals. Sam's summation of the situation he has returned to in Belfast is politically powerful, but perhaps overly didactic in tone:

> I fought in a war for two years, wakin up every mornin thinkin it was goin to be my last, because we thought it was worth fightin something as wrong as Fascism. But, now [...I]t makes me realise that this country's run by another bunch of fascists (MS Act I Scene I).

While another character – Eileen, who has joined Sam canvassing for the Labour Party – delivers an analysis that unpacks many of the play's inner dynamics in a manner that is equally direct:

> Sam I know the Protestant workin people are not to blame. If their leaders – the people they look up to and respect are gettin up and sayin that Catholics are lazy and disloyal and can't be trusted, well they're goin to believe them, aren't they? Well that's why I think I'm with the Labour Party cos yous are against bigotry and those men that are tryin to divide us (MS Act I Scene III).

The success of the tactics, as parsed by Eileen, to divide the North by mapping political loyalty onto confessional identity is revealed by the progressive shift of Bertha away from her fellow stall-holders. The Protestant Bertha has been friends with her Catholic neighbours on the stalls for years but her position radically shifts in the course of the play, as she reacts to the perceived threat to her identity represented not just by the leftist discourse of the Labour Party but the move by southern Ireland to declare a republic. Bertha's reaction is inflected with the increasingly polarizing language of contemporary Unionist politics: 'The bleedin body of Ulster is in danger of bein served up on the altar of a Gaelic Republic. Sir Basil Brooke said that!' (MS Act II Scene V). In the following scene we meet Bertha selling Unionist rosettes on her stall: 'Don't let the Green Men get us. Get your rosettes here. Stop the Pope and his men comin over our mountains. Wear the badge and save Ulster from the evil of Holy Water!' (MS Act II Scene VI). The impact of Bertha's pronouncements on her Catholic friends, summed up by one of them (Bridie), haunts the action and points to the piece's central argument: 'These spirits of destruction and evil she's talkin about. She means us! The people she's known all her life. Her only friends' (MS Act II Scene V). In all of this the audience is left in no doubt, the play's future is the audience's present. There is real heart in *Oul Delf and False Teeth*, and a serious-minded endeavour to examine the roots of the modern troubles in the North. But the overt politics of the play's subject matter led the group into a space that lacked the nuance and positive energy of *Lay Up Your Ends*. As a result, when in the piece's final moments the results of the election in the ward are announced (the Ulster Party candidate easily beats the Labour candidate: 6337 to

3599) the lack of possible alterity (while historically accurate) feels somehow over-determined and imaginatively restrictive.

In these terms we can read Charabanc's next production, *Now You're Talkin'* (1986, written by Marie Jones and the Company) as a reaction to the limitations of historical logic that regulated much of the action in *Oul Delf and False Teeth*. For the first time the group set their work in the contemporary moment (mid-eighties) and explicitly explored the inter-communal tensions that so powerfully regulated daily life in much of Northern Ireland. If historical distance provided a kind of safety zone for cultural production, the shift to a direct contemporaneity entailed new risks and pressures for Jones and Charabanc. Something of this is certainly at work in the dilemma posed by finding an ending that allowed for the alterity missing from *Oul Delf and False Teeth*. As Jones would later recall:

> In our third play [*Now You're Talkin'*] we couldn't find an ending. It was about the present. We were frightened of leaving it at a moment where people could say, 'Ah, that's what Charabanc thinks, that's a statement.' We invited people we trusted to come and see it and asked them what they thought of the ending. People made different suggestions, and we tried them (Interview in Martin 91).

Such a process relies heavily on the flexibility allowed by the collaborative approach that had served Charabanc so well; but it was also a high-wire act at times, as Eleanor Methven describes:

> One time I arrived at the show at quarter past seven and everyone said, 'Hurry up, hurry up, you're ending the show tonight, we'll rehearse during the interval.' We'd keep an ending for a week or two and then we'd change it again. Because we're writing our own stuff, it's never finished. We're always striving to make it better – to perfect it. It's a good opportunity that actors don't normally get. You normally get a script, and everything is basically laid down for you. We have a lot more freedom (Interview in Martin 91).

Indeed, while the issue of *Now You're Talkin*'s ending was never fully settled (one of the risks perhaps of the process described by Methven), the two main iterations explored by the company (see below) reveal much about Charabanc's ambitious new territory.

Now You're Talkin' was first performed on 17 March 1985 at the Civic Arts Centre, Belfast. As noted in Wei H. Kao's essay in this volume, it marks an important moment in the evolution of Jones as a playwright, whose writing skills were coming evermore to the fore in the group's inner-workings. It is a play dominated by Jones's ear for rapid-fire dialogue, local idioms, and her sense of comic timing. It is set in a residential centre for 'peace and reconciliation' where groups from different communities are invited to spend a few days living and talking together. As Kao points out in his piece, the play is a recognizable parody of the kind of peace and reconciliation residential centre made famous by the work of places such as the Corrymeela Community near Ballycastle (Co. Antrim). This is a setting that is ripe for dramatic conflict. The nature of the centre's work also means that the dialogue can openly bring the political subtexts of Charabanc's previous two plays to the surface: the women who are staying at the centre for the weekend have been invited there to discuss openly the 'Troubles' and its impact on their different communities. The group that are thrust together in *Now You're Talkin'* come from all parts of the Northern Irish political spectrum (nationalist / Republican; Unionist / Loyalist) and find themselves under the direction of a well-meaning but inept American facilitator named Carter. The fact that the latter shares his name with a recent American President only adds to the implicit critique of ill-informed external interventions into the complexity of Northern Irish affairs. Carter's techniques are often a highly comic mix of new-age mysticism and cod psychoanalysis, involving such disparate activities as Maypole dancing and Primal Scream Therapy. In a wonderfully comic example of theory removed from reality, for example, Carter establishes the goal of the Primal Scream session: 'I want you to relive and fully experience those unreal feelings of hate. Remember, the more pain you feel, the less you actually suffer' (20). Slightly earlier he had asked the women to look out the window on the majesty of the natural world, telling them they are 'All the same species ... we eat the same food, we live in the same land and, united as we are now, we can feel as one the joy and fulfilment of the beauty of nature'. Sitting in a circle holding hands, 'Carter *is feeling every moment of it*' while the '*women are bemused*' (7).

Unsurprisingly, tensions soon begin to emerge in the group; tensions that are only exasperated by Carter's well-meaning foolishness. Having asked what the word 'freedom' meant to the women, Carter feels on safe ground as they play along with the expected answers (concerning domestic duties, marriage commitments, gender roles etc.); but he clearly doesn't know how to handle Veronica, the hardline Republican in the group, when she declares 'Freedom for Ireland!' (6) The declaration breaks the veneer of polite falseness that the group had maintained up to this point and the full depths of what divides them quickly comes to the surface. The rupture proves to be fruitful in its way and the group unite to run Carter out of the room:

Yes! Yes! We do hate each other! We bloody well hate each other! That's what all this trouble is about. What the hell do you know about it? You don't know anything about it! Why don't you just fuck off? (Carter *runs off stage*) (23).

Thereafter the women choose to talk on their terms, terms that rely on blunt speaking in place of Carter's psycho-babble. Importantly the play offers no pat solutions or trite clichés. Open talk proves to be useful but resolution remains beyond the women's (and the play's) grasp. In a comic denouement the women's insistence on staying together to talk further on these newly honest and open terms is interpreted as a sit-in protest. There is much comedic potential in this set up and Jones and Charabanc are adept at exploiting it; but the play inexorably moves towards its more sombre conclusion. Just what this conclusion should, or could, be was, as we've seen, something that much occupied the group. In the play's first iteration, the lights go down on a scene where Veronica (the hardline Republican) and Jackie (who has been described as a moderate Protestant) stand looking out the window as other members of the group conduct a press conference outside. Neither is convinced that much has been achieved in the discussions and the attention their 'sit-in' has garnered:

> **JACKIE:** It is too late now ... (*Grabs* Veronica's *hand and leads her to the window.*) Look out there ... tell me what you see? ... Thelma, the true-blue Brit ... and there are thousands like her who are not going to give an inch ... how are you going to make people like that come with you into a new Ireland?
> **VERONICA** (*quietly*): What other choice do you have ... Fight to defend Ulster until every drop of Protestant blood has been spilt? (52-53)

That final stage image of the two women remaining to hold hands clearly left the group a little unsettled. The image, they knew, could be read as suggesting that Veronica could have persuaded Jackie to move from her Unionist position and thus be read as ideologically loaded in favour of a Republican agenda. In response, Charabanc tried out an alternative ending in which instead of holding hands the two women 'look at each other with nothing left to say' before leaving the stage separately. A more melancholic ending, undoubtedly, but also one that was more representative of Northern Ireland's political realities in 1985.

These years represent the zenith of Charabanc's creative energies and productivity. The following year would see the production of two new works: *Gold in the Streets* and *The Girls in the Big Picture*. Moreover, in terms of Jones the playwright, 1986 would be a particularly important year, as each of these plays would be credited more explicitly to her as writer: 'written by Marie Jones, devised by the Company'. *Gold in the Streets* was premiered in January 1986 at the Belfast Civic Arts Theatre and represents a summation of the group's interests and research up to that point. Rather than settling on one particular historical moment, *Gold in the Streets* moves through time to explore the thematic threads that link Belfast in 1912, 1950 and 1985.[4] Its three one-act pieces are self-contained but thematically connected through their examination of sectarianism and emigration. The first act, set in 1912 and returning us to territory very familiar from *Lay Up Your Ends*, tells the story of Agnes and John Joe, two Catholics who move to Belfast from the country to get work. John Joe is an expert hand-weaver but his skills are no longer needed in an increasingly mechanized industry. They arrive in the city to stay with Agnes's sister, Molly, who has married George, a Protestant from the Shankill Road. Unfortunately, their arrival is an unwanted surprise to George who is worried about the ramifications in the build-up to Ulster Day:

> **GEORGE:** He's not gonna get a job as a weaver up here. That's a skilled job. He's a Catholic.
> **MOLLY:** Could you not speak for him? You know Ernie Simpson, he's the foreman in the factory. He's in your lodge. Could you not vouch for him even though he's a Catholic?
> **GEORGE:** And get branded as a Fenian lover? I'd a hard enough time when I married you, love, but thank God you've done me proud. I'm not getting' myself into trouble. Ulster Day is coming up soon and I want to be able to hold my head up in these streets. (61)

To make ends meet, Agnes takes a job as house cleaner in one of the city's big houses: she has had to pretend to be Protestant to secure the position and she is finally 'caught out' in her pretence and is fired. In the end Agnes and John Joe are forced out of Belfast. They decide to go to England to escape from prejudice, but in the act's final moments the stage's soundscape is filled with English voices telling racist Irish jokes.

The second act, set in 1950, tells the story of Mary Connor (a Catholic) who has returned to Belfast from England with her daughter, Joan. Joan's father, an Englishman, was killed during the Second World War. A nervous Mary arrives home; she is clearly aware that some difficulties lie ahead but is unprepared for just how excluded she will be made feel. Mary and Joan's status as outcasts is brilliantly captured through Jones's skilful blending of the comic with pathos:

> **BERNIE:** My mummy says yous don't believe in God and are goin' to burn in the fires of hell like the black babies in Africa.

JOAN: No. My daddy is in heaven. The man in church said.
ELISH: He couldn't be; he's a Prod.
BERNIE: Even worse than that, he's English. He's bound to be in hell.
JOAN: But we believe in God as well.
ELISH: Well, God doesn't believe in you, so there! (84)

Rejected by her community, in an inversion of the sectarianism that marked the opening act, Mary is finally forced to leave Belfast once again to return to England.

The final act moves the action to 1985 and tells the story of Sharon McAllister. Sharon's husband Davy has been out of work for four years, since the collapse of the DeLorean car factory[5], and is clearly beginning to suffer from depression as a result. Desperate to change his situation, Davy joins the police (RUC). While Sharon sits at home night after night consumed with worry, Davy becomes ever more consumed with the camaraderie and 'friendship under fire' bonding of his new life. Totally oblivious to Sharon's worries, Davy returns home to regale her with stories of near-misses and the adrenalin rush of danger:

DAVY: [...] God, we'd a laugh the day. Big Ginger Donaldson – member I told you about him 'the Michelin Man', gets his uniforms made by Alec Simmons, me and him and Georgie McBride were all in the Landrover goin' up by Divis Flats when there was the sound of gunfire. So we stopped, all jumped out and took cover. Suddenly there was another burst of machine gun fire, silence, and then a psshh sound. As quick as a flask George pipes up 'Hey, Ginger, was that you or the back wheel?' We near pissed ourselves laughing (100).

It is clear to the audience, but not to Davy, that such stories are simply pushing Sharon further to the edge of a nervous breakdown. The ending is inevitable and echoes those of the preceding two acts: Sharon leaves with the children to live with her sister in London. While structurally different to the group's early work, there's a clear sense in which the piece rehearses Charabanc's central concerns: the relationship between the North's past and its present, and the presentation of those stories usually occluded from cultural production.

Both of these concerns are once again central to *The Girls in the Big Picture* (premiered at the Ardhowen Theatre, Enniskillen, September 1986). In other ways, though, the play marks an interesting change of tack for Charabanc. In place of the usual focus on the urban dynamics of Belfast, *The Girls in the Big Picture* has a rural setting and explores the politics of marriage and land in the early 1960s. The play tells the story of a group of women who are all, in their different ways, struggling to find a place for themselves in a social landscape heavily regulated by religious authority (in all its denominations), sexual repression, and the power entailed in holding property. *The Girls in the Big Picture* captures a fascinating moment in the development of modern Ireland (north and south). The rural world of the play, a world that in many ways has remained unchanged for decades, is being transformed by electrification and the creeping infiltration of a globalized cultural modernity (rock n roll music and dance-halls). It is a moment when one mode of social being is passing away while another is not fully formed and the play's younger characters are caught in an inter-generational waiting game: waiting to inherit the farm, to take over the local café, to inherit the village's clothes shop.

The imbrication of gender, property, and power is brilliantly exposed in one of the play's dramatic centre-pieces: the 'Basket Tea'. Mary-Jo, one of the three main female protagonists, explains the rural tradition to Pat (a visiting city-slicker who is more interested in rock n roll and the occasional fling):

> We have them every three months. You see, the women all make up big baskets of food, right? And Jamesie Bickerstaff, he's the auctioneer, he auctions them, and the men all bid for them. Whosoever basket you buy you stay with that person all night and you dance (136).

It is within these contours of social power that the women of the play live out their lives. Their visits to the local cinema thus become a way of escaping the constrictions of their day-to-day existence. These cinema scenes are accompanied by film soundtracks and the heightened melodramatic romantic intrigue of the movies cleverly counterpoints the more prosaic narratives of marriage and routine life discussed by the women. Just as importantly these on-stage cinema visits (the actresses face the audience as if watching the screen) open up a crucial meta-performative space: the women's engagement with culture as a mode of resistance amplifies Charabanc's theatrical project. The political dimensions of fantasy and reality, moreover, will be picked up again by Jones in future works such as *Somewhere Over the Balcony* and *Stones in His Pockets*. In the end, though, a complete escape remains unattainable, for now, and the women in *The Girls in the Big Picture* are left to deal with the realities of their claustrophobic existence. Unlike *Oul Delf and False Teeth*, however, the vitality of the language and vision in *The Girls in the Big Picture* opens up a space of possibility and perhaps even the promise of future alterity.

It is thus apt that the group's next piece *Somewhere Over the Balcony* should focus so fully on the relationship between language and the imagination, and on the possibility of 'otherness' offered by the fantastical. *Somewhere Over the Balcony* premiered at the Drill Hall Arts Centre (London) in September 1987 and marks the creative highpoint of the group's most fruitful period. *Somewhere Over the Balcony* tells the story of life in a Belfast tower block – although not specified, it becomes clear that the setting is the nationalist Divis flats in West Belfast – as it is observed by three women: Kate Tidy (devout Catholic in her thirties); Ceely Cash (irreverent widow in her thirties); Rose Marie Noble (mother of twins in her thirties). The play's setting thus creates a performative lens different to that deployed in the group's early work. While Charabanc had 'strained to remain detached from an exclusive association with any one community or political perspective, *Somewhere Over the Balcony* is written entirely from the perspective of the female nationalist population of Divis' (Maguire, *Making Theatre* 111). That Charabanc would bring the play with equal success to audiences from nationalist and unionist backgrounds is a testament to the integrity and honesty of its engagement with Belfast's communities. It is also a testament to the strength and incisiveness of Jones's writing by this stage of her career.

The formal style of the play was another key to its positive reception. The women occupy their viewpoint on the balconies and the events of the play are relayed to the audience through their interpretative narration. Through them the audience hears of the rushed wedding involving guests in disguise (because they're 'on the run'), a catering van getting blown up (while carrying the forty-five turkey dinners and trifles for the wedding reception) and the siege at the church as the army and police attempt to capture those guests of interest to them. As Claudia Harris puts it, *Somewhere over the Balcony* 'is an irrepressible pastiche of Belfast living. Highly entertaining, the play abounds in black comedy and ludicrous situations and wonderful music' (Review *Somewhere* 47). That said, while highly comedic, the play also adeptly sustains a tension, as Maria R. DiCenzo has it, 'between hilarity and horror; the comedy seduces the audience into the world of the play, but viewers are never allowed to lose sight of the violence (psychological and physical) done to the lives of women daily' (181-182). The play's reliance on fantasy is thus a safety-valve but not an abdication; as Eleanor Methven said of Belfast at that time, 'the parameters of normality have been stretched so much, that no matter what you put in, you will find a parallel for it in everyday normal life' (qtd. in DiCenzo

181). For Charabanc and Jones the conventions of realist theatre were simply not adequate to the task of representing a place where the borders of the 'real' and the 'unreal' had proven to be so permeable. *Somewhere Over the Balcony* represents the high-point of the group's engagement with performative techniques – anti-illusionist use of songs, direct audience address etc. – that had so informed their idea of community-based theatre practice from the outset.

This theatrical maturity is combined to great effect with the brilliance of Jones's comic dialogue, and the nuanced sense of its power to create meta-performative conceits, which is at work throughout *Somewhere Over the Balcony*. One of the women, Ceely, for example, has set up an illegal radio station in her flat and transmits to the local area with information, gossip, and a regular game of radio bingo. It is a clever device, revealing the power of communication (she mainly transmits to other women in the area) but also the sense of lives disconnected and trapped by the violence that surrounds them. In the face of real physical violence, it is the women of the play that truly understand the power of language to transform. We can see the pure joy of this language-play at work here, for instance, when Ceely broadcasts a request to find beds for visitors who have arrived to take part in the Internment commemorations:

> There are sixteen visitors sittin' over in that chapel, two arms the one length, and they still haven't been claimed yet. Now, I want them out and lodged before Charlene and Danny get married, right? Two 'Troops Out' from Manchester, men, middle aged. Two Basque Separatists; they want to stay together. Six of the Communist Party of Great Britain; they don't mind what way they're split up. Two Nicaraguan freedom strugglers and two 'Rock Against Racism' for anybody that likes a wee bit of a dance. And guess who? Valadimir the wee 'Solidarity' Polish fella. That cratur has been coming here on internment anniversary for three years, and he hasn't got a bed yet (191).

Thereafter the play culminates in a scene of high-farce (as reported to the audience via the three women on stage): the wedding church ends up under siege, with soldiers and police surrounding it demanding the surrender of the 'on the runs', turkey dinners are used as bargaining chips, a rival game of bingo breaks out amongst those trapped in the church (much to Ceely's annoyance), a baby threatens to be born before its parents can say their vows, and, finally, a stolen army helicopter is used to break out those of particular interest to the waiting police. The effect of all this is to seduce the audience into a space where the utterly bizarre takes on all the hallmarks of the everyday; as one of the women,

Kate, so eloquently sums it up at the end: 'That's what I love about this place. On a day like today you could be anywhere' (204).

Over the next number of years Charabanc would continue with Marie Jones working as its writer-in-residence, with scripts credited to her as the major author. The result would be four plays: *Terrible Twins Crazy Christmas* (1988); *Weddins, Weeins and Wakes* (1989); *Blind Fiddler of Glenaduach* (1990); and *The Hamster Wheel* (1990). The first of these, *Terrible Twins Crazy Christmas*, first performed in December 1988 at the Riverside Theatre (Coleraine), marked an interesting departure for Charabanc as it is a piece aimed specifically at younger audiences. A comic romp involving a fairy, a confused leprechaun (he's six foot), a giant, a witch, the Children of Lir, and a talking pigeon, *Terrible Twins Crazy Christmas* tells the story of the fight to save Christmas from the evil plots of Baron Begrudger. While a departure for Charabanc, the play did not come completely out of the blue in terms of Jones's interests. One-time Charabanc member, Brenda Winter, had in this same year founded Replay Theatre Company and from the outset Jones had connected with Replay's ambitions to bring quality drama to younger audiences, and would go on to work with Replay on many occasions in the years ahead (see interview with Winter in this volume).

Charabanc's next production, however, saw the group return to more familiar territory. *Weddins, Weeins and Wakes*, which was commissioned by the BBC and first performed at the Shankill Festival in 1989, went through two distinct iterations, starting out as a recognizably Charabanc-style play before being re-written as a musical. While perhaps not fully successful in either version, the piece was undoubtedly another example of Jones's ability to capture the everyday comic genius of a working-class Belfast community (in this case that of the Shankill Road). Equally, *Blind Fiddler of Glenaduach* is an interesting, but only partially successful, piece. As Wei H. Kao explores in his essay, it is a piece concerned with the debilitating effects of sectarianism on cultural production and the transmission of communal memory.

The most interesting of these final Jones / Charabanc plays is *The Hamster Wheel*. It is of particular note because it marks such a radical departure from the concerns that had so dominated Charabanc up to this point. While set in contemporary Northern Ireland, *The Hamster Wheel* has little to say about that place's ongoing political troubles. First produced at The Arts Theatre (Belfast) in February 1990, it focuses on a woman who finds herself as her husband's full-time-carer in the wake of his stroke. It is notable for just how successfully it captures the claustrophobic pressures that such a situation can so often bring to a home; it also reveals much about just how easily such households get forgotten about. While different in theme and tone to Charabanc's earlier plays, *The Hamster Wheel* still involved Jones and the group in the sort of preparatory work that had become their hallmark. As Maria R. DiCenzo notes: the 'production grew out of extensive research with voluntary and professional organizations and individuals in the Belfast community' (182). This commitment to social engagement was reflected in the play's part sponsorship by Belfast City Council. In place of the grand-narrative politics of the 'Northern situation', the play deals with the politics of the domestic, of the family, 'a set of troubles', as David Grant notes, 'as real and as serious as Northern Ireland's political ones, but which get nowhere near the same kind of attention' (Introduction *The Crack* xi). In terms of Jones's development as a writer, *The Hamster Wheel* is important exactly because it 'represents a significant move away from some by now slightly over-familiar tendencies in Northern Irish theatre' (Grant, Introduction *The Crack* viii). It is important in another way too, as it marked the last time Jones would work with Charabanc. While Charabanc would continue until 1995, Jones left the company in 1990 to pursue other creative projects. As the essays that follow demonstrate, Jones's subsequent career would be an extraordinary one; each in their own way also reveals just how important the early days of Charabanc were to the emergence of this remarkable voice in contemporary popular theatre.

---

[1] Marie Jones performed under the name Sarah Jones as there was already a Marie Jones registered as a member of Equity.

[2] The collaborative nature of the *Lay Up Your Ends* project in the end led to some ambiguity over just who should get the main writing credit. However, when the play was finally published in 2008, to mark its 25th anniversary, it was credited to 'Martin Lynch and the Charabanc Theatre Company', a move that seems to accurately reflect the collaborative nature of the play's evolution as well as the key role played by Lynch in its writing and structuring.

[3] The play's insight in this regard would establish one of the recurring concerns of Jones's work, namely not just the way people live but the way in which they are represented by and to others. These are certainly concerns that we read as informing later works such as *A Night in November*, *Stones in His Pockets*, and *Women on the Verge of HRT* (all explored more fully in the chapters that follow).

[4] In this regard we may read the play as performing a template for what would become a pattern in Northern Irish theatre from the 1990s of

multi-strand work, linked by a common set of concerns. See for example, multi-authored pieces like Tinderbox's *Convictions* in Crumlin Road Courthouse, or Big Telly's touring production of *Bog People*.

5 The DeLorean motor company was founded by John Delorean in the late 1970s and established a manufacturing plant in Belfast in the early 1980s. The controversial company produced cars in Belfast from 1981-82 but financial troubles led to the closure of the plant. The car is best remembered today as the vehicle converted to a time machine in the *Back to the Future* films.

4 | Finding her legs: *Lay Up Your Ends* and Marie Jones's international success.

Charlotte J. Headrick

Introduction

The story is now legendary: how a group of out-of-work actresses in Belfast in 1983 formed Charabanc Theatre Company, a company that, according to its historian and former board member, Claudia Harris, 'changed the face of theatre in Ireland.' The founding of Charabanc has been comprehensively covered in the preceding chapter but I would like to begin by noting the continued success of its five founders: Eleanor Methven is a respected actress across the island; Carol Scanlan (now Moore) continues to act, direct, and make award-winning films; Maureen Macaulay is a professional stage manager particularly with the theatre-in-education company Replay; Brenda Winter, who co-founded Replay and served as its artistic director, now lectures in Drama at Queen's University Belfast; and then there is Marie Jones. Of these founding members, it is Marie Jones who has made the strongest mark internationally as a dramatist, while maintaining a strong record as a performer in her own right. In this essay, I argue that the characteristics that have marked Jones's most successful works can be traced back to her time in Charabanc and in particular its first play, *Lay Up Your Ends*. I want also to explore how Charabanc's *Lay Up Your Ends* came to be produced in the United States, and how this reveals something of the obstacles that her work has faced in transferring beyond Northern Ireland. When Claudia Harris travelled from Brigham Young University to see the play's United States premiere at Oregon State University, she said to me, 'it has legs.'[1] She meant, of course, that the play can travel; it can have a life outside of its initial production. This essay traces how

Marie Jones found her legs and in so doing pursued the very same impulse as a writer that drove the establishment of Charabanc.

Lay Up Your Ends

Charabanc's first play, Lay Up Your Ends, was based in large part on the experiences of the women who had worked in the York Street Mills of Belfast in the earlier parts of the century. Brenda Winter writes of how a meeting with Sadie Patterson, a veteran trade union organizer, 'was seminal in motivating the women of Charabanc to tell the story of the 1911 mill-girls' strike' (That's Not Theatre 26). Marie Jones, indeed, would later recall how the leaders of the strike, and the nascent Trade Union movement in general, had been retained in the communal memory of Belfast's working-class communities:

> Growing up in Belfast, from a family whose bread and butter had been the linen mills, the shipyard and the rope works, I had heard the names of Sadie Patterson, Big Jim Larkin, wee Joe Beattie and David Bleakly. They were not called 'working class heroes' then or 'champions of the cause'; they were known simply as 'People who could spake for you' (People who could 129).

That idea of 'People who could spake for you' went to the very heart of the early Charabanc project. If the women of the 1911 mill strike had wrestled with the inequality built into the city's industrial modes of production, the women of Charabanc drew on their story to challenge the cultural modes of production in 1983 Northern Ireland. David Grant, moreover, suggests that *Lay Up Your Ends*,

> addressed an issue that seemed to the Company of far more fundamental importance to women in Belfast than 'The Troubles' – the experience of women whom they interviewed of life in the 1930s linen industry, of the coming of Trades Unions, and by extension of the role of women in Northern Ireland life in general. The production was a triumph. (Introduction *The Crack* xi).

Winter has acknowledged how these out-of-work actresses felt a deep kinship with the women of the mills: 'Charabanc was now seeking, whether they consciously realized it or not, to create a piece of political theatre' (That's Not Theatre 27). Of note too, however, is her clear sense of how the actresses eschewed the use of labels such as Marxist or feminist:

> The company sought to tell their story to all communities and felt that labels would limit that ability. The play's subsequent success with working-class audiences justified the strategic necessity of this approach at that time (That's Not Theatre 33).

Having hit upon their subject-matter the five founders quickly developed a pattern of working that would shape not just this production but Charabanc's output for the rest of the decade. After the initial idea was hit upon, what followed was 'extensive research – recording interviews, finding documents, viewing records of all sorts', out of which the final play was crafted 'during the writing, rewriting, and rehearsal stages' (Harris, Introduction *Four Plays* xi). The interviews and archival research were really the key components in this process, out of them emerged the characters and incidents around which the play's structure would be wound. The entire process was collaborative and fluid. But if *Lay Up Your Ends* was the result of an unstructured process, there is little doubt that Marie Jones began to emerge as a significant presence in the writing stages.

Indeed we can see just how finely tuned Jones was to the issue of language and its performative subtexts when she recounts her memory of the interviews that formed the basis of *Lay Up Your Ends*:

> We spoke to mill workers – obviously they weren't around in 1911, only one or two – but the mill situation hasn't really changed that much. We spoke to women in their 70s and 80s. We took these women's perceptions of men and used that in our play. When they talked about their lives, the men really weren't mentioned very much except things like, 'He really wasn't home very much, and he got drunk, and he gave me a hayden [hit] every now and again.' But the men didn't figure very much in their lives; they were just there to bring the money home. That was how they saw it, so that's how we portrayed the men (qtd. in Martin 1).

The memory also indicates a key characteristic of what would become Charabanc's 'house style' in the years ahead. While shying away from what they saw as potentially divisive labels presenting the company as programmatically feminist, Charabanc's founders were nonetheless very clear in their sense of a theatre that constructed narratives from the perspective of those who had been most radically occluded. If the male characters in *Lay Up Your Ends* are at times peripheral to the action, it is because this is how they appeared to the women at the centre of the action. When it came to staging the material, it was also decided that the actresses would take on the male as well as the female roles. As with much else with Charabanc in its early days, the decision was largely driven by practical rather than theoretical considerations: there simply weren't enough male actors around who qualified for funding under the scheme through which Charabanc had secured some seed-funding. To qualify for funding a person had to have been out of work for at least six months: the fact that the five female founders all qualified for this, while they struggled to find male actors who did, is another telling indication of the conditions that the women battled against in early 1980s Belfast. Financial constraints meant that Charabanc also embraced minimalist (or non-existent) scenery and props, with their aesthetic emerging as a response to necessity. As well as insisting that all characters be played by female actors, for example, the stage directions on the original script for *Lay Up Your Ends* also suggest that the 'set should be minimal – e.g. six beer boxes'.[2]

The drive that informed Charabanc, and arguably all of Jones's writing subsequently, is articulated in her first role for Charabanc as Belle, the ringleader of the wildcat strikers, a role she reprised in the 2009 revival. In one of the most stirring speeches in the play, done as a direct address to the audience, Belle captures the anger at the social injustice and abuse of the women in the mills: 'Well, I don't give a damn. No one man shud have all that money when the ones that made it for him haven't even got what wud put a meal's mate on the table ... Well, that's not fair' (74). Here, then, one can see the first beginnings of the threads that are consistent throughout her work: an emphasis on telling stories of the forgotten, the underdogs, and her attempt to represent both communities in Northern Ireland, complete with humour, and a keen awareness of economic power.

In their encounter with the former mill workers, Charabanc happened upon a specific process of making plays: gathering stories through interviews, taking that material into workshops, and from there fashioning it into a script. For the first play, the actresses called in dramatist Martin Lynch to help them with this project. Claudia Harris writes that in the initial meeting with Lynch, his suggestion that the women should write their own play was met by 'an instant silence, followed by laughter' (Introduction *Four Plays* xvii). In the summer of 1996, Martin Lynch laughed in turn as he recalled to me how inexperienced and at times awful some of the first attempts at writing were, but he also commented that it was Marie Jones who showed something in those first sketches.

As noted above, the original production was marked by its minimalism, using, within an otherwise empty space, a series of beer crates, a few props, signs, mime, and simple costumes with pieces added and removed. It invited its audiences to see for themselves the mill, the mill owners' wives in their fancy parlours, the streets of Belfast, the charabanc ride and other scenes. While the design achieved a Brechtian simplicity and the economy of a classic piece of agit-prop, it was also pragmatic; the play was meant to tour on a limited budget.

Such an approach to staging was characteristic of the early work of Charabanc, first with *Lay Up Your Ends*, then with *Somewhere Over the Balcony*, and with much of the work that followed. A further dimension of the work established here was the pride taken by the company on being able to take their work into any area of Belfast and into any community. The stories they told reclaimed Northern Irish women's history and avoided isolating audiences politically or along sectarian lines. Martin Lynch recalled the first nights of the play: 'The night I sat in a packed Arts Theatre as the audience gave a standing ovation to *Lay Up Your Ends* was a highlight. In the next two nights we packed out the old Shankill Stadium Centre and the Andersonstown Leisure Centre, reassuring us that our work was relevant to both sides of our community' (Why This Play? 146).

The reception of the original production by the Belfast public and the critical attention the company received through it and other subsequent productions (discussed below) did not lead, however, to its inclusion within the professional theatrical repertoire in Ireland or elsewhere. Indeed, it was not until 2008 that the script of *Lay Up Your Ends* was finally published. Brenda Winter writes that if the play had not been published, there was a fear that the script would only be 'a fondly remembered, dog-eared manuscript on the shelves of the Theatre Archive of the Linenhall Library, Belfast – freely available, but only to those who knew where it was to be found' (That's Not theatre 35). Winter continues that the play was not published to be a scholarly text, a document to some past event, but that 'A play is only ever completely realized in production ... that revivals of *Lay Up Your Ends* will still have much to say to a twenty-first century audience' (35-36).

What the play might say to a contemporary audience was tested in August 2009 with the first professional revival of the play at Belfast's Grand Opera House and then on tour. It was directed by Ian McElhinney and produced by Martin Lynch.[3] The glowing reviews of the original 1983 *Lay Up Your Ends* production are in contrast to the mixed reviews of the 2009 revival in Belfast. One of the chief criticisms was that the production suffered from its venue. Deborah Douglas writes, 'There is no denying that a quarter of a century ago this work enticed people to the theatre who might not have been there otherwise, but modern audiences, particularly the young, would struggle to engage with the piece.' Later in her review, she says, 'Perhaps a more intimate setting would have added to the atmosphere.' In his review, Ian Hill echoes much of what Douglas writes, concluding that the production 'missed out on an intimacy which could never be redeemed.'

In 2013, there was a student production at Queen's University by the Queen's University Players. Again, the chief complaint about that production was that the venue was not suitable for the play. Ryan T. Crown, while praising that the play still resonates with modern audiences, noted the venue worked against the production saying that the 'setting in the Elmwood Hall: a cathedral of consumption in the salubrious suburbs of south Belfast contrasts jarringly with the stage world of poverty and penury and despite a talented ensemble cast, the production gets lost in the sheer size and scale of its space.' On 14 March of that same year, founding member of Charabanc Carol Moore staged a rehearsed reading of *Lay Up Your Ends* in Belfast City Hall.

It is interesting to note the contrast between the history of revivals and reproductions of *Lay Up Your Ends* and that of Brian Friel's *Dancing at Lughnasa*, for example. The latter has been remounted repeatedly by professional companies, in amateur productions and in colleges and universities. Turning to my own context as a university professor, in the United States, college and university theatres are in dire need of plays that utilize their strong actress pool. They turn frequently to Friel's play. This begs the question as to why *Lay Up Your Ends* has not been revived more. In the next sections, I explore this very issue by examining the first production of the play in the United States and then charting the history of Jones's later works internationally.

The United States premiere of *Lay Up Your Ends*:

In the 1980s, anyone who was interested in women dramatists in Ireland (North and South) was aware of Charabanc's work. In the United States, Helen Lojek and Claudia Harris were pioneering in publishing and presenting academic papers on Irish female dramatists at conferences such as the American Conference for Irish Studies and the International Association for the Study of Irish Literatures. In the summer of 1995, the American Conference for Irish Studies held its annual conference at Queens University in Belfast.[4] At that conference, several companies showcased their work. Eleanor Methven and Carol Moore performed a section of a Charabanc piece, and Dubbeljoint, with whom Jones was now affiliated, presented a section of *A Night in November*, directed by Pam Brighton. It was through Claudia Harris that I was introduced to Carol Moore and Eleanor Methven. Keen to see if the stories they had told might translate to an audience in Corvallis, Oregon where I teach at Oregon State University, I asked them which Charabanc play was suitable for a college production. They both agreed it should be *Lay Up Your Ends*. In what follows below I detail that 1997 production to draw out some of the issues that we encountered and how they may shed light on the play's production history more generally.

Just as in the Charabanc production, scenic pieces and properties were kept at a minimum; the Oregon version tried to mirror the original approach, keeping the setting to basics. A series of beer crates were used for all the scenes and rough clothes trees on either side of the stage were hung with costume pieces for various scenes. Costumes were created by William Earl; particularly useful were the pieces that were added for the Gilbert and Sullivan 'ladies' as they rehearse 'Three Little Maids from School' from *The Mikado* (the society women are rehearsing for a social event). Earl created hats and matching shawls for the wealthy matrons of Belfast. Costume additions and discards were completed in full view of the audience. With the addition of a hat, an apron, a man's jacket, the actresses made their transitions into the various characters, always coming back to the character's basic costume.

What was significantly different was the use of painted scenery. The Main Stage of the University Theatre at Oregon State is a 360-seat thrust house. Scene designer Richard George built a façade of Belfast brick doors upstage, and certain entrances and exits were made through these doors as well as the standard exits stage left and right. In keeping with the Brechtian mode of the play, George built a larger than life frieze of three mill owners looming over the stage. There was no doubt that these were the 'fat cat' mill owners complete with black bowler hats. Although the scenery was needed to mask the back of the thrust stage, the action of the play was mostly downstage on the apron of the thrust trying to keep with the spirit of the original production, being as close to the audience as possible.

Due to copyright issues, Moore suggested that new music be composed for the opening song. Oregon State University was fortunate at that time to have composer and ethnomusicologist Michael Coolen. For this production, Coolen wrote a piece of music based on traditional work chants, and he taught the actresses the song for that first song 'Belfast Mill.' All of the other songs in the production were learned from Moore's singing on cassette tape. There was also a live fiddle and percussionist on stage throughout and appropriate period music was used as transitions between scenes.

Obviously, one of the challenges for the production was the reproduction of Belfast vernacular. Indeed, Deborah Douglas's review of the 2009 revival would note that even for a Belfast audience, 'Heavy use of the vernacular makes some dialogue difficult to understand for some theatregoers'. For the Oregon State production, Martin Hannigan, a graduate student and native of Belfast, worked tirelessly coaching the actresses in the dialect. For him, it became a matter of home-town pride that these actresses would sound like they came from Northern Ireland. Many reviewers and audience members on seeing the performances commented on the dialect work in the play. Paul Farber, distinguished Professor Emeritus of History, wrote after the performance, 'I don't think I have ever seen accent work that good at OSU ever before, and I'm not sure I've seen ensemble work that good either. You've done a great service by bringing such a strong and interesting play to campus' (Note to author). After watching a video of the production, Carol Moore wrote to me to say, 'I think you did a fantastic job. I was incredibly impressed at the accents – the tone, and rhythms were right, so the general sound felt very northern' (Note to author).

As well as introducing its audiences to the play, the production also had a role in developing interest in and knowledge of Belfast and Irish women's history. The production was accompanied by a one-day interdisciplinary conference on Irish Women's Voices, which brought together United States scholars of Irish theatre, literature and history. On his memory of the play, Paul Farber wrote:

> *Lay Up Your Ends* brought home to me the plight of the Irish working class in the textile mills. I knew something about the American labor story, and the mill strike in the play showed me that such struggles were going on in Europe at the same time. The production was very moving and told a lot about daily life, the class system, and the abysmal conditions of the working class. (Note to author)

In a review in the local paper, the *Gazette-Times*, of the Oregon State University production entitled 'Story of Irish mill strike plays well in U.S. premiere', Natalie Daley wrote that the play 'is a celebration of working women's determination to survive in a man's world, in the world of the wealthy, in a world of small and great cruelty. With its fine music, energy and enthusiasm, it is a surprisingly interesting night at the theater.'

The test for the production then was that it would remain faithful to the Charabanc original while engaging an audience far removed from its original Belfast context. That the Oregon State production succeeded in staying true to the spirit of the original is seen in the comments of Carol Moore on the quality of the set and music, ending her letter saying, 'All in all the production had integrity, commitment and passion for the subject matter, so one can't ask for much more than that. You should be proud of yourselves' (Note to author). Claudia Harris commented also that the original was perhaps grittier and certainly more 'agit-prop', and she thought that the American production showed a bit more reverence to the subject matter because by now the importance of Charabanc was well known.

So, the reasons for the play's neglect cannot be to do with any sense of its context, the specificity of its subject matter, or the minimalist approach to its staging. The Oregon audience coped with the play's broad vernacular and the strongly positive response demonstrated that there was a life for the play outside of Northern Ireland and Ireland. Yet while *Lay Up Your Ends* is ideal for college campuses, as with so many pieces of new theatre, without a Broadway or professional regional theatre production, it has remained largely undiscovered internationally. This neglect of the play's potential for production matches its wider neglect within academic discussion, with each mutually reinforcing the other. This is despite the success of Charabanc in touring beyond Northern Ireland and Jones's subsequent success as a playwright whose work and reputation were to cross the Atlantic successfully. These successes demonstrate effectively the relationship between mainstream commercial success and international transfer and revival. This was something that Jones as a playwright outside of Charabanc was to become more aware of: her adaptation of Gogol's *The Government Inspector* in 1993 toured extensively across Ireland and transferred to The Tricycle Theatre (London), establishing a pattern for much of her work with DubbelJoint.

It is important to note, too, the negative impact on transfer of having a script that remained unpublished until the twenty-fifth anniversary of the original production. It wasn't until 2006 that Claudia Harris's long-term project to publish an anthology of Charabanc's plays came to fruition, although *Somewhere Over the Balcony* was included in an anthology of postcolonial plays edited by Helen Gilbert in 2001. By contrast, in her work as an individual playwright the importance of that relationship between the wide availability of a printed edition of the script and the extension of the life of a play was something that Marie Jones came to recognize. It was of course also facilitated since her rights as sole writer were easier to negotiate than the rights to any collaboratively devised piece. *The Hamster Wheel* was to be included in an anthology edited by David Grant; Samuel French have produced an acting edition of *The Blind Fiddler* and *Women on the Verge of HRT*; *A Night in November* was published initially on its own by New Island Books, then jointly in an edition with *Stones in His Pockets* by Nick

Hern Books. In 2010 Nick Hern also published the anthology that includes *The Milliner and The Weaver*. The precise relationship between publication and success is difficult to gauge, but it is interesting to note Antony Roche's comment that Jones 'broke through in the 1990s to an unprecedented level of success for a contemporary woman playwright with *Women on the Verge of HRT*, *A Night in November* and *Stones in His Pockets*, all enjoying long runs in London and New York' (179) – all published scripts.

Jones's oeuvre after Charabanc

The Hamster Wheel (1990) marked an important moment in Jones's career as a playwright and in her relationship with Charabanc. As discussed in the preceding chapter, *The Hamster Wheel* would be Jones's final play with Charabanc; interestingly, it is also a play for which she received sole writing credit. David Grant believes that *The Hamster Wheel* was a 'quantum leap away from previous Charabanc productions ... ' (Introduction *The Crack* xi). According to Grant, this work 'asserts Marie Jones's position as a playwright of the first order' noting that in the play, she draws fully developed and emotionally deep characterizations, as the 'characters are individual, but they are also tellingly typical' (xii). The original production had a very wide tour, including to Glasgow's Mayfest in 1990.

Yet, with its naturalistic idiom, single room setting and adherence to the conventions of the 'well-made' play, *The Hamster Wheel* was a significant departure for both Jones and Charabanc. Subsequently, she was to return to the inventive theatricality that so marked the production of *Lay Up Your Ends*. In Jones's two most famous pieces, *A Night in November* and *Stones in His Pockets*, the influence of her work with Charabanc and in particular her work on *Lay Up Your Ends* are readily seen. Each involves the performers presenting multiple characters, both male and female; direct audience address; minimalist costume and set; and a mix of dramatic modes. Just as importantly Charabanc's black comedy is seen repeatedly in Jones's work in these well-known pieces.

Stones in His Pockets, *Women on the Verge of HRT*, and her recent *Fly Me to the Moon*, demonstrate the accessibility of her work to audiences within and outside Northern Ireland, irrespective of their background or politics. This is not the case for *A Night in November*. While the play has had a very positive response in both its initial production and subsequent revivals, it has also proved to be the most divisive of Jones's plays. Former members of the Peace People,[5] a long time worker in reconciliation in Belfast, and others, including a number of critics, have found the play to be problematic (see Maguire, *Making Theatre*). Fintan O'Toole claims, 'It is equally insulting to both sides, the only difference being that it insults the identity of Protestants and the intelligence of Catholics' (Insulting both sides 159).

Despite this criticism, the play has had an extended life following its initial production at the West Belfast Festival, demonstrating the power of Jones as a writer supported by a commercial production sensibility and a widely available script. It transferred to London's Tricycle Theatre and subsequently to the Douglas Fairbanks Theater in New York. Dan Gordon reprised the role in a remount for the Lyric Theatre in Belfast in 2002 and on tour to the Perth Festival a year later. Significantly, the play has had repeated success in the United States. In 2001 Marty Maguire starred in a production at the Los Angeles Celtic Arts Theater that then transferred to the Falcon Theater, Los Angeles. This production in turn toured back to the Tricycle Theatre, the Edinburgh Fringe, and to Dublin. In 2006, Maguire returned to play Kenneth McCallister at the Tricycle and the Irish Arts Centre, New York. The following year, Patrick Kielty starred in a production directed by Ian McElhinney in Belfast's Grand Opera House, which transferred to London's Trafalgar Studios. There have been further productions at the ADC Theatre in Cambridge (2010) and at Dublin's Tivoli Theatre (2011).

The same effects can be seen in the production history of *Stones in his Pockets*, particularly in the United States. In researching this piece, I discovered a note from Dr. John Byrne, President Emeritus of Oregon State University attached to a flyer for the New York production of *Stones in his Pockets*. On 7 June 2001, having seen the production on Broadway, he wrote, 'Shirley and I saw this in New York last evening. It was marvelous. I laughed uproariously and wept alternately throughout the second act' (Note to Author). Three months later, the attack on the World Trade Towers happened. Jones's play was one of a number to close shortly after, having run for 201 performances with 11 previews and received three Tony Award nominations. From the initial Broadway production until the present, the play has been performed all over the United States. With the two-person cast, its theatricality, and the simplicity of the set, the play has proved to be popular with regional professional companies all over the country. In 2002, American actors, Bronson Pinchot and Christopher Burns embarked on a US national tour after doing a season in the West End, while previous incumbents in the West End run, Sean Sloan and Louis Dempsey launched a world tour of the show in Australia. In the past three years the play has been in production in the United States almost continuously. It has been produced in the 2013-2014 season in Key West, Florida, Yale Repertory Theatre, Boston, MA, Baltimore, MD, Berkeley, CA, Skokie, IL, outside of Chicago, Fort Worth, TX, South Carolina, and New York State, and this list is not complete. Now, it is being seen on college campuses and community theatres and there have been productions where a woman is cross-dressed to portray one of the two men in the script.

In an interview with Christine Ehren for *Playbill* in March of 2001, Ehren questioned Jones about the rumour that there was to be a film made of the play. Ehren asked if Jones was doing the film script: Jones replied, 'No, I'm not. I don't even go to the movies. I'm not a movie person. I only act in them or write about them. I don't go watch them, for God's sake!' In September of 2013, Maureen Coleman relates that Jones is involved in turning the play into a film. She writes that Jones 'is adapting *Stones* herself for the big screen and her husband, Ian McElhinney, will reprise his role as director.' Coleman also reports that Jones was 'initially reluctant to adapt the play for the big movie screen. However, she is now said to be "very excited" about the project'.

Patrick Lonergan's *Theatre and Globalization* includes an examination of the worldwide franchise phenomenon that *Stones in His Pockets* has become:

> The play itself shows Jones's awareness of the interrelationships of cultural and economic globalization, and she neatly satirizes the resultant development of celebrity culture. Its international success is also an example of globalization, not simply because its themes are relevant to audiences internationally, but also because its commercial success was achieved by the use of business strategies that were first developed by multinational corporations. It is a play that raises questions about how national identity can be exploited as a commodity on international markets, but Jones herself shows an awareness that such values as authenticity and liveness are particularly appreciated by theatre goers throughout the West. (16)

Lonergan's point is well made. Jones's abilities as a writer may have been honed since those early efforts on *Lay Up Your Ends*, but the most critical factor in ensuring that her work would have legs has been the development of business strategies to ensure that she would reach the widest possible audience. These include agreements to transfer shows even as they go into production and a canny approach to publication. *Stones in His Pockets* is about a movie crew invading a small Irish town. Soon, a real movie crew might be invading an Irish town to film the movie version of the play. In a manner not unlike her two characters, Jake and Charlie, Jones seems willing to exploit the very industry she has critiqued. Yet the impulse to do this is exactly the same impulse that led to the creation of Charabanc: a working-class Belfast woman taking control of her own means of production to open doors that would have remained closed to her if she had not worked on her own initiative and with others.

Conclusion

From Somewhere Over the Balcony to The Hamster Wheel, to A Night in November to Stones in His Pockets to Fly Me to the Moon, the legacy of Jones and her work on Lay Up Your Ends can be seen. Charabanc and Jones's emphasis of telling stories of the forgotten, the underdogs and their attempts to represent both communities in Northern Ireland, complete with humour, at times very dark humour, can be seen in the work throughout her career. Lyn Gardner of The Guardian says of the dramatist: 'Jones writes the kind of plays that make theatre critics sneer and ordinary audiences cheer. She writes about what she knows – the Belfast community where she was born and bred.' (The Guardian, 11 August 2004). Of her own writing, Jones states, 'I still write plays about us. I haven't moved away from my background and culture' (The Guardian, 11 August 2004). Dramatists have been long-encouraged to write what they know, and in doing this, writing from the specific, they will find the universal. This mantra is readily seen in Jones's canon of plays. In writing about her own community, Jones has won international recognition and acclaim but her writing is anchored in Belfast. With Broadway and London productions, productions in translation, productions in regional theatres, Jones has earned her international standing as a writer. It all began with Lay Up Your Ends, but the lessons she learnt there about playwriting had to be accompanied by lessons learnt later about the business of being a playwright before such success could be assured.

---

[1] To my knowledge, Harris is the only person who saw the original production on Botanic Avenue and the American premiere in Corvallis, Oregon. She wrote dramaturgy notes for the play.
[2] For original script see, Linen Hall Theatre Archive, Charabanc Collection, box 25.
[3] Lynch had by this point become an established producer of popular theatre revivals including of Jones's *A Night in November* and *Fly Me to*

    the Moon, as well as new plays such as *Dancing Shoes – the George Best Story* (2010).
4 It was at this conference that the news of Charabanc's dissolution was announced. As noted, Marie Jones was now with Dubbeljoint. In conversation, Claudia Harris has said that the summer of 1995 was a bittersweet time for Charabanc, as financial problems led the board to disband the company. Christopher Murray has said of Charabanc: 'Its demise in 1995 was surely premature' (195).
5 The Peace People was a grass-roots organization that set out to campaign for peace in Northern Ireland, founded in 1976 at the height of the Troubles. Founding members Betty Maguire and Mairead Corrigan were recognised with the award of the Nobel Prize for Peace in 1977. The organisation continues its work today.

5 | Brenda Winter

Interviewed by Eugene McNulty

In this interview with Eugene Mc Nulty, Brenda recounts the very early days of Charabanc and her subsequent professional collaborations with Marie Jones.

EMN: I guess the most obvious place to begin is at the beginning. Can you remember the first time you encountered Marie Jones?

BW: In a way it was inevitable that we'd meet. We were both working as actors in Belfast and it was a very small, close-knit community. As for the first time: I think I first met Marie through Andy Hinds – which is interesting really because of a company that's been forgotten to a certain extent (but deserves to be better remembered), Playzone. Marie worked with Andy in Playzone, along with Frank Brennan, Stephen Rea, and Bill Morrison the playwright. There are some really important connections there – that was the first time I heard about community touring for example, they were going into schools, nursing homes and so on. Andy was a friend of mine at university and so I got to know Marie. After that we both ended up involved in pantomimes and things at the Arts Theatre; and then, of course, we both got involved in this idea for an 'Actors' Centre'. We tried to establish an Actors' Centre in Belfast: myself, Marie, Ian Mc Elhinney, Eleanor, Carol, Maureen – actually all the Charabanc girls were involved. We just weren't getting anywhere in town at that stage – one of the main reasons was the cast policy at the Lyric at that time ....

We were all quite like-minded; we all shared a sense of the ridiculous, making jokes that made us laugh, taking the mickey out of Ian Mc Elhinney! Carol and Eleanor had been talking about doing something together, and at the same time Marie, Carol and Maureen and I were involved in a pantomime at the Arts Theatre – it was getting near the end of the contract, and, as we used to say at the time, we were in the Jo Depressos (because we knew there was no work out there). So there's no doubt that ideas were beginning to percolate between us. We'd also all seen Martin's *Dockers* – I mean I'll never forget the first night I saw *Dockers*, just to hear your own language and the way you spoke up on the stage at the Lyric Theatre – it was just brilliant. So we thought, right we'll go to Martin to see if he'll write a few skits for us to perform. Of course Martin said write it yourself, and the rest is history! As it turned out, over the next couple of years I was privileged to witness Marie emerge and develop as a writer.

EMN: It's great that you've brought up that idea of a creative journey, as it's really one of the stories we want to tell.

BW: She did it (begin to write) because she's fearless, absolutely fearless. Although I've written since, at the time I very much would have seen myself as an actress – I knew that was what I was good at. But Marie was never afraid to plunge in; she'd a great sense of herself and who she was – and a real sense of her class as well – that's what Pam Brighton used to say about her – 'Marie has an impeccable sense of class.' And so she just took it on, and she really thrived. Martin encouraged her, and Pam Brighton encouraged her; Carol was writing as well but I think by the end of *Lay Up Your Ends* it was Marie who was emerging as a (writing) talent. She had (and has) a fantastic facility with one-liners, and she also had an instinctive understanding of the women who we were trying to bring to life on stage. We all contributed, we all threw in ideas, but she was the one who was actually able to go and translate those into a written script. I always maintain that's the key skill, actors can throw up all sorts of wonderful ideas in the rehearsal room but it's the person who actually has to sit down at the computer and mould those into a cohesive script, that's where the craft is, and that's where she began her craft.

EMN: Just on that transition – what kind of actor was she when you first met her? I guess I'm wondering could you begin to see the development of a writer in her approach to acting.

BW: No, not at all. I really couldn't have seen that any of us would have gone further in that direction. I think in that regard that we have to pay our dues to both Martin Lynch and Pam Brighton. We took off pretty quickly once the input went in, but the nurturing we got was instrumental. In terms of acting, it was a question of the rawness being knocked out of us – but also of being given a language, because none of us really knew about the whole popular political theatre – John

McGrath etc. – I mean we know all about that now but at the time we thought we'd invented it. In any case we took to it like ducks to water. But I don't think there was anything about Marie the actress that suggested she would go on to be the writer that she became. That said, she was such a quick learner, so smart, she learned really quickly.

EMN: Just before we move the story forward, I wonder could we go back a little. I'm interested in Playzone and the sense that it may have provided a kind of model for Charabanc. Would you say that's fair?

BW: There's certainly a lot in that. Now we went in a different direction (to Playzone), in terms of the type of theatre we did, but if it comes to influences I'd say there are three main ones: the first would be Martin Lynch's popular political theatre and the second would be Andy Hinds's notion (as demonstrated in Playzone) that you could take theatre out into the community. Martin tended to work in Turf Lodge within his community, but what Playzone provided was this idea that it was actually possible to take plays out into various communities. Now I know they'd been doing it in England – but we're talking about a time in Belfast when theatre was extremely traditional and centred on the Lyric and what was going on there. And the third influence, then, was Pam Brighton when she came. She brought with her that whole language of popular political theatre as per John McGrath, 7:84, Hull Truck etc. It's funny, when I went back to university and started to read about McGrath and the whole popular political theatre movement, I kept thinking 'we did that, and that, and that!'. You see Pam had worked so closely with McGrath that she had really absorbed it all and brought it with her.

You know, while we're talking about contexts and influences and so on, there's a thing we need to knock on the head. People said Charabanc and Field Day were in direct competition – not a bit of it, we were that busy doing our own thing we didn't have time to be minding them. We were faintly aware of these boyos up in Derry doing their thing, but we weren't set up in opposition. That idea, that I read about sometimes, is a lot of nonsense.

EMN: There are interesting comparisons to be made between the two though.

BW: Oh yes, and I've written about that myself, but the idea of opposition or competition is just silly. Now I'm not saying it didn't rankle later on when Field Day got all the kudos and there was definitely that sense that they were the big boys and we were the feisty young fillies. And Field Day were maybe blissfully unaware of us, let's be honest.

EMN: That sense of Charabanc really doing its own thing is interesting; I guess it reminds us of just how different it was to the prevailing sense of theatre that dominated Belfast's mainstream scene at that time. What are your recollections of that time; was mainstream theatre as exclusive, and as exclusionary, as it sounds?

BW: Well that's certainly how we perceived it. What we saw was that actresses were being brought over from London ... but you know, looking back at it now, and trying to be fair to Leon Rubin, I think when he took over the Lyric he actually had a tough job to deal with the established figures that had so dominated it from the beginning. I think he had a challenge to break up that coterie; but in breaking up that coterie he also managed to exclude all the young, hungry, talent that was coming up in the city. That talent had to find an outlet – and it found the outlet in Charabanc (and later in Tinderbox, Big Telly etc.). It was a pretty grim place to work at the time. The only other bastion of hope was the Arts Theatre, but they had to do a lot just to survive, they did a lot of musicals and if you weren't all singing all dancing (as an actor / actress) then that was a problem. As it happens I did get a lot of work on their children's shows, which was really useful when I started Replay, because I had worked a lot with younger audiences. Add to all that the fact that the troubles made everything difficult in Belfast in the early 80s, and you have a real sense of just what a tough place it was to be an actress. That was really how the idea of the Actors' Centre came about – it was an act of desperation really.

EMN: Where was that based?

BW: We didn't have a base; well, it was Marie's house! That was another important thing about Marie; that house became a real base for innovative theatre in the city.

EMN: It's certainly a house that seems to have played a big part in the making of *Lay Up Your Ends* – I wonder what are your memories of that time?

BW: The whole process was alive but pretty haphazard. A lot of talking and working through went on in that house; but not in the sense of improvisation – people think we used a lot of improvisation but we didn't really. You know – this is a slight aside I know – but people think the decision to only use women on stage was an ideological one – it really wasn't. We were given some funding, but to qualify you had to have been unemployed as an actor for at least six months – we all qualified but we couldn't find any male actors in the city who did! So it was Pam who said 'Ah play all the parts yourselves' – which seemed a very odd idea to me at the time – but looking back I can see the link between that idea and the work that Pam had done with Monstrous Regiment of Women. As it turned out it became a kind of highlight of what we did in the early days but there was no ideological reason – you know if someone like Des McAleer had been available we would have snapped him up! But back to the house – a lot of the work was done sitting round a table, talking through scenes; someone would have written something (it may have been Martin or Marie or Carol) and we'd all talk it through and the person who wrote it would go off and re-draft it. This process was repeated over and over again – draft, discussion, re-draft, discussion, and on it went. A week before we were due to go into the Arts Theatre we finally got a script – and then when we went out on the road the script kept changing. It was never finished in a way, and really fluid. Sometimes if you went home a bit early, you'd come back the next day to discover your scene was cut! I can remember being handed a speech one night backstage at 7pm and being told it was going in that night! If I did that to an actor now there'd be trouble!

EMN: Was it the sense of co-ownership that made such things OK?

BW: Absolutely; but in a way that was hard too because you were really expected to do everything all the time. But the craic made it all worthwhile you know; we all talked at once – that's my major memory – all of us talking at once, provoking, making each other laugh. There was just a sense of vibrancy, there really was. It was a very special time. And then when *Lay Up Your Ends* was such a success...

EMN: The opening night sounds amazing from the descriptions of it.

BW: It was epic; we were such underdogs and here we were with a hit on our hands. And then mad tours round Ireland, Scotland, Russia – it was wonderful. Then with the second play (*Oul Delf and False Teeth*,1984) ... there's a brilliant play waiting there to get out – but to be honest none of us are happy with it as it is.

EMN: I'd have to say that was my reaction to it – it's almost there but not quite. I suppose my sense was that there's something rather over-determined about it as a piece.

BW: I'd have to say that Pam Brighton's greatest strength is also sometimes a weakness – and that is her commitment to left-wing politics, which sometimes over-rides everything in a problematic way. There's a heart in that play that's waiting to get out. It's an important play though because it was really the time when Marie took over as the group's main writer. It was also the end of my involvement – my second child had arrived and that put the touring out of me – I had to bow out and it was awful.

EMN: It was a really hard decision to move away from Charabanc then?

BW: Absolutely. I had to go see *Somewhere Over the Balcony* in Dublin and it broke my heart because they were just so wonderful. You know Marie is a great collaborator, she's very generous – she takes from people but she gives to people as well. And I think she and Peter Sheridan (who directed *Somewhere*) were just a marriage of minds. Both have that off-beat, anarchic, sense of humour. For me *Somewhere Over the Balcony* is the culmination of everything. I'd have given my eye-teeth to be in it.

EMN: It is a brilliant play – it's kind of got everything that's good about Charabanc in it.

BW: It is a brilliant piece – and you know the other one that's a brilliant piece is the first version of *Weddins, Weeins and Wakes*.

EMN: That's interesting that you'd single that out; perhaps not one I would have when thinking about Charabanc's work around that time.

BW: It was turned into a musical whereas that first version is a brilliantly observed comedy about the culture of the Shankill. It's funny, sharp as hell, and black, black as your boot. The musical version was hugely popular but for me the original one is the one with the real bite.

EMN: I suppose that takes us near to the point when Marie Jones left Charabanc.

BW: That was a difficult time – like with any group of creative people it can often end in rather combustible situations and artistic differences certainly played their part.

EMN: As it happens that time also coincided with the emergence of your company Replay.

BW: Yes, Marie and I had stayed close friends down through the years so it was natural that I'd ask her to write something for Replay. Also, you know, I'd originally conceived Replay as a kind of Charabanc for schools. In other words, it was to be a group that privileged the language of this place, the culture and history of this place – and brought that work into the schools. And so Marie really was the ideal person and she wrote the first play (*Under Napoleon's Nose*, 1988) and then several more in the years to come.

EMN: I wonder should we set the scene for that work a little more broadly. Replay is often referred to as a Theatre in Education (TIE) company – but what does that mean, what sort of project does that encapsulate?

BW: That's an interesting one because TIE has largely been defined by the British model – actor in role, hot-seating, workshops and so on –

but I simply wanted to bring good theatre to schools. So I suppose in many ways Replay was more of an educational theatre company rather than a TIE company (if defined by the British model of such). Replay really set out to bring theatre into primary, secondary, and special needs schools – and then eventually into other spaces like Museums. It did theatre in an educational context in other words. I was never really a workshop person; I was much more a production person. So we'd take a show into a school and we may have had an accompanying pack or they might do the odd workshop or two but Replay was only really Theatre in Education because it did theatre in an educational setting, so it wasn't a TIE company as such. I went into Replay determined to get the best, the best writers, directors, actors – and I did. So, again, it was natural that I would start with Marie.

EMN: Why do you think her voice worked so well within that context?

BW: It was that mixture of popular political theatre – you know the things that popular audiences like that McGrath talks about in *A Good Night Out* [directness, comedy, music, emotion, variety, effect, immediacy, localism (space), localism (identity)] – well it happens that school children like those things too. You know we went into some tough schools, but we never had an unruly audience.

EMN: So your careers and lives have intersected and intertwined for many decades now.

BW: Oh totally; while all that other stuff was going on throughout those years you know we'd also be working together as actors on whatever things came up (theatre, telly). It's been a real privilege to work with her; and I hope she'd say the same about me. It's been good, very good.

6 | Purchasing Power: Material Culture and the Function of America in Marie Jones's post Charabanc plays

Deirdre O'Leary

Introduction

A consideration of Marie Jones's plays written after her departure from Charabanc Theatre Company in 1990 reveals a consistent interrogation of the material culture and unprecedented consumerism that was a defining characteristic of the Irish and Northern Irish economies of the 1990s and early 2000s. Specifically, she considers how the forces of global capitalism, largely realized onstage by either American character(s) or references to American popular culture, both shape the representational apparatus of Ireland and Northern Ireland, as well as the Irish complicity in such a representation. Jones's post-Charabanc plays not only acknowledge this consumerism, but also interrogate how global capitalism both liberates and reifies notions of the Irish and Northern Irish identities. As Jones uses economic class as the primary distinguishing feature of Northern Irish characters rather than religion or politics, this conspicuous consumption serves to interrogate and dismantle notions of identity, religion and nationalism seen formerly as static. At the same time, Jones warns that this consumption is an artificial construct, re-inscribing a postmodern sensibility onto urban sectarianism that does little to alter economic disparity. America, in Jones's plays, is both a neocolonial force as well as a postmodern space where sectarian differences collapse in favour of a generically imagined 'Irish' brand.

The context

The extraordinary socio-economic events of the 1990s in Ireland: divorce legalized, homosexuality decriminalized, and the explosive growth of what has been termed the Celtic Tiger Economy, paired with economic surge and a sustainable peace agreement in Northern Ireland allowed for the unprecedented international visibility of 'Irish' popular culture, a means to engage the Irish and diasporic consumer with material goods and culture from home more forcefully than ever (for more see Lonergan, *Theatre and Globalisation*). As emigration in the Republic and Northern Ireland exceeded immigration totals until the 1990s, the diaspora that exists worldwide allows, through multiple generations removed from the land, a participation in a quasi-invented communitas, a mixture of family history, blended cultures, memory and cultural materialism. The journeying home of expats back to the Republic and North in record numbers during the late 1990s to the mid-2000s, along with the influx of refugees, workers and asylum seekers from outside the European Union, forced, in Mark Phelan's words, a 'theatrical revolution ... as the foundational grand narratives of nationalism, history and modernity have fragmented under the pressure of a superheated 'Tiger economy'' (Fantasy of post-nationalism 89).

Marie Jones has acknowledged how technology and material culture have provided a new way for generations of diaspora to participate in an imagined Ulster and Ireland. As Eberhard Bort points out in 'Come on You Boys in Green: Irish Football, Irish Theatre, and the 'Irish Diaspora'', Jones's post-Charabanc career coincided with the election of Mary Robinson in 1990 as the first woman President of Ireland, and echoes her public extension of Irishness beyond the boundaries of the island. In her 1995 address, 'Cherishing the Diaspora: Address to the Houses of Oireachtas,' Robinson urged people to think of Irishness as 'not simply territorial,' and urged a national embracing of the diaspora as a fundamental part of the Irish culture and identity. She remarked, 'I have become more convinced each year that this great narrative of dispossession and belonging, which so often had its origins in sorrow and leave-taking, has become – with a certain amount of historical irony – one of the treasures of our society'. Her words serve the needs of a nation identifying itself as increasingly international, but also signal a canny acknowledgment of the economic benefits to be reaped from the diasporic marketplace.

The economic effects of the Celtic Tiger in the Republic were belatedly felt in Northern Ireland, and were more stimulated by political developments, including the visit to Belfast by then President of the United States, Bill Clinton, in 1995; the IRA ceasefires of 1994 and 1997; and the first meetings of Gerry Adams and Ian Paisley. These culminated in the 1998 Belfast (or Good Friday) Agreement that articulated an explicit willingness by Republican and Unionist politicians to work within a devolved legislature in which power would be shared between parties. This agreement was brokered in large part through the involvement of the United States government, through the efforts of a team led by Senator George Mitchell. Yet as Mark Phelan notes, cultural and theatrical developments that were the result of the economic boom have been largely confined to the south of Ireland and have not been enjoyed, in the same scale, north of the border. He writes, 'Belfast has not experienced anything like the same extraordinary efflorescence of young independent theatre companies that sprang up in Dublin from the early 1990s onwards, and which may one day be regarded as something of a second dramatic Renaissance' (Fantasy of post-nationalism 90). Phelan identifies what he sees as mitigating factors preventing Belfast and other Northern cities from developing and sustaining the kind of varied, flourishing theatre scenes like those in many cities in the Republic. Such conditions include, 'paltry levels of funding (vis-à-vis comparative levels in the UK and in the Republic) and perforce dependence on lottery funding; the chronic lack of theatre spaces in Belfast; the absence of any kind of consistent Arts Council policy or Arts Plan; combined with the inherent instability of local government and a culture resistant to theatre – all provide deep-seated political and practical difficulties that profoundly affect theatrical practice' (Fantasy of post-nationalism 90-91).[1] Of course such constraints, while limiting, haven't stopped the development and success of such innovative Northern theatre companies as Tinderbox (founded in 1988), and Kabosh (founded in 1994) or the publication and production of works by Northern writers including Gary Mitchell, Darragh Carville, Martin Lynch and Marie Jones, among others. All of the writers and companies listed have received critical attention from scholars focused on contemporary theatre in Northern Ireland. However, the unique challenge for those discussing Marie Jones's works emerges when one considers her identity *as* a Northern playwright, and by extension, how her plays comment or do not comment on the Troubles. While there is no binding assumption that a Northern playwright *must* address the socio-political conflict, it is with no small amount of irony that practitioners and scholars of Northern Irish theatre concede that the most commercially successful play by a

Northern Irish writer to date is not set in the North but in the Republic of Ireland, and is concerned not with the socio-political Troubles, but with the comic goings on of disenfranchised Irish extras on an American financed movie set along the Kerry coast. The long shadow cast by *Stones in his Pockets* has thus eclipsed most discussions of Jones's post Charabanc playwriting career, which has been dismissed by many as apolitical at best, and at worst only superficially engaged with the politics of Northern Ireland. The burden of representation, to document and respond theatrically to life in Northern Ireland is perhaps best articulated by Frank McGuinness's admission, 'The North is the North is the North, anyone who tells you they have left it is lying' (qtd. in Foley 108).

Yet this criticism does not acknowledge how Jones's interrogation of material culture could be read as a democratic means to imagine a new type of identity politics, one that has particular potency for working class audiences. For those inhabitants of east and west Belfast who feel that they have little political agency and even less voice in their representation across a range of media outlets, the idea of material culture as a means to achieve agency is particularly vital and immediate.

America, placelessness and consumerism

Tony Kushner writes in *Angels in America* that 'You do not live in America, no such place exists' (10), and Una Chaudhuri notes that the splitting of the modern unified subject position is made thematically relevant in the very placelessness of America in the modern theatre: '[America] ... is a principal of dispersal, of dissolution, the site where the erasure of spatial particularity is possible' (32). Brian Singleton applies Chaudhuri's notes to a specifically Irish theatrical context to observe that the American has replaced the Englishman as the dominant Other in contemporary Irish drama. The figure of America then, according to Chaudhuri and Singleton, serves the drama by its very placelessness: both 'a betrayal of place' and 'a muted celebration of placelessness' (Chaudhuri 15).

According to Timothy Brennan, Chaudhuri's American 'placelessness' also conveys the consequential fracturing of native culture against the threat of the imperialist forces of globalization. This privileged hybridity of identity, thanks to globalization, in fact occludes cultural difference into the construction of a single social space: 'Rather than the hybridity that is widely acclaimed as being on the rise, we are instead seeing the violent incorporation of global difference into a single national project that is, importantly, even vitally, not perceived as such' (Development to Globalization 127). The economic and cultural distinctions are, according to Brennan, dismissed in favour of a broadly drawn class, linked by manufactured images of place and nationalism rather than by race, religion or birthright.

While *Stones in His Pockets* (1996) is perhaps the most obvious example of Jones's dramaturgical preoccupation with unchecked consumerism and American representation/misrepresentation of Ireland, the topic has long resonated in her work. Carter, the pompous, overweening conflict resolution specialist in *Now You're Talking* (1985) is an obvious example of the stereotypical American whose understanding of sectarianism is superficial at best. Guided by misplaced enthusiasm for drama therapy and temporary reconciliation rather than any sophisticated understanding of the demographics, history or geopolitical rhetoric of Northern Ireland, he attempts to engage a disparate group of republican and unionist women in an array of 'team building' exercises and sing-a-longs, all of which fail. His sole success in guiding the women to any measure of understanding is met when they temporarily unite and throw him out of the room. Her 1989 production for Replay youth theatre company, *It's a Waste of Time, Tracy* uses an American fast food magnet as the opposition against which a nascent Irish eco-consciousness emerges. Terrified by a vision of Belfast as an environmental disaster in the future, young adult Tracy galvanizes disparate communities in Belfast to save the local youth centre from the clutches of the Tasty Texan Maxi Bap.

Of course arrogance and comic self-interest are not character traits solely reserved for Americans in Jones's plays. *Christmas Eve Can Kill You* (1994) charts the chaotic and humorous night shift of taxicab driver Mackers, as he shuttles assorted passengers around Belfast on Christmas Eve. Among the many customers he meets is English actor Daniel Demonte, who is about to start filming a network movie set in the Maze Prison. His level of ignorance of Belfast's history and geography is comically displayed when he expresses his wish to have Mackers drive him around the Falls Road, so that he can view 'authentic working class loyalists.'[2] When Mackers questions whether Daniel's posh BBC accent will pass muster when he plays the head of a loyalist paramilitary group, Daniel answers that the need for authenticity is in direct proportion to the size of the potential audience market: 'Well, if you take the whole of the UK and then perhaps an American release and probably a lot of European sales then here is only a mere drop in the ocean ... the problem is if you get Belfast actors no one can understand them' (*Christmas Eve* 9).

This idea that people in Belfast are not in charge of its representation is made explicit later in the play when a letter is sent to a young British army officer stationed in Belfast from his girlfriend, Debbie, living in England. The officer shares the letter with Mackers. While Debbie explains in the letter that she is breaking up with the officer, the post script reads as follows: 'P.S. I have just watched *Derby* [sic] *O'Gill and the Little People* and somehow I felt closer to you as I wrote this letter and even a little jealous of you being there' (*Christmas Eve* 44). The line gets a huge laugh from the audience, though the story of the actual film's development even more clearly demonstrates Jones's point about limited cinematic representation. The film's development began with Walt Disney visiting Ireland in the hopes of financing a picture with the cooperation of the Irish Folklore Commission in 1947. The Disney Company continued to communicate with the Commission over the next decade and expressed their desire to use Irish folklore as the basis of a film. However, Disney eventually decided to make an adaptation of American writer Hermione Templeton Kavanagh's 1903 collection of stories *Darbie O'Gill and the Good People*. So, in Jones's joke, a young English woman watches a 1959 American-financed film based on an American collection of stories about leprechauns and Irish villagers and assumes that there is nothing to distinguish that mise-en-scène from contemporary urban Belfast.

Jones's next play, *Eddie Bottom's Dream* (1996) is a comic fable warning against rampant commercialism, but problematically posits that Ireland really *is* the land where enchanted fairies roam. Eddie Bottom, a foreman on a new Donegal golf course currently under construction, uncovers a fairy thorn bush while overseeing the development of a new fairway and must decide if the bush should be preserved or destroyed in the name of commercial progress. Eddie's co-worker Charlie shares his concern over the rush towards development at the expense of a problematically narrow definition of 'Irish authenticity': 'this used to be a part of us ... you know, the sheep, the hills and the bogs and soon it will look like something you would see anywhere, you know all them golf courses luk [sic] the same' (*Eddie Bottom's Dream* 2). The field, like Ireland as a whole, is in danger of becoming what Augé terms a 'non-place' where local people, 'don't recognize themselves in it, or cease to recognize themselves in it, or have not yet recognized themselves in it' (Augé 9). Eddie opines that the rush to consume material goods, a trait he largely associates with his wife Helen, is symptomatic of an emerging Irish commodifying instinct that sacrifices local culture in the rush for the new:

> nothing is special unless it costs money. Nothing has any meaning, if it's done throw it out, she takes pleasure out of showing what she has to people who have nothing, that is the only thing that gives us pleasure, makes us somebody, doing somebody else down, lifts us up, we only see value in things, not in people, not in land, not in anything' (37).

Jones's play cautions against rampant commercialization, but ultimately works to preserve a problematic, essentialist fiction, that Ireland is a land defined entirely as rural and enchanted. O'Brien, the fairy king, offers a more pragmatic assessment of the delicate balance between preserving an idealized past and embracing a commercial future: 'So, we save the land and what do we suggest these people do to earn a living, eh? There is nothing else ... this damned golf course will bring tourists ... that will bring these people a living ... all we are doing is playing for time ... that's all and time naturally progresses, moves on' (51).

The concern with the lived experience of Northern Ireland as an actual place, distinct from its commodification was taken up by Jones again in her contribution to *Convictions*, a site-specific collaborative theatre project produced as part of the 2000 Belfast Theatre Festival.[3] The production, composed of eight short plays and one artistic exhibit, was written by eight playwrights and set in various locations in the Crumlin Road Courthouse. In Jones's piece, *Court Number Two*, marketing executives Karen Daly, Claire Cathcart and musician Fabian Morrissey are discussing plans to turn the now disused building into a contemporary reconciliation centre/educational facility for children. They quickly disagree over their different visions, which rely more on cinematic clichés than any nuanced study of the economic or cultural complexities surrounding the judicial process at the Crumlin Road. Karen imagines an unrepentant Catholic republican on trial, whose appearance and demeanour will frighten children, while Fabian envisions a sympathetic republican who 'look[s] like George Clooney' (11). The marketability of the violent history of the site is made explicit in Karen's suggestion that a gift shop be installed in the Crumlin Road Courthouse, where children and tourists can purchase mugs and pencils with pictures of gallows on them.

Material Culture and Global Capital

Convictions and *Christmas Eve Can Kill You* were significant for their interrogation of mediatized representation of Northern Ireland, but it is *A Night in November* (1995) and *Stones in His Pockets* (1996) that most forcefully interrogate the intersections of material culture and global capitalism. While material culture allows for participation in a liminal fictive Ireland, the forces of global capitalism so limit the scope of representation that what emerges is, as Timothy Brennan writes, 'a single social space' (123). In *A Night in November*, Kenneth decides to journey to New York City to watch the Republic of Ireland football team play in the World Cup. At Dublin airport he is given an Irish football t-shirt and he changes onstage.

The change in his physical appearance, where he is visibly marked by the trappings of a materialist consumer culture, occurs at the same time that he admits to 'finding' his Irishness. The enormous success of the play, particularly in the United States, can be specifically interrogated as to the effectiveness of a 'commodity Irishness'.[4] Fintan O'Toole, in his review of the original production, called it 'the most successful Irish play of 1994 and 1995' and suggested the play is 'another type of Irish Revival, with dissatisfied Protestants inventing a Catholic Other to fill in the gaps in their own desires' (*Critical Moments* 70). O'Toole's point is well made, but doesn't consider the *means* by which such a transformation can occur. While the character articulates a growing dissatisfaction with his life, his onstage 'conversion,' is made possible by consumerism. Kenneth does not wear the shirt because he *is* Irish, he wears the shirt so that he can *become* Irish. According to Bourdieu, 'the possession of cultural capital is accumulated through a long process of acquisition or inculcation which includes the pedagogical action of the family or group members (family education), educated members of the social formation (diffuse education) and social institutions (institutionalized education)' (7). Here, however, Kenneth acquires a kind of material capital which subverts or renders irrelevant any necessary cultural knowledge for his transformation. While this may represent an expansion of Irish identity beyond a narrow ethnicity, for Kenneth participation in the Irish communitas at Dublin airport is made possible only by enthusiastic consumerism. This suggests a more fluid yet superficial understanding of cultural transformation, a forerunner of a sociocultural trend this century that John Seabrook identifies as 'nobrow culture' where the old distinctions between elite culture and commercial culture are torn down and the new arbiters' value of what is 'good' is defined in terms of what is 'popular.' Nobrow culture is not without hierarchy, but status is achieved and identity is informed by the consumption or acquisition of material goods, not by birthright or education. Perhaps not surprisingly, Seabrook identifies the pre-eminent land of materialist nobrow culture as America, but its global dominance of mass culture spreads far beyond its boundaries.

Brian Singleton and Eamonn Jordan have suggested that the success of *A Night in November* is largely due to the play's conceit that one actor plays every role. The monological drama, according to Singleton, offers a stirring critique of the static narrative of Ulster identity through actor Dan Gordon's seamless transitioning between characters. Jordan notes the degree of theatrical agency the solo performance allows, arguing that the very markers of identity are demonstrated in the play as performative. He cites Kenneth's noticing a scared, thinly disguised Republican supporter at the game and whispers the words to 'The Sash My Father Wore' so that he might better pass as unionist spectator (Kicking with both feet 52). This suggests an expansive if temporary definition of Irishness or Ulsterism to include any person who can literally and metaphorically sing the songs or wear the requisite jerseys.[5] Ireland's changing demographics in the 1990s supported an increasingly international brand identity, demonstrated by the members of the Republic's football team, drawn from across the Irish diaspora and managed by Jack Charlton, a member of England's World Cup winning team in 1966. Yet Jones's Northern Ireland is represented as so homogenous that at the match Ernie is shocked at the sight of three black players on the field for the Republic, and though he doesn't name him specifically, he calls out to the 'big Gorilla' on the field – almost certainly Paul McGrath – Ireland's most popular player in the early 1990s. It's hard to believe that a football fan like Ernie wouldn't know who Paul McGrath is. He was born in England and famously played in the top flight of English football for Manchester United and Aston Villa, but what is more interesting is Ernie's comical inability to incorporate race into his dialogue on Irish identity: Paul McGrath's father was Nigerian, his mother Irish. Driving to the game Ernie yells at a car with a Republic of Ireland license plate, but reserves more disdain for foreign players who claim Irish citizenship and play under the Republic's flag. Ernie is obviously unaware that one of the leaders of the Easter Rising, and the first Prime Minister of Ireland, was Eamon DeValera, born in New York to a Spanish father and Irish mother.

Kenneth's post-match transformation in a quest to know and understand Catholic Republicans is one of the biggest challenges in the play. As Mark Phelan notes, the danger in this reductionist dramaturgy is that as easily as a jersey can be put on, it can be removed and the cultural traditions that inform Ulster Protestantism run the risk of disappearing in Kenneth's enthusiastic shopping spree for the Irish brand. While it can be noted that Kenneth's disavowal of sectarian violence at the play's end is life-affirming, it is sustained and inspired by common stereotype: a boozy camaraderie where everyone's a mate or a relative. In fact, Kenneth stays in New York City by exploiting the same diaspora that had enabled Ernie's hated 'pseudo Irish' footballers to wear the jersey. While Kenneth's declaration that he is 'an Irish man' is as much about the inclusiveness of that identity to him as it is redefined through sport (and performance), it is also a sign of the commodification of identity politics. If Kenneth's Ireland is informed primarily by the spectatorship of a football match and the opportunity to be something other an unhappily married man, then audiences must question how lasting this transformation will be.

The last line of the play provides little indication of what Kenneth will do next. The play fails to suggest how this temporary Ireland-of-the imagination, a kind of Erin Disneyland, can provide Kenneth with anything more than a good time away from his marriage and a football match. Ultimately the transformation he undergoes must be intensely personal, but can it be sustained outside the temporary holiday surrounding a soccer match? The play does not say. Mark Phelan argues that the apparent inclusivity of his new position is undermined by the fact that it is based on a politics of absorption rather than inclusion, of negation rather than negotiation (Fantasy of post-nationalism 103).

Jones's *Stones in His Pockets* revisits these issues to suggest the means by which Irishmen revise the trope of representation, and warn of the dire consequences of a nation's people buying too heavily into material simulacra knowingly packaged as authentic national culture. Rather than a football match, the playing field in *Stones* is an American film production shooting on location in the west of Ireland. The backdrop is merely a strip of celluloid, with a light blue sky and clouds. The cinematic image is juxtaposed with thirty odd pairs of worn shoes, presumably belonging to the characters Jake and Charlie routinely inhabit. The actors metaphorically step into these shoes, and the play deals with the contrast between the reality of the local Irish and the dream world of Hollywood, and by extension, America. The production only serves to complicate the two worlds by having two actors play all of the roles in the play, changing moment to moment. In their multiple and seamlessly changing roles, accomplished only with changes in voice, posture and gesture, the two actors provide commentary on the misunderstandings and disruptions that occur. In one intricate piece of stage performance an Irish male actor plays a female American trying (and failing) to play an Irish landowner. As in *A Night in November,* the performance gymnastics of actors playing roles across gender and ethnic identities reveals them as performative, but also points out the superficial nature of culturally mining a community to represent it commercially.

Piped in before the show and during intermission is the orchestrated score from *The Quiet Man*, intertextually referencing John Ford's 1952 film shot in Ireland, starring John Wayne and Maureen O'Hara. *The Quiet Man* is arguably the most famous film shot in Ireland and with knowing irony, the film being shot in Jones's play is titled *The Quiet Valley*, suggesting, according to Jacqueline E. Bixler, a move 'from individual to mass passivity' (433) in terms of Ireland's allowing and participating in the breaking down of national, cultural and economic borders, mapping the local to more broadly reflect the global. The action of the play spans a few days spent on the film set. Jake and Charlie's primary interest in being film extras is financial. Charlie has recently lost all of his money in a failed video store venture that ultimately could not compete with the larger video chain conglomerate, aptly named Extra Vision. Jake, having recently returned to Ireland from a prolonged stay in the United States, is on unemployment and living with his mother. They are the locals; Jake is from the town where the film takes place and Charlie is from Northern Ireland, yet are both rendered alien and Other to their own surroundings as they easily concede authority and spatial jurisdiction to the American film crew and star. The proprietors of the local bed and breakfast, the audience learns, have rented out their own living quarters to film crew members and are sleeping in a caravan parked in their driveway. They have willingly given up their personal space for the sake of economic advancement, but metaphorically their actions speak to the town's and, by extension, the country's willingness to allow the cultural apparatus of the globalized Hollywood film industry inhabit their land and determine the most effective, and thus most narrowly defined, representational strategy.

Representations of the Irish in the film are comically juxtaposed with the presentation of the Irish extras on set, who inhabit a thoroughly late twentieth century Western consumerist lifestyle, yet routinely perform, for money, the familiar role of disenfranchised nineteenth-century Irish peasants in the film. Hilariously unable to maintain a sufficiently 'dispossessed' look of a turf digging peasant, the extras routinely puncture the liminal realm of representation, questioning the passivity of the peasant characters, laughing at the superficiality of the production set up, and challenging the hackneyed strategy of the stereotypical representation. Not that most members of the film crew are particularly concerned about the authenticity of the film. The lead actress Caroline Giovanni's Irish accent, bad as it is, is hardly a concern, and in a line reminiscent of Daniel Delmonte in *Christmas Eve Can Kill You*, the accent coach explains, 'Ireland is only 1% of the market' (*Stones* 13). Yet the presentation of a quasi-familiar Irish product to the global market is of the utmost importance, as new cows must be brought in because the native Kerry cows, 'Don't look Irish enough' (*Stones* 28).

The play takes aim at not just Ireland's tourist industry, that sustains quaintly bucolic homogeneity despite Ireland's growing multicultural population, and is complicit with the Hollywood producers' neatly packaged marketing scheme little changed since *The Quiet Man*. Of course, the film company's presence in the town greatly enhances the town's potential as a tourist destination and increase the cultural capital of the pub and restaurants. Just as with O'Brien in *Eddie Bottom's Dream*, the town inhabitants are more than willing to comply with any cinematic packaging of Ireland, so long as it financially benefits them. Restaurant proprietors clamour after Caroline, trying to get her to take a bite of an offered sandwich so as to be able to advertise: Caroline Giovanni was served here. Perhaps then it is not so unreasonable that Caroline, a vain, seemingly untalented yet internationally famous movie star falls in love with what she perceives to be Ireland: 'Look around this place … God it's just heaven on earth … I love this place … I'm third generation you know, on my mother's side … I do get a real feeling of belonging here, you know that. You people are so simple, uncomplicated, contented' (15).

Irish and Irish American audiences can laugh at this display of enthusiasm, built on nothing but idealized projection. Nonetheless, Caroline's idealization of the Irish and Ireland is really not very different from Kenneth McCallister's Irish football frenzy, and Jones posits his 'transformation' complete whereas Caroline's is comic fodder. Granted, Kenneth has the benefit of living on the island, while Caroline is an American celebrity in Ireland temporarily; yet, each displays little knowledge of Ireland's geography, history or culture beyond enthusiastic first impressions and tourist-projected wish fulfillment.

Their engagement with other Irish people is equally limited: Kenneth's first and only trip across the border into the Republic of Ireland is to Dublin airport, yet he declares himself 'an Irish man' at the play's end, based on his experiences in New York City. Caroline's assertion that her being 'third generation [Irish] on her mother's side,' allows, in her mind, some measure of emotional ownership of the landscape and culture. Yet when it comes to engaging with other Irish people, her relationship is marked by getting town native Sean Harkin thrown out of his local pub. Turned away physically and emotionally from the Hollywood dream world that was to be his salvation, Sean Harkin commits suicide by drowning. Sean Harkin's death and the film company's refusal to halt production for the funeral mobilizes the extras to rebel against the director and production crew. The rebellion takes numerous forms but largely includes characters getting drunk at Sean's wake, explaining that it's out of respect for Sean and for Irish tradition. Mickey, the veteran extra, returns to the set drunk from the funeral and not surprisingly is ordered off the premises. The name Mickey is also used by Jones in *A Night in November* as the forename of Kenneth's Irish drinking buddy in the New York pub. The name, long a generic slander against the Irish, evokes a familiar image of an untrustworthy, drunken, violent Irishman. Mickey's behaviour only confirms the negatively held stereotype, allowing Simon to affirm his disposability: 'there are three hundred and fifty of you ... nobody is even going to notice [you]' (*Stones* 53).

The play's triumphal end has Jake and Charlie resolutely trying to write their own screenplay, playing the American capitalist game, with, the audience believes, the benefit of local knowledge. They set up a production company, Canvas Productions, named for Charlie's sole belonging, and pitch their idea to the director who rejects them. Undeterred, Jake and Charlie decide to write the script anyway, armed with little more than their belief in their ideas and each other. The audience takes pleasure in noting that the extras in this movie will be the stars, turning the cameras onto what is, for them, ostensibly real and authentic. Yet the image that Jake and Charlie end on is cows, the same image that is so thoroughly familiar to Irish heritage and cinematic representation that Martin McDonagh chose it to comically comment on the banal and claustrophobic Irish existence in his 1996 play *The Beauty Queen of Leenane*: 'Ireland is fecking boring, that's what it is. Just look at your window and you'll see Ireland. (looks out window) There goes a cow' (55).

Come Together: The liminal space as communitas

In the previous examples Jones explores how global capitalism forces a renegotiation of Irish and Northern Irish identity such that what is represented is more simulacrum than anything else. Yet there is also a significant tension in Jones's plays whereby popular culture, particularly American popular culture, provides a liminal space of participation and rapprochement for characters long distanced from each other. The New York City bar Eamon Doran's in *A Night in November* is a Rabelaisian carnival space to support Kenneth's new identity as Irish football supporter. A man's life is defined solely by his love of Frank Sinatra and the song 'Fly Me to the Moon' replaces the requisite hymns in his makeshift, cross community funeral in *Fly Me to the Moon* (2012). In *The Wedding Community Play* (2000), a marriage ceremony of a Protestant bride and Catholic groom is marked by the temporary creation of community not by the acceptance of the marriage, but by the singing of American pop music.

The Wedding Community Play[6] (2000) was a collaborative, site-specific theatre project that ultimately involved over ninety people and was fifteen months in the making. The project began in September of 1998, when six Belfast community theatre groups from across sectarian lines met to develop a community play based on an idea by producer Jo Egan and playwright Martin Lynch. All of the community theatre groups were situated in west and east Belfast, and were committed to creating a collaborative drama about the marriage between a Protestant bride (Nicola) and a Catholic groom (Damian). The production required that the audience move between the Nationalist Short Strand area of east Belfast to the Catholic groom's house, then the Protestant bride's house on the Loyalist Templemore Avenue, a short distance away, then on to the church in the city centre for the ceremony and then finally to a pub on the banks of the Lagan river for the reception.[7] The production not only cast the city of Belfast as a particular theatre landscape, but used theatre to suggest the possibility of re-mapping the political geography of Belfast to allow for contrapuntal discussions on identity, politics, religion, and cross communal marriage in Northern Ireland.[8]

The Wedding Community Play project addresses the apparently stubborn divisions of the Belfast inner city where streets are physically closed off from each other by the physical barriers of so-called Peace Walls, and territories marked by political murals, all under a highly militarized system of surveillance. It is not surprising that the two characters in the play have grown up two streets away from one another and never met; the political impositions on the geography, which has then enforced cultural and social discrimination, has made such an encounter highly unlikely, despite the advances of the Peace Agreement and ceasefires. A line was worked into the play that Damian and Nicola met at a U2 concert in the city centre. This is a reference to the famous May 1998 concert at Belfast's Waterfront Hall where lead singer Bono escorted unionist political leader, David Trimble and his nationalist counterpart, John Hume, onstage for a photo opportunity to drum up youth support for the Good Friday Agreement. It was the first time Trimble and Hume had made a joint appearance since April, when they and six other party leaders struck a compromise accord on how Northern Ireland should be governed. The photo ran on the front pages of the international papers for days.

In the play the mixed marriage is hardly embraced by both families. Cassie, the Protestant grandmother of the bride, purposefully wears a red, white, and blue corsage to the church and reception, saying that 'God will protect [her] against the Romans' (5). The groom's parents convey the same concern for not just the safety of the couple but the chances their marriage has at lasting. However, here it is the wedding ceremony that is of particular interest. The wedding ceremony was staged at the First Presbyterian Church in Rosemary Street, the oldest in the city, established in 1644.[9] The scene begins traditionally with the bride walking down the aisle to the bridal march by Wagner, then with a change of lighting and the introduction of American popular music, the ceremony turns into an interactive song and dance number about gender politics and sectarianism. The bride is greeted by characters sitting in the pews frozen in emotionally expressive tableaux, some aghast, some thrilled, all pointing at her walking down the aisle. While the metatheatricality of the ceremony is purposefully alienating, the only sense of community is created by the use of pop standards, which both Protestants and Catholics join in enthusiastically. If the music of U2 brought the bride and groom together initially, this idea of communitas is developed further by the ceremony sing-along, which humorously punctuates moments in the service, including 'Take Another Little Piece of My Heart,' 'Shout!' 'R.E.S.P.E.C.T.,' 'Goin to the Chapel' and 'Everlasting Love.' At one point during the reciting of the vows, all of the women in the church sing 'Take Another Little Piece of My Heart' to their respective husbands. Such a number, while imposing a heteronormative model that doesn't necessarily include everyone, goes some way towards fostering a sense of community among the disparate members of the congregation, wedding party, and audience. Additionally, as the audience had earlier been divided into different groups seeing concurrent scenes at the different sites, the wedding ceremony is the first time that the audience and company at large share a space. Audience members sing along while characters dance in the church. In some ways, Jones is using popular music so that *everyone* is able to participate in the celebration of this cross communal marriage. Exploiting the reach of American popular culture, it is perhaps not surprising that the moments of people coming together in the church do not involve sectarian or religious songs, but American pop classics. The musical performances both herald the triumphant, celebratory nature of the service, as well as engage everyone present in the shared language of song. Unlike in *A Night in November*, no one is needed to whisper the words in our ears so that we might feel as though we belong.

While the wedding ceremony doesn't have quite the same kind of raucous, carnivalesque quality to Kenneth McCallister's transformative night at Eamon Doran's, it does suggest a way to cultivate a liminal space of community that acquires much of its emotional power by its very temporary nature. If identity is shaped more by acquisition of material goods and shared popular culture, then the potential exists for identity in Jones's plays to be defined not as fixed, but amorphous, constantly changing, absorbing new products and adding new members who put on new shirts and sing new songs and make their own films. In some ways this advocates a kind of cultural disposability – people linked by their shared superficial desire to consume the same material goods and cultural reference and discard as they go. Jones dispenses with the grand narratives of nationalism and modernity and fixed notions of race and religion and politics.

As cultural theorists examine the role of culture in the reproduction of existing social and economic structures, Marie Jones asks us to think about how material culture and global capitalism both shapes the representation of Irish and Northern Irish identity, as well as suggesting ways in which its scope may expand to include those not bound by geography or religion or politics. In some ways this is a radical approach to imagining a new kind of identity politics and diasporic participation in Ireland and Northern Ireland.

---

[1] Despite Phelan's pessimistic overview, there are in 2014 more producing companies across Northern Ireland than ever before and an established circuit of regional touring venues, with a renovated Lyric Theatre and new Metropolitan Arts Centre in Belfast itself; while in 2013 Derry-Londonderry celebrated a year as the inaugural UK City of Culture. The

expansion of theatrical performances outside of institutional theatre venues has been a marked development in the work of Kabosh and Big Telly, for example.

2 The Falls Road has been the heartland of the Republican community in West Belfast since the outbreak of the Troubles.

3 The courthouse had become notorious during the Troubles as the site where suspected terrorists were tried under the Diplock courts without a jury, often on the basis of testimony supplied by paid informants. It ceased to be used in 1998, under the provisions of the Good Friday Agreement, and until *Convictions*, had remained derelict. The production was a site-specific promenade performance in which the theatregoer walked through the rooms, watching scenes about both specific crimes and victims, as well as scenes about what to do with the Courthouse itself. For further discussion of the production, see for example, Michael McKinnie, 'The state of this place: *Convictions*, the courthouse, and the geography of performance in Belfast (Tinderbox-Theatre-Company).'

4 For a further discussion of the shift in conception of Irish identity from ethnicity to commodity see, for example, Luke Gibbons's, *Beyond the Pale: Race Ethnicity and Irish Culture.*'

5 This relationship between clothing and identity is explored further in 'Maguire's "You're Only Putting It On": Dressing Up, Identity and Subversion in Northern Irish Drama.' Jones uses costume changes again in *The Milliner and the Weaver* (2010), discussed in more detail in Dawn Fowler's essay in this volume. While Henrietta and Elspeth are separated by economics, class and material culture, changing clothing can offer each of them some measure of protection, albeit temporarily.

6 For detailed description of the production and play text, see Deirdre O'Leary, 'No Go/New Show: Staging Belfast in *The Wedding Community Play* and *Convictions*.'

7 For many members of the cast and crew, as well as members of the audience, the journey across the thresholds into Catholic and Protestant homes in the Short Strand was the first time they had ever entered the homes and neighborhoods of the other political community, despite their proximity.

8 The Belfast production grew out of a desire to examine the incredibly low percentage of interfaith marriages in Northern Ireland, as well as take advantage of the site specific opportunities newly available in east Belfast thanks to the ceasefire and 1998 Good Friday Agreement.

9 The church has also served as the venue for other theatre productions, most notably the revival of Stewart Parker's *Northern Star* in November 1998.

7 | An Alternative Peace Process: Violence and Reconciliation in Marie Jones's Plays.

Wei H. Kao

Introduction

Despite Marie Jones having (co-)authored or adapted over 30 plays since 1984, (co-)founded two theatre companies, and having had a powerful impact on several companies that have come in the wake of this work,[1] she has not been given the kind of critical attention that such achievements surely merit. When Jones's work has been addressed, moreover, it has often been to position it within the satirical tradition of Irish Protestant writers.[2] One could argue that a major problem for critics has been that only a very limited number of Jones's plays have been published; it was not until 2006 that a small selection were collected with a critical introduction by Claudia W. Harris under the title *Four Plays by the Charabanc Theatre Company: Inventing Women's Work*. The reasons for this situation are myriad and complex, but it is certainly the case that most mainstream publishers are unused to publishing scripts with a collaborative writing style that is 'radically different from the primarily text-based theatre tradition' (Jordan 5).

It should also be noted that although some critics have maintained that Irish male dramatists, for instance Sean O'Casey, J.M. Synge, Brian Friel and Tom Murphy, have created strong female characters that are 'splendid ... complex [and] subtle' (Harris, Introduction *Four Plays* 116), their portraits of Irish life derive mainly from male observations. Thus, so this line of argument continues, the perspective 'that is exclusively female is very seldom represented on stage' (O'Toole, *Light Heart* 10). Focusing more specifically on Northern Irish drama, this phenomenon may be attributed to the fact that public discourses around identity in Northern Ireland have been largely conditioned by the male-oriented nature of Republicanism and Loyalism, which circumscribe 'both the experience of the Troubles and the representation of such experience on the stage' (Maguire, *Making Theatre* 95). Consequently, different perceptions of the Troubles via the different positionalities of men and women are underrepresented or can only be understood 'within a narrow range of gendered stereotypes' (Maguire, *Making Theatre* 97).

Rather surprisingly, perhaps, this sense of occlusion was reinforced by many feminist scholars, who at times dismissed Charabanc and DubbelJoint from their critical purview, or only gave them a few lines of description, such as that the founders of the two theatre companies 'were initially reluctant to use the term feminist' to label their works (Lojek, *Playing Politics* 89).[3] Such institutionalized neglect is probably rooted in a broader social hesitancy towards female theatre practitioners and their work. What Jones sought to challenge, one could argue, was a theatrical culture that had largely kept male-centric conventions intact.

This essay will therefore examine how Jones deconstructs gendered ideologies through the eyes of politically complex characters. In an attempt to assess the political boundaries that Jones crosses, this essay will consider a selection of her plays that deal, either directly or more obliquely, with the Troubles. Among the plays which disclose an alternative, or at least less represented, facet of Northern Irish life are *Now You're Talkin'* (1985), *Somewhere Over the Balcony* (1987), *The Blind Fiddler* (1990 / 2004), *A Night in November* (1994), and *The Wedding Community Play* (1999). This comparative study of these plays, centering on male and female experiences considered separately, aims to demonstrate Jones's appeal for justice and peace in a region where quite fraught tensions still exist.

Now You're Talkin': Let's Talk about Barriers

A central aim of *Now You're Talkin'* (Charabanc, 1985), I wish to argue here, was to encourage audience members to see sectarian boundaries, their position within them, and the possibility of moving across or beyond them. With this commitment the play was performed in more than thirty venues in Northern Ireland and the Republic of Ireland between 1985 and 1986, attracting working-class audiences who were most likely 'unaccustomed to theatre-going' (Lojek, Troubling Perspective 333). The play features two Protestant and three Catholic women from Belfast who are either misled or are self-motivated to join a cross-community peace-making programme. Its original audiences would have easily recognized the setting as a satire of endeavours such as the Corrymeela Community (located near Ballycastle on the north Antrim coast). The programme is to be conducted over a weekend by an American facilitator at a reconciliation centre based in a seaside town.

Unlike most contemporary mainstream Irish drama, which is still dominated by the idea of the single authoring voice of a playwright, *Now You're Talkin'* is a collaboratively written play that has its origins in a series of workshops, with members drawn from across Northern Ireland's communities. In the wake of these sessions Marie Jones was largely responsible for bringing the resultant ideas to the stage as a coherent whole. The play opens with a series of scenes in which the American facilitator uses various ploys designed to make the women become friendly with, and open up to, each other. As he puts it, he wants them to 'find out new things in an atmosphere that's ... conducive' (6). For instance, they are taken to the seashore to collect shells and to join in a collaborative exercise based around maypole dancing. All of this, as he tells them, so as to 'liberate our minds from the futility of personality' (13). Though not all of them follow the dance willingly and squabbles occur – mainly about the sectarian significance of the colours of the ribbons on the maypole – they are in a sense trapped within the confines of the reconciliation centre and forced to participate. It is ironic, moreover, that the American character never attempts to understand the historical roots of the sectarian violence in Northern Ireland but, as a complacent outsider, tries to de-contextualize these women through irrelevant dancing and role play, rather than observing their individual and collective troubles.

The climax of the play is shaped by the way in which a news agency deals with the information about 'a group of women [who] have barricaded themselves in a room ... [at] a reconciliation centre in Portrock ... these women ... are not believed to be armed' (37). One reporter breaks through the 'barricade' to interview the women, who do not actually have any views in common, about the search for peace in Northern Ireland. Special notice should be taken of the fact that this collaborative play, involving as it does the cross-community efforts of Charabanc's members and the various groups with which they worked, does not throw light on any possible process of conciliation but instead lays bare the difficulty of peacemaking at the reconciliation centre – a space that ironically becomes the epitome of the divided society in which these characters live. The reconciliation centre is thus a parallel arena that reflects the sectarian communities in which these women and their families live out their lives. It may be argued, as I think this play does, that a feasible solution for sectarian conflicts can emerge only if the audience members are able to recognize themselves and hear the voices of the antagonistic Other on the stage.

It is interesting to note, indeed, that the highly politicized atmosphere of the play created difficulties for the Charabanc members when it came to settling on an appropriate ending. According to Jones herself, for example, all the members worried that Charabanc would be read as 'making a statement' and this would back the group into a too closely defined ideological corner (qtd. in Foley 50). Their wariness at making a firm statement resulted in two different endings that – while critical of the violence used within and around Protestant and Catholic communities – were nuanced in slightly different ways. The two endings both demonstrate the quandaries that these women, and the communities from which they come, are forced into. One ending shows Veronica, a die-hard republican disclosing her antipathy towards sectarian arbitrariness: 'Jesus, don't think that I want to live in a priest-ridden Ireland, but I can't live in one run by Union Jack waving bigots!' (53). The other ending illuminates the despair of Jackie, a Protestant woman, in seeing revenge established as a normative practice: 'The people whose husbands are being shot dead because they join a police force to protect it. They believe in their cause just as much as you believe in yours cos there's 20 ordinary Joes standin' by to take the place of every policeman that's killed' (53). Specifically, the two commentaries which appear in the alternative endings not only exhibit the paradoxes in both Unionist and Republican ideologies but confront audiences with the possible futures to which the communal divide will take Northern Ireland.

More significantly, the fact that *Now You're Talkin'* can be seen as a political satire is implied in the play from the allusion to the Dirty Protest at the all-women Armagh Prison in 1980-81. The play includes, for example, a moment of scatological performance when Thelma relieves herself (on stage) during their sit-in protest at the reconciliation centre. It is an event that may remind the audience of the 'no wash' protests of women republican prisoners – tactics borrowed from male prisoners at Long Kesh Prison in protests that began in the late 1970s. The fact too that Veronica, the play's uncompromising Republican character, is tied to the bed by force and gagged with a scarf by this mixed group of Belfast women, indexes the deprivation of freedom of speech as well as other human rights during the Troubles. Despite the fact that these scenes are performed, to some extent, in a light-hearted way, they illustrate 'a strikingly ironic performance of barbarity' against the official criminalization of the disobedient Other, or the Northern Ireland nationalist minority (Pilkington 63). In other words, Jones and her team reproduced this nauseating image of the Dirty Protest in contrast to the civility of the privileged rulers in order to dissect how violence has resulted in a vicious circle from which no individual can escape and has given rise to social unrest in the wider world outside the reconciliation centre.

It can be claimed that *Now You're Talkin'* reveals a strategy shared by many Irish playwrights by refashioning the public memory of notable events in an attempt to elicit a less polarized perspective in a politically divided society. By dramatizing Catholic and Protestant women in Belfast and identifying their shared problems, it may help in breaking down the sectarian barriers between hostile groups. The following section will focus further on working class women who are trapped and under surveillance in the nationalist Divis Flats in *Somewhere Over the Balcony*, and how Jones 'forges a meta-reality, a world of illusion' in order to rattle the barriers through the use of dark humour (Foley 45).

Somewhere Over the Balcony: Satirizing An Armed Patriarchy

There can be little doubt that sectarian violence has left lingering effects at all levels of Northern Irish society. *Somewhere Over the Balcony* reveals how violence has been internalized in the everyday life of this particular West Belfast Catholic community. It is a play that is often thought to mark Charabanc's 'height of creativity,' exemplifying, as it does, Charabanc's 'new aesthetic' that blurred the 'borderlines between the surreal and the real, between sanity and madness' (Foley 46). Indeed this play, I wish to argue, marks an artistic breakthrough that allows for deep-set critiques of sectarian violence and gender inequality through an experimental dramaturgy.

The play unfolds on stage with three women protagonists working together like three embedded journalists providing an interpretive lens through which the audience *hears* the absurdities happening around Belfast's Divis Flats. Acting as 'modern-day Cassandra[s]', they allow the audience to experience the raids and chaos that envelop these women who are usually silent and regarded as loyal supporters of republican causes (Harris, Introduction *Four Plays* xliv). Differently from Charabanc's other productions, *Somewhere Over the Balcony* initially derived from, according to Helen Lojek's interview with Carol

Moore, 'a surreal dream which Eleanor Methven had about the Troubles' (In Conversation 346), followed by a series of interviews with women living in Divis Flats. Situated between black comedy and political drama, between other balconies above and below, between hovering helicopters and a siege on the ground, between a wedding and a funeral, between watching and being watched, the play presents an unusual perspective, namely that of those 'Cassandras' who are trapped in the Divis Flats.

With a husband or male family member who is either dead, on the run, or under detention, each of these women attempt to make fun of their isolation in the community. Indeed their humour – which they use to distance themselves from the tumult around them – builds up a kind of 'Brechtian alienation' to be observed by the audience (Lonergan, Marie Jones 167). The technique produces a central irony for the performance: these female protagonists do not see themselves as alienated as they observe a succession of surreal events, whereas, without witnessing the actual raids and riots and only eavesdropping on the descriptions, the audience is conscious of how these women characters are confined to the balcony and unable to move elsewhere. The balcony is therefore symbolic of the margin of the public sphere where women in the Divis Flats are given limited standing room.

Differing from the stereotypes about West Belfast lives lived in perpetual misery during the Troubles, *Somewhere Over the Balcony* satirically questions this perception through the perspectives of local people. For example, when Kate Tidy appears on stage, 'carrying a large tin rubbish bin ... plonk[ing] the bin down and sit[ting] on it,' (*Somewhere* 447), she subverts the traditional role assigned to Catholic Republican women of alerting menfolk to approaching danger by banging the lid of the bin. For Kate, the bin is symbolic of her precious time alone every morning: 'If it wasn't for me having my own bin I wouldn't know peace and quiet ... I can hold my bin out 'til my heart's content' (447). The rubbish bin has been an object that incites arguments amongst critics. Megan Sullivan believes that, through this prop, Kate is 'constructed by its political significance and her relation to the state' (qtd. in Owicki, Rattle Away 162). While Eleanor Owicki argues that Sullivan overlooks '[how] Kate actively uses the prop to resist [an] overly determined role' assigned to Republican women in the Divis Flats (Rattle Away 61). That a group of German tourists – visiting Belfast 'on their holidays ... for the internment anniversary' – want to purchase a bid lid from Kate for ten pounds also subverts the often sensational perception of the Troubles (*Somewhere* 447-8). The bin lid is no longer an alarm device but a souvenir to be retailed with make-believe significance: 'That was the first bin lid ever banged on internment morning ... was handed down from my granny. It is a collector's item. It's worth ... two hundred pounds' (450).

A critical perspective of Northern Irish sectarianism is also introduced through Kate's observation of how foreign media misguide the public's reception / perception of the Troubles. When a child falls from one of the balconies and swings two floors above the ground on a TV aerial, no one comes to his rescue but the child is asked by a German photographer 'to hang out of an empty flat with a tricolour in his hand,' so that they can take news photos for the anniversary of Internment (450). The fact that the desired photograph is of a child hanging over a balcony with a Republican flag succinctly indexes the kinds of stereotyped images constructed by external media agencies.

The subversive nature of *Somewhere Over the Balcony* also lies partially in the presentation of female sexuality that is rarely given explicit attention in the 'armed patriarchy' that one could argue was hegemonic during the Northern Irish troubles (for more see Galligan). When long-lens cameras are pointing everywhere to keep the Divis Flats under surveillance, these women take erotic pleasure in peeping through binoculars at the 'hot and sweaty' British soldiers who are sunbathing on one of the observation towers (*Somewhere* 448). The besieged wedding scenario at the heart of the play is similarly subversive. In a series of carnivalesque inversions the women describe undercover Priests, disguised nuns, and a best-man who turns out to be wanted by the British authorities.

Somewhere Over the Balcony certainly provides plenty of evidence that the prolonged Troubles have enormously 'stretched the parameters of normality in Northern Ireland over the past few decades' (Bort, Female Voices 274). It is perhaps curious, then, that only a limited number of Irish women dramatists – for instance, Anne Devlin and Christina Reid – have combined political satire and black comedy to analyse sectarianism – as is the case with these characters in *Somewhere Over the Balcony*. Notably, this half surreal and half comic play aims at reaching political neutrality while also striving to show how sectarian barriers could be brought down through the power of humour.

The Blind Fiddler: Irish Music as A Lost Cause?

Along with *Somewhere Over the Balcony*, *The Blind Fiddler* is a Jones play that demonstrates how sectarian barriers may be breached by non-vociferous but no less effective dramaturgy. This play does not feature political tensions as explicitly as do *Now You're Talkin'* and *Somewhere Over the Balcony*, but instead introduces a retrospective view of the eve of the Troubles in the 1960s. It is also a memorable play that has been staged, in different iterations, several times from 1990 to 2004, during different stages of the peace process.[4] *The Blind Fiddler* focuses on the transition of one family from a humble rural background to the security, but restrictiveness, of a middle-class Belfast existence. In particular, the daughter of the family, Kathleen, has been traumatized by her mother's insistence that she should have nothing to do with the world from which her father came. He was a great fiddler, and she showed signs of the same ability – but her mother wants to keep this, as she sees it, ideologically suspect activity hidden from her Protestant neighbours. For years Kathleen had believed that her father disappeared once a year to go on a pilgrimage to Lough Derg. It is only when he has died that she discovers he in fact went back to his County Tyrone home-place, to play the fiddle and be true to himself. Set in the present-day, the play casts its audience back (through a series of flashback scenes) to the years just before the outbreak of the troubles. While a slight piece, it has interesting things to say about the relationship between culture, politics and class.

Its genesis is also interesting. Originally a one-act play produced by Charabanc in 1990 (*The Blind Fiddler of Glenadaugh*), Jones returned to the idea for a re-worked, and lengthened version, in 2004 (now titled *The Blind Fiddler*). The 2004 version did much to reveal the central concerns, and the power of their consequences, that lay at the heart of the earlier piece – as in this exchange between the mother and father (Mary and Pat):

> **MARY:** I'd thank you not to fill her head with stories about drinking and dancing and people starving ... I don't want either of the two of them children thinking that to put a bite on the table all you have to do is dance to a bloody fiddle with a lot of oul drunken farmers.
> **PAT:** I want her to know about her family ... my background.
> **MARY:** Did you tell her you were sent up here with hardly a shoe on your foot and one ten shilling note ... oh aye we all had a great time being poor and starving ... that's no fairy story ... I want my children to feel important, I want them children thinking that there [sic] as good as them that come from money ... My children are going to be something ... not like us... (*Blind Fiddler* 8)

Such family secrets were possible because the mother intentionally barred her children from any cultural practices too closely aligned with nationalism. Not only are the children forced to imitate the accent of well-to-do Protestants, but Kathleen's brother, Joe, is sent to a prestigious music school and thus into a world of classical music far removed from the fiddle playing of his father. As for Kathleen, she was forced to learn ballet when she was a child. To fulfill her mother's wishes, Kathleen passes the exams to become a civil servant. To ensure her children an advanced social position in the future, Mary chooses to leave her husband to run a pub on his own, while she moves with her children to Cave Hill, a respectable Protestant area of Belfast. The father, forbidden by his wife to play the fiddle at home, invents the idea of an annual retreat in Lough Derg when in reality he makes a pilgrimage to Drumquin, his hometown in County Tyrone, to enjoy the company of local musicians. As he puts it: 'there I'm a young buck again' (33).

As for the mother, her desire to disguise her children into appearing more Protestant than Catholic, and her over-dominance at home, reveal how a sectarian society has given her a strong sense of insecurity about being a Catholic. Her over-protective attitude towards her children is symptomatic of a paranoia induced by the grind of daily sectarianism. Distrust, fear, and a sense of uncertainty have become common feelings among ordinary people, and this devastates the creativity and artistry needed for the sustainability of a tradition. It can thus be argued that *The Blind Fiddler* is an attempt to visualize life in a politically polarized society.

A Night in November: A Loyalist Insider and Outsider's Odyssey

Apart from the fact that Charabanc often experiments with various styles in their productions, the depiction of chaos in reality and in the fictional world has been a notable feature of this theatre company. A focus on the chaotic may explain why *Somewhere Over the Balcony* is intertwined with surreal elements. What we might describe as a nonlinear approach to the Troubles is further demonstrated in *A Night in November*, a monodrama in which a Protestant male character finds ways to cure his conflicted political selfhood. *A Night in November* presents the journey of self-discovery made by an Ulster Protestant minor civil servant, Kenneth, who is surrounded by, and also sometimes participates in, sectarian attitudes to Catholics. Life is unremarkable for him until the World Cup qualifier match (November 1993) in which the football teams of Northern Ireland and the Republic met in Belfast. The match resulted in a draw, but this was enough for the Republic to qualify for the 1994 World Cup in the United States.

This series of sports events form the fulcrum around which Kenneth re-examines the (institutionalized) bigotry that has so marked his life in Northern Ireland up until this point. His journey to New York to cheer for the Republic of Ireland, without telling any of his friends and family in advance, becomes a personal odyssey in which he peruses the connotations of being Irish/British and the possibility of living out his identity in a different manner. The play illustrates how the opposing fortunes of the two football teams came to be an ideological locus for many of the die-hard fans: 'it's not about who wins, it's about who doesn't win' (*Night* 72). Of greater significance, however, is how this minimalist play – in which the set is only a rostrum with three differently coloured levels, and a single actor – lays bare the inter-communal antagonism while simultaneously illuminating Kenneth's epiphany regarding the possibilities for the nascent peace process. The theatrical subtlety which Jones achieves through Kenneth's monologue on a minimalist stage speaks for the silenced who suffered trauma throughout the Troubles. Tellingly, Kenneth experiences not only a split between his private and public selves, but also between the nation and the individual in a fragmented society. It is of even greater significance that Jones does not employ a woman, or a group of characters, to demonstrate these points but chooses to focus on a male character from her own Protestant community.[5] The focus on a Protestant man's traumatic experience – portrayed in an autobiographical manner by a female playwright – can be seen as a strident critique of Northern Irish politics. That is, the sectarian ethos not only prevents communication between two individual beings but also damages the prospects for inter/cross communal exchange.

One interesting but less discussed facet of the play is the characterization of Deborah, Kenneth's wife, a relatively minor role whose presence at home as an over-dominant, puritanical Protestant always distresses her husband. Despite Jones's characterization of Deborah being more one-sided than that given to Kenneth, it implies the underrepresentation of Unionist women who have, as some critics argue, 'a greater problem when it comes to confronting their oppression as women' (Ward and McGivern 71). They are often stereotyped as people who are 'more deeply imbedded than is the case within Republicanism' (Ward and McGivern 71). Arguably, Deborah may be seen as a victim of an armed patriarchy in which women are subjugated by the patrilineal order imposed on them by family, religion and community. Not being conscious of the oppression of her fellow womenfolk in the Unionist community, her constant demand on Kenneth that he acquire a golf club membership is not only for the purpose of reconfirming the privileged, Protestant position of her entire family but also for a firm recognition that she is following the proper male-centered order which her fundamentalist father has inherited without question.

The premiere of *A Night in November* in 1994 was, as Ian Hill recalls, 'a revelation' with 'the audience sitting in a semi-circle,' while they were 'marveling at the Gordon-Jones ensemble' (Welcome Return 16). The revelation may partially be on account of the design of the theatrical set through which each audience member can, during the performance, develop his/her view of the protagonist and his troubles from a unique position in a multidimensional space. A private perspective may thus be cultivated in order to view Kenneth not from an individual viewpoint but in connection with other audiences that have politically and religiously sectarian backgrounds. In other words, they do not have to take on the prepared perspective of the playwright but can view Kenneth from the perspective of being both an insider and outsider of his community, and have a chance to see that 'not every Prod is a tight-tush, not every Taig a free Celtic spirit' (Hill, Welcome Return 16). Even more significantly, Kenneth's odyssey of self-discovery both mirrors and encourages the shifts in social attitudes in Northern Ireland in the post-Troubles period of the late 1990s. The transformation of Kenneth is therefore a revelation of the break from bigotry to pluralism in the years to come.

The Wedding Community Play: Let's Untie The Knot

Jones, among her contemporaries in Northern Ireland, may be the most versatile in trying different theatrical expressions to stage the various facets of the Troubles, although her productions have not always received positive reviews. *The Wedding Community Play*, a piece of site-specific theatre (also known as environment theatre), was a cross-communal production with Jo Egan and Martin Lynch in 1999. This project unprecedentedly put together six community theatre groups which involved at least ninety people ranging in age from ten to sixty-five, and across sectarian lines, over a year from September 1998 (O'Leary, 'Staging the City').[6] According to Maggie Taggart, a BBC journalist, this play attracted about seven hundred audience members in Greater Belfast with eight shows fully booked out.[7]

Site-specific theatre, as devised by Richard Schechner, has been active since at least the late 1960s in the US. However, 'until the ceasefire [it] would not have been safe' for theatre practitioners in Northern Ireland to draw heavily on its spatial and performative possibilities, and no 'community theatre groups had [ever] worked together' in quite this way (Moriarty 15).[8] The performances of this play thus did not take place in any regular theatre venue but 'the real homes of Geordie and Jean Marshall (Templemore Avenue) and Margaret and Sammy Todd (Short Strand)'; the audience 'board[ed] a bus in downtown Belfast and travel[led] to both homes to eavesdrop on the happenings, tensions and joys on the day of a mixed marriage,' as advertised in local newspapers (qtd. in Moriarty 14). Witnessing the marriage of a Protestant bride and a Catholic groom later in a real church, the audience got to meet at a pub for the reception.

Dramaturgically, apart from adopting the principles of site-specific theatre, the piece also drew on Augusto Boal's 'Theatre of the Oppressed' concept, and by so doing transformed silent and usually passive audiences into active participants. In this connection, workshops and the interactions that followed between on-the-spot 'spect-actors' and real actors in a domestic setting were able to ignite a cultural intimacy across sectarian lines. Through storytelling, brainstorming, questioning, rehearsing and experimentation, both formal and informal, a democratic process was (re-)installed. It may thus be deduced that by abandoning the convention of a proscenium theatre, *The Wedding Community Play* brings together theatre practitioners from different communities to share their own experiences in a workshop setting.[9] During the workshop, an opportunity is created for audiences to observe the problems and difficulties that face a couple in a mixed marriage and their families. Furthermore, for some audience members who had never entered a home that was the opposite of their own religious tradition, they were immediately prompted to take on the role of 'spect-actors' – spontaneously being both insiders and outsiders – while they were also observing their own experiences in the community they belonged to.

However, the making of *The Wedding Community Play* which was co-written by Jones and Lynch, a Protestant and a Catholic respectively, was not always in a totally benign manner. As Jones has described herself as a 'Nationalist', regardless of her Protestant working-class background, her works have 'not [been] considered representative by large parts of Protestant communities in the North' (Urban 253). To reduce suspicions from paramilitary groups, the project coordinators had to seek understandings from these groups prior to the workshops: '[t]here are certain things that you don't do in Belfast without doing something else first,' explained Maureen Harkins, a community theatre director based in Belfast (see O'Leary, Staging the City).

Their experiences may explain why staging this play in private homes, as opposed to in a standard theatre, did not happen earlier in Northern Ireland, despite this dramaturgy becoming gradually more popular in the 1960s in the US and some European countries. Such theatre can, after all, be seen as a form of resistance to the conventions, regulations and taboos that endow a public space. *The Wedding Community Play* to some extent liberates participants from the drawbacks of a proscenium theatre in which interactions (between the performers and audience members) are limited. As mixed marriages in Northern Ireland used to be discouraged, two private homes – one from the Catholic community and the other Protestant – potentially form the bases of communal and individual exchange by opening doors to those off-limits areas in Belfast. It could therefore be suggested that what Jones and her team intended to evoke here was a micro-conversation in the area of political discourse. Community theatre practitioners such as Jones and Lynch, then, were clearly attempting to establish a platform that would initiate inter-communal dialogues, and allow audiences to observe or take a chance to be at peace with themselves.[10]

With its humorous touches, *The Wedding Community Play* invited audience members to be both intruders from the public sphere and inhabitants of a private home during the performance. They were prompted to observe closely a cross-sectarian event involving the power struggles, discrimination and prejudice that condition the mixed reactions of two families. Interestingly, the audience became part of the script in which they were not only bused from the different locations of East and West Belfast but had drinks together at a pub during the interval before they were taken to the next performance venue. The intention of the playwrights was for the audience to be both observers and participants in the drama – the hope being that this might lead to improvisations in every performance that were based on the reactions of the audiences. Although busing a mixed audience group across the sectarian divide (during the evening) was not without risk in the post-Troubles period, a wedding celebration portends a different route for the peace process in which sectarian differences are tolerated and understood. The success of the production partially stemmed from 'the agreements from the paramilitaries,' both republican and loyalist, before the show was put on (O'Leary, Staging the City).

Conclusion

Despite the fact that Marie Jones has only written a limited number of plays that are directly engaged with the Northern Ireland Troubles and their aftermath, they have been deliberately created to demonstrate the largely ignored experiences of Protestant and Catholic individuals, especially those deemed politically and religiously nonconformist. It should also be noted that Jones adopts a distinctive strategy by revealing hidden yet unsettling aspects of Northern Irish life. When asked about her working class upbringing in east Belfast, Jones replied: '[i]t is what I am. My background is important to me ... Nearly every time I've known who I was writing for. It's very focused. It frees you to do what you want. It makes the plays more vivid.' (qtd. in Johnston 203). In this connection, these plays visualize a theatrical space which allows Jones to present how sectarian violence leads to political absurdities (and vice versa) and hampers interpersonal relationships. By not endorsing any specific political persuasion in Northern Ireland but instead dramatizing the everyday difficulties of living in a deeply divided society, Jones questions the over-celebration of masculinity in Nationalist / Republican and Unionist / Loyalist discourses that has unrelentingly oppressed both genders regardless of whether they are on the social margin or seemingly within the mainstream.

---

[1] Companies such as Big Telly and Tinderbox, it is largely acknowledged, 'owe a debt to Charabanc' for its pioneering work in dramatizing women's issues and concerns that were socially marginalised (DiCenzo 184).

[2] For instance, Jones's frequent application of black humour may have its roots in the works of Jonathan Swift, and she has been likened to George Bernard Shaw for employing 'literary laughing gas to mask the painful messages' (Hill, *Marie's Game* 19). Jones is also often compared with male Ulster dramatists such as Sam Cree, Sam Thompson and Stewart Parker, because they all explore the causes and effects of sectarian divides yet cloak their wishes for reconciliation in comedy. For details, see Philip Johnston's *The Lost Tribe in the Mirror: Four Playwrights of Northern Ireland* and Eamonn Jordan's 'Kicking with both Feet?: Marie Jones's *A Night in November*.'

[3] Helen Lojek, in her 'Playing Politics with Belfast's Charabanc Theatre Company', criticises Anthony Roche's *Contemporary Irish Drama: From Beckett to McGuinness* (1994) and Christopher Murray's *20th-century Irish Drama: Mirror Up to The Nation* (1997) for limiting their references to Charabanc to no more than one page. The 2009 revised version of Roche's *Contemporary Irish Drama* did not rectify this problem. Other examples include Lionel Pilkington's *Theatre and the State in Twentieth-century Ireland: Cultivating the People* (2001), *The Cambridge Companion to Twentieth-Century Irish Drama* (2004), and

D.E.S. Maxwell's often-cited article, 'Northern Ireland's Political Drama' (1990).

4 Premiered by Charabanc in 1990, the play was entitled *The Blind Fiddler of Glenadaugh*. It was reproduced by Lane Theatre Company as part of the Edinburgh Fringe Festival in 2004 with the revised title, *The Blind Fiddler*.

5 Deborah R. Geis argues that the reason why female playwrights tend to be 'drawn to the monologue form' is in part to demonstrate the 'conquest of narrative space [to] be viewed as a reification of the feminine subject in-process' (119). Obviously, Jones intends not to use such a convenient pattern to narrate the communal experience of Loyalists. It should also be noted that Irish women playwrights have produced works that are autobiographical (eg. Anne Devlin's *After Easter*), ethnographic (eg. Christina Reid's *The Belle of the Belfast City* and Dolores Walshe's *In the Talking Dark*), and/or political (eg. Mary Kenny's *Allegiance: Winston Churchill and Michael Collins: 1921-22*.)

6 Six community theatre groups were involved in the production, including Ballybeen, Stone Chair, Doc Ward, Tongue and Cheek, Shankill and Real Wood. According to Gerri Moriarty, there were 150 participants in the making of the play from September 1998 to October 1999 (14).

7 One may argue that the success – with all the tickets being sold and the play being awarded the 2000 Belfast Arts Award for Best Drama and Arts Partnership – was due to the calmer political atmosphere occasioned by the Good Friday Agreement that had been signed in 1998. The script is archived at the Linen Hall Library, Belfast. Part of the script is available on the BBC website 'Eyewitness':

8 Gerri Moriarty was the key narrator in *The Wedding Community Play*. She recalled how this play was workshopped for fifteen months and the ways in which the audiences participated in the development of the performance on different sites. For details, see her article 'The Wedding Community Play Project: A Cross-community Production in Northern Ireland.'

9 Based upon Richard Schechner's principles, Paulo Freire's *Pedagogy of the Oppressed* and Augusto Boal's *Theatre of the Oppressed* were applied during the workshop for *The Wedding Community Play*.

10 For instance, Playzone, founded as a touring community theatre in 1977 by director Andy Hinds, a graduate of Queen's University Belfast, and Frank Brennan, a Dubliner, was the precursor of Charabanc. According to Winter, 'it was the Playzone model which allowed the Charabanc actresses to recognise that it was possible to tour theatre to community centres.' (That's Not Theatre 21). Jones and Stephen Rea were both members of Playzone.

8 | Marie Jones and the DubbelJoint Theatre Company: Performance, Practice, and Controversy

Fiona Coffey

Introduction

DubbelJoint Theatre Company was founded by Marie Jones, Pam Brighton, and Mark Lambert in 1991. Jones and Brighton had worked together previously with Charabanc Theatre Company. As discussed elsewhere in this volume, Charabanc had proven a fertile training ground for Jones as a writer and Charabanc's focus on community and working-class theatre served significantly to inform DubbelJoint's mission. DubbelJoint was initially conceived as a cross-border project to tour productions throughout Northern Ireland and the Republic. Prior to this cross-border collaborative theatre projects between companies and cross-border touring were limited in part due to complex issues regarding arts council funding and equity rules and the impact of the Troubles on mobility.[1] However, during the 1980s, Charabanc had joined Field Day to break new ground by mounting cross-border tours. With this model of success, Jones, Brighton and Lambert believed that theatre could connect to establish common ground between the two states to ease cross-border tension and to connect theatre and drama north and south. As Eileen Pollack, a Board Member of DubbelJoint, explained, 'DubbelJoint represents Dublin and Belfast joined, and its aim is to express the absence of boundaries in theatre' (qtd. *Irish Independent* 7 July 1998).

In addition to its cross-border model, the company focused on producing plays that reflected the lives of ordinary people with the desire to highlight the dignity and honour of everyday struggles. Pollack described the company as 'devoted to producing plays that reflect the worth of everyday lives. Theatre shouldn't necessarily be some kind of escapist activity; people should be able to see appreciations of their own lives on stage, too' (qtd. *Irish Independent* 7 July 1998). In contrast to the Abbey Theatre in Dublin or the Lyric Theatre in Belfast, DubbelJoint prided itself on producing theatre that would be accessible and meaningful to those beyond a narrow cultural elite. In a 2003 play programme, the company described itself as having 'a strong commitment to community venues, particularly in areas that suffer from social, economic, and cultural disadvantage and to local writing, and through these, strives to democratize theatre and make it accessible to all' (Moore, Programme *Black Taxis*). With this mission, DubbelJoint's tenure was defined by cross-border touring of politically engaged work, performing in areas without access to theatre, and supportive of community and women's theatre groups.

Whereas Charabanc had encountered resistance in the late 1980s and early 1990s as it tried to grow and diversify its offerings, DubbelJoint was a new enterprise with an unproven record and no critical or audience expectations against which to chafe. This freedom allowed the company to experiment initially with a range of productions, mounting both original plays by Jones and adaptations of classics. The company was immediately successful with audiences embracing a wide-range of challenging original plays, commercial 'holiday hits' as well as European classics. One of the company's first productions was an original piece, *Hang All the Harpers* (1991), co-written by Jones and Shane Connaughton. The play examined the role of Irish music in the formation of national identity. In contrast, the next year, the company premiered *Christmas Eve Can Kill You* (1992) at the Old Museum Arts Centre, a production that would prove to be a commercial success for both DubbelJoint and later the Lyric Theatre. One year later, they switched focus again, producing Terry Eagleton's *The White, the Gold and the Gangrene* (1993) about the 1916 Easter Rising, as well as performing Jones's much-lauded adaptation of Nikolai Gogol's *The Government Inspector* (1993). Audience acceptance of such diverse offerings along with the transfer of a DubbelJoint production to the Lyric signals how quickly the company established itself and how the reputations of Jones and Brighton garnered opportunities for their new company.

It was Jones's success in adapting Gogol's *The Government Inspector* that solidified DubbelJoint's reputation for high-quality theatre. The play premiered in August 1993 at Féile an Phobail, the

West Belfast Festival. This initiated what would become the company's tradition of premiering new work at the annual summer festival. Field Day had already demonstrated the possibilities offered by the transposition of a classic script into a Northern Irish setting in both Tom Paulin's *The Riot Act* (a version of Sophocles' *Antigone*) and Derek Mahon's *High Time* (based on Molière's *School for Husbands*) to great critical acclaim. These productions served as a model for how foreign classic work could illuminate politics and violence in Northern Ireland. Jones reset *The Government Inspector* in a small rural town on the proposed border, should Ireland be partitioned. The local corrupt Unionist politicians mistake a young English lothario for the government inspector sent by the English crown. By this resetting, Jones embraced a similar goal to that of Field Day: to disrupt old narratives about the conflict and show parallels between the North and other societies. The play captures the hysteria of the local politicians who fear their power will be diminished if Ireland is divided. Theatre critic Peter Cromer described the production as 'a new play about the prejudices revealed by the threat of partition'. The unionists in the town are concerned that their land and farms will end up on the wrong side of partition, making them a unionist minority in the Irish Free State rather than a powerful majority in a unionist-controlled North. When they hear that the English Queen is sending an inspector to town, the unionists become panicked because they have been illegally evicting Catholic tenants from their land and deporting them to America. The Protestants have been using the newly abandoned land to raise cattle, which they have been exporting to Europe without paying tax to the British crown. Afraid the inspector will report their tax fraud, the play revolves around the ways in which the townspeople bribe and cajole the man they think is an inspector into keeping their secret.

Although transposing it to Ireland, for the most part Jones retained Gogol's original plot. She did, however, make a significant change to the ending to infuse it with a contemporary feminist slant. Although the mayor's wife and daughter both try to seduce the inspector, they are not the flighty, foolish females of Gogol's original. In fact, the daughter is the first to see through the impostor's affectations: she realizes that he is recycling the poems of Yeats and Merriman and claiming them as his own.[2] The wife and daughter each reveal at the end of the play that they knew the lothario was a fake all along, and they blackmail the con-artist into returning all the bribes the town had given him, thus saving the day. Therefore, Jones positions the daughter and wife as intelligent and educated women who do not fall prey to the same phony charms and seduction that had taken in the male officials. As Cromer wrote of the production, 'Adapter Marie Jones's main change is in making the female characters the only honest voices amongst a horde of ineffectual, cowardly and bullying hypocrites.' Despite the mother and daughter's intelligent wit, however, the town's corrupt unionist hypocrites do not learn their lesson. When the real inspector arrives the next day, the unionists, not wanting to be duped again, treat the man as another impostor. They tie him to a chair, harass him, and proceed to humorously confess their sins of tax evasion and eviction of the Catholics, guaranteeing their own downfall.

The production was highly satirical and Brighton's direction made much use of a highly visual comedy, using double-takes, stage tableaux, stage tricks and grotesque exaggeration reminiscent of the Marx Brothers' slapstick. Reviews from both Irish and English critics were overwhelmingly positive. Most agreed that Jones had successfully written a highly provocative and politically astute satire of partition, British-Irish stereotypes, cultural misunderstandings, and unionist corruption while making it accessible and enjoyable through a fast-paced, physical production that used humour to critique society's ills. In addition to exploring the dishonesty of local unionist leaders in a comedic way, the play also satirized stereotypes of the Irish long-established within English imperial culture.[3] In one scene, the false inspector becomes convinced that the Irish are cannibals, believing that Jonathan Swift's *A Modest Proposal* (1729) has been written into law. Throughout the play, the locals serve the inspector and his assistant their best beef, which results in panicked hysteria as the British conmen believe that they have been served human flesh. The play also used unapologetically bawdy humour. The Anglophile unionists in town are enthralled by anything British; since the inspector comes from London, this gives him an air of glamour and sexual allure for the women of the village who attempt to seduce him and his assistant at every turn.[4] In one of the funniest scenes in the play, the mayor's wife has orgasms just listening to the impostor recite poetry.

While the play is replete with comic observations about rural Irish life, it does not shy away from revealing a dark unionist history that systematically abused Catholics: massive numbers of Catholics in the town are hanging themselves because they have been evicted or can no longer afford to pay rent. The town officials grumble about the number of corpses which are piling up since the Catholics cannot afford to bury their families. Thus, the primary plotline (the humorous, lavish entertainment of the inspector) is counterpointed by constant reminders of death, poverty, and suicide caused by the greedy corruption and widespread abuse of the Catholic population by the unionists. This riotous humour in juxtaposition with serious political and social commentary would become a hallmark of Jones's work, and the plays she wrote for DubbelJoint are built on this model. After its premiere at Féile an Phobail, *The Government Inspector* toured across the island in early 1994, playing in Derry/Londonderry, Newtownabbey, Hollywood, Armagh, Sligo, and Galway. In addition, it played at the Grand Opera House, then Belfast's largest commercial receiving house, demonstrating the production's wide appeal. Glowing reviews and ticket sales allowed the play to transfer to the Tricycle Theatre in London later that year for an English run. These tours provided DubbelJoint with a reputation as a new theatrical force emerging from Northern Ireland.

Women on the Verge of HRT

Reflecting the company's mission to capture the lives of everyday Irish people, Jones wrote another play for the company in 1995 that highlighted a population often marginalized in Irish culture. *Women on the Verge of HRT,* which premiered at Féile an Phobail in August 1995, explores the sexual politics of womanhood.[5] The play follows the increasing frustrations of two lonely middle-aged women from East Belfast as they grow older, divorce and experience menopause. Desperate to find a romantic and sexual connection with men, the women use humour and fantasy to confront limiting social norms that de-sex women once they have passed the age of childbearing. Jones joined the cast, playing the role of Vera, a middle-aged woman whose ex-husband has just married a woman in her twenties. The play takes place in a hotel room at the Viking House in Kincasslagh, Donegal. Vera and her best friend Anna (originally performed by Eileen Pollock) have escaped their mundane lives in East Belfast and travelled to Kincasslagh in order to meet the famous singer, Daniel O'Donnell. Thus, Jones returns to her concern with border-crossing within the narrative of the play, not just in the touring of it. The real-life Irish celebrity had an annual tradition of inviting fans to his mother's cottage in Kincasslagh for a cup of tea, and every year, hundreds of women travelled to Donegal for the event. After a day standing in line and meeting their idol, the two female characters are ensconced in their hotel room for the night where they discuss the injustice of society's double-standard: while older women are supposed to gracefully retreat from society and live asexual lives quietly at home, older men often get to have romantic and sexually fulfilling second-acts with younger women. Vera bemoans the fact that once women pass their child-bearing years, they cease to be viewed as sexually appealing by men and by society at large. As she puts it, 'How do you prepare yourself for being on the sexual scrap heap?' (5) Throughout the play, Jones exposes the sexist notion that women's emotions, desires and dreams are not legitimate or reasonable but are instead controlled by the hormones caused by Pre-Menstrual Syndrome or menopause that render women's emotions invalid.

While Vera is enraged by her ex-husband's marriage to a younger woman, Anna is trapped in an unhappy marriage with Dessie who no longer loves her. Unlike Vera, Anna accepts her fate in a resigned manner. Exasperated, Vera exclaims, 'You have just accepted that you are not sexy anymore. You have accepted that when you walk into a room nobody will notice you. Anna? Anna who? You have just accepted that you are invisible' (15). For both Vera and Anna, Daniel O'Donnell is the projection of the romantic fantasy that they searched for but never achieved in their lives. Throughout the play, Fergal, the room service clerk, magically transforms into various people from the women's lives, allowing Vera and Anna to humorously confront their husbands while also giving the men a chance to explain their perspective on why their marriages have failed. When Fergal transforms into Vera's ex-husband, Dessie argues that Vera was never very interested in being his wife or in forging a life together. 'Self, self, self, Vera,' Dessie says, 'The only person you ever thought about' (25). By including Dessie's point of view, Jones provides a more nuanced picture of an unhappy marriage in which both parties share some responsibility. The audience thus hears multiple perspectives so the play never slips into a one-sided polemic.

Ultimately, *Women on the Verge of HRT* confronts and breaks down the stereotypes and myths about older women's sexuality, giving voice to a taboo subject on the public stage. The play ends with a defiant rallying song to the women of the audience, urging them to stand up against pressure to hide their bodies and repress their sexuality:

> We're women on the verge
> And we won't take ignorin'
> No sex hospice for us
> We're still up for scoring
>
> So come on sisters
> Don't let them win
> We may be over forty
> But we can still sin, sin, sin, sin.

We won't go down easy; we'll go down protestin'
The rest of our life is too long for restin'
All we're askin' is the right to reply
When we're told our passion must lie down and die. (39-40)

Women on the Verge of HRT toured extensively throughout Northern Ireland and the Republic. It had extended runs in Dublin, first at the Andrews Lane Theatre for one week in 1995, returning for a two-week run at the Gaiety Theatre there a year later. It was also performed at Mayfest in Glasgow in 1996.[6] Programmes for the productions were filled with quotations and excerpts from newspaper articles regarding women's looks, sexuality, and aging. One quotation from a woman interviewed by *The Guardian* stated, 'I don't worry about it in terms of vanity, but aging is bad professionally for women. I need to carve out a niche for myself where I am hired for myself as a total entity' (qtd. in Programme for *Women on the Verge* 1995). This quotation was accompanied by a question to the reader: 'Do you worry about aging?' By including provocative quotations and excerpts from articles, audience members were asked to immerse themselves in societal expectations of women and to question their fairness before the play began. This strategy invited the spectators to identify with the material in the play programme, to support their relationship with the characters of Vera and Anna, potentially transforming the play's protagonists into a mirror of the audience itself. This play, then, realized one of DubbelJoint's primary goals: to express the lives of ordinary people and to highlight those who are often marginalized: in this case, older women who are made to feel invisible after menopause.

Reviews were positive with most critics and audience members grateful that Jones had managed to shed light on a taboo subject in such an accessible and humorous way. The *Electronic Telegraph* wrote *Women on the Verge of HRT* 'is a banshee screech against the injustice of a society which stamps women with a sexual sell-by date' (Dickson 8 March 1997). Newspaper critic Joyce McMillan wrote that the production is a 'brave, bold, beautifully performed and searingly honest piece of theatre that looks the existential horror of this experience squarely in the face, rages inconsolably against the dying of the light, accepts no platitudinous answers ... but still emerges with a wry grin on its face' (*A Night to Remember*). Several reviewers remarked with surprise at how deftly Jones was able to balance the controversy of sexual politics with comedy. The *Sunday Telegraph* was relieved that the play 'wrap[ped] up its polemical points in a good deal of fantasy and charm' (8 March 1997) and *The Herald* wrote, '...the rough-cut Belfast humour and a strong cast fashion this into a surprisingly substantial dramatic offering than one would imagined [sic] associated with O'Donnell' (7 May 1996). While a few critics complained the play devolved in a didactic rant, most felt that the play balanced its message with humour, charm, and good writing. While extremely different in terms of genre and subject matter, *The Government Inspector* and *Women on the Verge of HRT* demonstrate the range of Jones' writing style as well as her ability to address complex political issues on both the state and individual levels.

Success with DubbelJoint

With its strong positioning in the Irish theatre sector and its diverse range of offerings, DubbelJoint allowed Jones to mature as a dramatist and to produce her most successful work. *A Night in November* premiered at Féile an Phobail in August 1994. The Provisional IRA had declared a three-day cease-fire that July and as the play premiered there was mounting expectation that a second ceasefire would be declared. That ceasefire was confirmed just as the play went out on tour. The one-man play, originally performed by Dan Gordon, centres on the fictionalized retelling by the narrator, Kenneth McCallister, of the real-life events of 17 November 1993, when the Northern Ireland and Republic football teams met at a World Cup qualifying match in Windsor Park, Belfast. The play toured the island, later being played in London and New York, and has been performed by a number of companies in Ireland and abroad, including, a production by Martin Lynch's GBL Productions with stand-up comic Patrick Kielty in 2007. Crucially, the play sustains the same border-crossing trope that the company sought to fulfil in its own touring.

    Two years after *A Night in November*, Jones wrote for DubbelJoint the first version of what would become an international hit: *Stones in His Pockets* (1996). The play, which Jones reworked in 1999, ran in the West End from 2000 to 2003 and on Broadway for 198 performances in 2001. The comedic two-man play follows a series of movie extras on the west coast of Ireland where an American film crew is making a movie. The extremely comedic play is marked by tragedy when a young local man drowns himself in the ocean due to poverty and lack of opportunity in the rural West. The play shows that the idealistic and romantic rural Ireland depicted by Hollywood often does not represent the destitution and isolation that can characterize real life in the West.

DubbelJoint and Nationalism

While Jones remained committed to the Charabanc model that crossed sectarian boundaries in both what was represented and the audiences to which they toured, Brighton began to direct a series of increasingly nationalist plays in the mid-to-late 1990s. In 1996 and 1997, DubbelJoint helped several women from west Belfast to form the JustUs Community Theatre Company. Together, DubbelJoint and JustUs staged several highly controversial productions. In 1995, they produced *Just a Prisoner's Wife*: a four-person monologue play that explored nationalist women's experiences of supporting family members in prison. Jones stepped in to play a part in that production. In 1997, DubbelJoint co-produced *Binlids* which traced the history of west Belfast through a series of loosely-connected vignettes. The play was based on documentary material and verbatim accounts and charted the repression of the nationalist community by politicians, police, and military.[7] The production generated controversy as many in the Unionist community accused it of being one-sided, polemical, and antagonistic while also justifying republican violence. In the most controversial and shocking scene of the play (and also the one most cited by Unionist critics), a group of Catholic women lured an 18-year-old British soldier to his death. In the scene, the women strike up a friendly conversation and convince the young, inexperienced soldier to relax and sit down. Once he does so, they stealthily take his gun, and an IRA man enters the scene and shoots him point blank in the head. For the audience, the scene begins with the women emotionally connecting to and mothering the young solider; it then unexpectedly turns into a cold execution. This section of the play is complex because the scene takes care to humanize this Welsh soldier from an impoverished town only to then show no mercy for the life of this young, inexperienced man. Interpretation of the scene is further complicated by being sandwiched between two scenes of a young Catholic man being brutally tortured by the RUC.

The controversy was played out in the court of public opinion and in newspaper and media outlets across the North. The production called into question the role and purpose of the arts within the conflict and questioned whether funding should be given to a clearly sectarian production. Brighton defended the show arguing that the nationalist community had a right to present its stories in a manner that reflected its own experiences and understanding of the past. Additionally, it is important to remember that *Binlids* was performed in the months leading up to the signing of the Belfast Agreement. Many Catholics during this period feared their stories and histories would be lost to the dominant peace process narrative, which called for calm and peaceful speech, reconciliation, and leaving the past behind. DubbelJoint argued that *Binlids* was purposefully polemical with an aim to educate audiences, to give voice to an underrepresented portion of the population, and to make sure the history of Catholic repression was not swept aside or forgotten in the eagerness for peace.

Controversy exploded again over the next joint production, *Forced Upon Us* (1999), which went back in time to cover the early part of the twentieth century during the building of the Titanic, the signing of the Ulster Covenant, and the formation of the Ulster Volunteer Force. The opening scenes in particular provoked outrage: the first scene featured a young Catholic girl who was too frightened of the Royal Ulster Constabulary to report her rape and the second scene followed a group of Protestant ship workers who attacked a Catholic worker, tied him to a lamppost, poured paint thinner over him, and set him on fire. Many critics called the production highly offensive, grotesquely exaggerated, and sectarian in nature. Malachi O'Doherty, writing in *Fortnight Magazine*, stated: 'This is a disappointing play. It is nasty and sectarian. If it is supposed to be evidence of reflective thinking in a more politically mature republican culture, then we are in trouble ...' (September 1999). In another article he argued that the play presented Northern Irish history in a reductive and simplistic manner; he summed up the majority unionist view succinctly, saying, 'It is a sectarian play which sees all modern history in Northern Ireland as the suppression of Good Catholics by Bad Protestants' (Play-acting 10). DubbelJoint and JustUs again defended their work as the stories and perspectives of the subjugated Catholic community and argued that not all theatre had to be balanced or non-sectarian in order to be valid. The theatre, they argued, provided a unique and vital opportunity to empower and validate a minority experience that had been repressed by the British and Northern governments and the unionist-controlled media. Terence O'Neill, who wrote the songs to the show, told the New York based Irish-American newspaper, *The Irish Echo,* 'There's a challenge for recognition involved even to the extent of admitting that we even have a story to tell here. We constantly have to keep proving that we're real and that what we're doing is authentic, and that we have a place in the scheme of things' (Hurley *Irish Echo*). It is also interesting to note that the production was performed within a political climate (in the direct aftermath of the Belfast Agreement) that again called for moderation, calm, and non-incendiary speech. The play, however, was extremely controversial, taking an uncompromising and often shocking look at injustice against the Catholic community. The play was thus interpreted by some as counterproductive to the larger political project of peace that permeated the country; in contrast, it was defended by the Catholic press as preserving the authentic history of a brutally repressed minority.

Divisions intensified after the Arts Council of Northern Ireland arguably bowed to increasing public pressure and withdrew its funding for the production *Forced Upon Us*. DubbelJoint promptly sued the Arts Council claiming censorship, and debate over whether sectarian art should be publically funded consumed the press. The Arts Council ultimately denied any wrongdoing, arguing that its decision was based purely on artistic merit. Damien Smyth of the Arts Council defended the organization's decision, saying that the script 'was deemed not of a sufficiently high artistic standard to warrant a huge injection of public subsidy' (Shots in the Arts 22). This contention put forth by the council that the 'quality of the writing was as bad as anything the assessors had ever read' (Moroney) was wholly rejected by the Catholic community who instead argued censorship. Eoin O'Broin from the nationalist newspaper, *An Phoblacht*, defended the production in his article entitled, 'A Clear Case of Political Censorship.' He argued that the play 'does not pretend to be an objective historical document of the complex and turbulent period it deals with. Rather it offers the audience an interpretation in tune with the feelings and historical memory of the community who will make up its primary audience' (22). On 30 July 1999 several important writers and artists such as Shane Connaughton, Marina Carr, Frank McGuinness, Peter Sheridan, Trevor Griffiths and Marie Jones, published an open letter in the *Irish Times* that called the withdrawal of funding a political act that trampled on freedom of expression. Despite the lack of Arts Council funding, the show toured across the island playing to packed houses.

To further strain relations, in the same year as *Forced Upon Us* DubbelJoint also produced Pearse Elliot's four-person monologue play, *A Mother's Heart*. This original work explored the emotional and psychological journey of four women (two Catholic and two Protestant) whose children had been killed during the Troubles. Three of the four actresses in the production were ex-republican prisoners: Brenda Murphy, Bridie McMahon, and Rosena Brown. Brown was especially notorious because in 1992 she had lured a prison officer with the promise of sex into a trap where the IRA executed him. Brown had been sentenced to twenty years in prison in 1993 but was released only a few years later under the Belfast Agreement. Public outrage, which was already high over her early release, was exacerbated when she agreed to appear on the public stage acting the role of a loyalist mother grieving over her dead child. Jim Rodgers, an Ulster Unionist Party Councillor for Belfast, reflected community outrage saying, 'This is absolutely disgusting. For Rosena Brown to play this role when the real victims of terrorism are having to come to terms with the early release of prisoners shows she has no conscience' (Harnden, *Daily Telegraph* 22 February 1999). Rodgers expressed further indignation that none of the victims in the play died at the hands of the IRA, creating an arguably skewed representation of Troubles violence. Many critics found the play to be unbalanced and highly polemical, threatening DubbelJoint's reputation for producing complex and even-handed work. Jane Coyle of the *Belfast Telegraph* wrote, 'Now that DubbelJoint's vision has become more closely aligned with a republican agenda, the days when it produced fine and politically astute work like *The Government Inspector* and *A Night in November* are fading into fond and distant memory' (Terminator's All Greased Up). DubbelJoint again vigorously defended the production arguing that this was the first time that a play took grieving women out from behind the private curtain of mourning and explored the impact of Troubles violence on motherhood. Actress Brenda Murphy, who played one of the mothers, said, 'It is the first play during my lifetime, during the war, that has addressed the issues that women have kept hidden, and this play allows them to become public' (Kelly, A Mother's Heart 15). The playwright, Pearse Elliot, added to this sentiment, saying, 'This play is a real first. I don't think there has ever been a play like it, that articulates women's rage and humanity, done by women who have lived through it and have something to say' (Kelly, A Mother's Heart 15). DubbelJoint viewed the play as an important therapeutic tool to heal and empower family members of sectarian violence in a manner that also was cathartic for the whole community.

The controversy did much to damage DubbelJoint's reputation and calls for the cessation of funding to the company increased. The combination of these four highly provocative productions allowed critics to claim that DubbelJoint was a sectarian theatre company and question its claim to public subsidy. Despite the controversy, the company continued to produce material that dealt with the nationalist experience under Brighton's leadership; these included Brian Campbell's *Des* (2000) about the work of a radical priest in west Belfast and *The Laughter of Our Children* (2001) about the 1981 hunger strikes, written by ex-Republican prisoners Brian Campbell and Laurence McKeown. Jones, who never wanted the company associated with a sectarian affiliation, became increasingly uncomfortable with the reputation of the company and Brighton's work.

Jones the solo artist

The progression of the company towards material dealing only with a single identity on the one hand, alongside her growing independent success on the other, contributed to Jones's distance from the company in the late 1990s. She began to focus on touring her two most successful plays. *A Night in November* played throughout Ireland in 1994, 1995, and 1998. In 1995, the production transferred to the Tricycle Theatre in London, and in 1998, it played off-Broadway at the Douglas Fairbanks Theatre in New York City. In 2001, another production originated in Los Angeles and then toured to London, Dublin, and the Edinburgh Fringe Festival. In 1999, Jones reworked her 1996 version of *Stones in His Pockets* and staged a new version at the Lyric Theatre without DubbelJoint's involvement. The revised play was a critical sensation and a financial success. *Stones in His Pockets* ran in the West End for four years and on Broadway for one year, elevating Jones' reputation internationally and securing her standing as one of Ireland's leading playwrights. The play won the 2000 London *Evening Standard* Theatre Award for Best Comedy, the 2001 Laurence Olivier Award for Best New Comedy, and received three Tony nominations including Best Play. In 2001, Brighton sued Jones, arguing that her role as a dramaturg and director for the original 1996 version of *Stones in his Pockets* had shaped the current play to such a degree that she should be considered a joint-author. She also argued that DubbelJoint was owed royalties as the original producer of the work. Jones paid royalties to DubbelJoint, but Brighton ultimately lost her bid for co-authorship in 2004.[8]

Conclusion

Overall, between 1991 and 1998, Jones wrote seven shows for DubbelJoint: *Hang all the Harpers* (1991, co-written with Shane Connaughton), *Christmas Eve Can Kill You* (1992), *The Government Inspector* (1993), *A Night in November* (1994), *Women on the Verge of HRT* (1995), *Eddie Bottom's Dream* (1996), and *Stones in His Pockets* (1996).

These plays addressed issues of cultural and national identity, tackled taboo subjects such as sexuality, bigotry, and sectarianism, and highlighted important social issues such as poverty, unemployment, and suicide. Furthermore, the company addressed these issues in a manner that engaged the entire island, emphasizing commonality rather than difference between the two sides of the border. Ultimately, Jones's tenure at DubbelJoint was among her most prolific and fruitful periods of writing; she won numerous awards for her plays and secured an international reputation as one of Ireland's leading playwrights.

Although DubbelJoint became associated with a nationalist voice, it stayed constant to the founding tenets set by Jones, Brighton, and Lambert. Throughout its existence, the company remained committed to touring politically engaged work, highlighting the stories of ordinary people, performing in locations without access to theatre, and engaging the North and South in a cross-border model that helped to maintain a cultural link throughout the entire island. Its success was instrumental to the formation of a strong independent theatre sector in Northern Ireland and its diverse repertoire of classic, serious, and comedic offerings served as a model for what other Irish theatre companies could achieve. Whereas many politicians and state officials had failed to make a lasting impact on the sectarian conflict, the company's cross-border and community-based paradigm served as inspiration for what the performing arts could accomplish both within the Troubles and beyond.

---

[1] The historical reasons for infrequent collaboration between companies on either side of the border are complex involving political, historical, and financial issues. Each arts council, for example, faced constraints on the jurisdictions in which it could disburse funding; while Equity operated two different organizations on the island, one for the UK, including Northern Ireland, and a separate one for the Republic. Nonetheless, Field Day had already established a practice of all-island touring that was to be followed up by DubbelJoint, Big Telly and others. The arts councils have since the late 1990s collaborated to run a joint fund to support North-South touring, with the latest initiative announced in 2014.

[2] Jones returns to this motif in *Stones in His Pockets* where one of her characters is caught out passing off Seamus Heaney's poetry as his own.

[3] The acme of the stereotype was to emerge, of course, in the figure of the stage Irishman. See for example, Maureen Waters's *The Comic Irishman* and Nicholas Grene's *The Politics of Irish Drama: Plays in Context from Boucicault to Friel*.

[4] One might also read this as an allusion to Synge's *The Playboy of the Western World*.

[5] The HRT of the title refers to the hormone replace therapy that in the UK is routinely prescribed for women to ease the symptoms of the menopause.

6 Based on the success of this show, Jones wrote a sequel in 2000 entitled *Women on the Verge...Get a Life!* in which Vera and Anna travel on vacation to Gambia and find love.

7 For a further discussion of the context and controversy over the production, see Tom Maguire's essay '*Binlids* at The Boundaries of Being: A West Belfast community stages an authentic self.'

8 Although Jones ceased to be associated with the company after 2000, DubbelJoint continued to produce shows, including many with nationalist leanings such as *Working Class Heroes* (2003) by Brenda Murphy, *In a Cold House* by Laurence McKeown and Brian Campbell (2003), and *Black Taxi* by Brian Moore (2003). The company's last two major seasons included *The Session* by Brian Moore and *Voyage of No Return* by Brian Campbell in 2005 and *The Ballad of Malachy Mulligan* by Brian Moore and *Remnants of Fear* by Gary Mitchell in 2006.

9 | Tim Loane

Interviewed by Tom Maguire

In this interview with Tom Maguire, Tim outlines the context for the creation and reception of Marie Jones's work from the early 1990s; the professional networks that she developed and which supported her own development; and something of the influence she has had.

TM: When you started working professionally what was the theatre scene in Belfast and Northern Ireland like?

TL: I left Queens in 1987 and there were a few of us got together who had gained an ambition for ourselves as individuals. We hadn't really understood how to put those ambitions together in terms of where we were. We were convinced we wanted to start a theatre company and to produce plays. That's all we wanted. We worked out how to do that through trial and error. We looked around and we could see very little in the way of precedents, very little in the way of infrastructure that could accommodate us.

We did at a very early stage arrange to meet up with Marie Jones and Eleanor Methven to tell them what we were planning to do and to take their advice on it. They were extremely helpful from the very beginning as they [Charabanc] were the only independent company we were really aware of. We were aware of Field Day and used to go and see all the Field Day plays but in many ways they felt like a different country – I'm being playful saying it like that – but they were untouchable – they were operating in a different sphere ... whereas Charabanc and Eleanor and Marie were so much more approachable – we were playing on the same team, kind of thing. They were very quick to point out how tough it was going to be to start a new company. I still remember going into their kitchen – they shared a house in Ravenhill – and they were very encouraging all the same and they were very clear that they knew who their audience was, who they were producing Charabanc plays for: they urged us to have a think about that.

TM: And had you even seen any of Charabanc's work then?

TL: No, not in the early days. We were coming out of university and, I think, the whole arts scene was segregated in many ways. We used to go and see plays at the Lyric, occasionally we'd go and see Field Day at the Opera House, and the Belfast Festival was a big thing for us, going to see the RSC and the National, the Abbey and Rough Magic and Druid. All the big 'international' stuff, that excited us terribly, but we got one month of it. The rest of the year there wasn't really anything for us, though we tried to support any local companies that were there. We perceived Charabanc to have a very particular purpose and to be something separate from us. We were never aware of the plays unless they were ... I remember *Somewhere Over the Balcony* was part of the Festival, at the Arts Theatre. But Charabanc, because they were not in your obvious theatres, not in the city centre most of the time, we were aware of them but not in terms of their practice.

Once Tinderbox had been going for a year or so, we had been speaking to a couple of writers and they were expressing frustration with the Lyric, a gap, because there was nobody doing new stuff that wasn't written for their own companies; nobody who would read plays and do readings of plays. So, we thought we'd give that a go and we did a festival of new Irish writing, which was 1989 ... And that was where we accessed our audience, we found an audience that was interested in new work as well. This was absolutely everything to do with place and we sat down with writers from Belfast and across the country who had something to say about where we were. We saw ourselves as a conduit, an organ, for writers.

TM: I'm getting a sense of a broken tradition here. The generation that went before, Stewart Parker, Anne Devlin and so on, they weren't really featuring at all?

TL: No, they'd been and gone, not gone perhaps, but the heyday of the Lyric in the early 80s of Martin Lynch, Stewart Parker and the two Reids [Christina and Graham], there wasn't any of their stuff going on that we could see. We were early twenties by this stage.

TM: Yet if I go to something like *Caught Red-Handed*, I would recognize in that a distinctive kind of Ulster comedy, not a kitchen comedy, but a real sense of an engaged comedy. I'm wondering where that came out of ? Clearly when you're working with someone like Dan Gordon [the lead in *Caught Red-Handed*] whose own development is influenced by that ...

TL: That's interesting. There were a couple of years when Marie, Dan Gordon, Pam Brighton and myself worked very closely together on a couple of things.

At one stage I was on a film set, me and Marie were whiling away the very long boring hours while we were filming something as actors and we came up with the idea for what became *Christmas Eve Can Kill You*. We devised the notion of that together and neither of us had very much coming up at that particular time so Marie said, 'Alright, I'll write it, but only on condition that you produce it.' And I said, 'OK, You write it and I'll make it happen.' So she did and we got Pam Brighton on board. At this particular time, I think it was pre-DubbleJoint ... this was never a DubbelJoint show, I produced it first for the Old Museum. Marie wrote it, I produced it and Pam directed it. And Dan Gordon was in it. I directed him in the Dario Fo [*Can't Pay, Won't Pay* for Tinderbox]. I had also worked with Dan on a god-awful tv programme *The Show*, a sketch show. So I knew how funny Dan was, I knew how talented he was. I had cast him in multi-role stuff in the Dario Fo. When it came to *Christmas Eve Can Kill You*, Marie agreed with me. She had seen *Can't Pay, Won't Pay*, but I don't think she had worked with Dan before. That was the time that that triumvirate was created, where Dan and Pam and Marie became a team.[1]

TM: Where did the appetite for this work from Northern Ireland come from?

TL: Well when we did *Christmas Eve* in the Old Museum we did it to only 100 people a night. But there was always a sense that Marie had an audience; the Belfast audience knew Marie.

TM: But she hadn't had that commercial success at that point? And to go to the West Belfast Festival that wasn't a mainstream theatre audience. She hadn't established herself as a writer in mainstream venues.

TL: Well, there was *The Government Inspector* – I was in the first production of it as well, also at the West Belfast Festival.

TM: And it toured?

TL: Yes it went off to the Tricycle, I wasn't involved in that part. It toured all of Ireland first, then they revived it a year later and took it to the Tricycle.

TM: When you toured it, did you have any sense of that tour as in any way being ground-breaking – people from the North going south, of Northern Irish theatre going out?

TL: In a sense, except we, Tinderbox, had been doing it for years before that. Once Tinderbox started the new writing, then touring was very important to us. The Arts Council [of Northern Ireland] wanted us to tour ... But Charabanc had been doing that too.

TM: How would you say Marie Jones contributed to the emergence of new writing in Northern Ireland, particularly by women?

TL: There is no question that Marie broke the mould: she was absolutely a pioneer as a female theatre writer and actress who was, apart from anything, determined to deal with very serious issues in a comic fashion. She was the first that I'm aware of and she set the bar so high.

TM: What would your expectation be of a new play by Marie Jones?

TL: I'd be very glad for a start because it's been too many years since we've seen it. I'd expect it to be funny – always. It's always going to be irreverent – something I've always loved. I'd hope that it's going to be challenging in a sense that it's not going to be offering the audience what they want. When Marie – like so many comic writers – has presented comedy that the audience is comfortable with, that's disappointing.

TM: As someone who has acted in her work, do you see her as an actorly writer?

TL: It's very funny: when you see a script that's come straight from her [computer] – it used to be an Amstrad as far as I can recall – it certainly didn't look the prettiest piece of writing on the page. You read it and some of it being phonetically written, you'd think, 'Ach this isn't going to work.' You'd read it a couple of times and then you'd either stumble upon it or Marie or somebody else would point it out, 'Look, this is the way it's meant to be.' She writes very precisely. It might seem to be informal in how it's written but it's actually very precise in Marie's mind. She's writing dialogue in a way that fits actors' tongues very nicely. I don't remember ever making any significant script changes, maybe cutting a few lines here or there or re-ordering scenes in *Christmas Eve Can Kill You* or in *The Government Inspector*. I was in a few radio plays as well, let me see, *Blind Fiddler*, the radio version of that. Not that she would be precious, because if there was a way of improving a line, Marie would grab it, no question. But it just didn't seem to come up very often because it was always very precise.

---

[1] Gordon appeared in a number of productions of Jones's plays including the original and revivals of *A Night in November, A Very Weird Manor* (Lyric, Belfast, 2005) as well as in Loane's *Caught Red-Handed* and its follow-up *To Be Sure* (Lyric, Belfast, 2007). Through these he gained a reputation for playing multiple roles, something that audiences came increasingly to expect.

10 | 'I am a Protestant Man, I'm an Irish Man': Politics, Identity, and A Night in November in Performance

Eleanor Owicki

Introduction

A man stands, mouth open and arms outstretched, as though he is cheering. He wears a white button-up shirt, black trousers, and a Union Jack tie. The shirt and trousers imply a certain level of formality, but the pose and the tie undercut any reading of the man as serious and dignified. The background features the familiar crosses of the Union Jack, but with a difference; instead of red, white, and blue, they are green, white, and orange. This suggests a melding of British and Irish identities – the shape of the British flag, with the colours of the Irish tricolour. These two flags have long served as symbols for enemies, so the combination is striking and unexpected. There is yet another layer to the background. The top of the flag has been cut away to create the silhouette of a cityscape, suggesting a kind of cosmopolitanism one would, perhaps, not normally associate with the North of Ireland.

This is the poster for the 2007 Grand Opera House production of Marie Jones's one-man play *A Night in November*, which starred comedian Patrick Kielty and was directed by Ian McElhinney. The poster hints at a great deal about both the play and this particular production. It emphasizes the charisma and excitement of the play's lone performer, and also puts him in a context of hybrid national identity. This is particularly evident in the blending of the tricolour and the union flag. In Northern Ireland, these two flags carry deep significance – they signal community identity, religion, and national allegiance. They are also generally viewed as fundamentally in conflict.

The depth of the feelings attached to the flags was made visible in December 2012, when riots followed the Belfast City Council's decision to stop flying the union flag over City Hall every day. Belfast unionists and loyalists saw this as an attack on their community's traditions and on Northern Ireland's continued connection with Great Britain. Thus, the blended flag on the *Night in November* poster offered a radical revision of the traditional view that the flags, and by extension Britishness and Irishness, are fundamentally in conflict. Instead, it suggested that some kind of fusion of the two identities is possible.

Haunting and Ghosting *A Night in November*

This chapter examines the social and artistic contexts for two productions of *A Night in November*: the 2007 Grand Opera House production and the 1994 premiere staged by the DubbelJoint theatre company. The 1994 production starred prominent Belfast actor Dan Gordon and was directed by Pam Brighton. The thirteen years that separated the productions saw massive changes in Northern Ireland, and each production was a product of its particular moment. As I discuss each of the productions, I work to highlight the contexts that would have shaped audience understandings of them. Many theatre theorists have worked to build methodologies for understanding audience reactions to plays in cases where specific data is lacking. Since few theatres conduct surveys or interviews with their audiences to identify how audience members understood the play, these alternative methodologies can prove extremely useful. For example, Susan Bennett's seminal text *Theatre Audiences: A Theory of Production and Reception* (1997) argues 'As the artist works within the technical means available and within the scope of aesthetic convention, so audiences read according to the scope and means of culturally and aesthetically constituted interpretive processes' (99). In other words, an audience's understanding of a performance is shaped by the cultural and aesthetic training they have received. Many other scholars have developed these themes; this chapter offers examples of the ways methodologies developed by Marvin Carlson and Bruce McConachie can be used to theorize the audience reactions to each of these productions.

Carlson and McConachie approach the issue from different directions, but arrive at similar and complementary conclusions. In *The Haunted Stage: Theatre as Memory Machine* (2001) Carlson draws on critical theory, particularly semiotics, to argue that audiences use their previous relationships with the various elements of theatre – text, actors, design, and venue – to understand a new production. In contrast, in his essay 'Doing Things with Image Schemas: The Cognitive Turn in Theatre Studies and the Problem of Experience for Historians' (2001), McConachie builds on cognitive science to argue that a 'cognitive unconsciousness' is always at work as the human brain makes sense of the world, and that this cognitive unconsciousness uses the 'image schemas' or 'primary metaphors' with which it is familiar to complete this process (577). McConachie then argues that, by understanding the image schemas at work within a particular theatrical context, a historian can understand the ways audiences at these productions would have mentally processed the works.

I begin with an analysis of the script of *A Night in November*, paying particular attention to the ways it has been received by critics. I then apply each of these theorists in order to identify the differences between the two productions. Drawing from Carlson, I analyze the tangible elements of the productions, particularly the differences in venue and in the identity of the play's one actor. Then, drawing from McConachie, I read each production in light of a dominant narrative of its particular moment. In the case of the 1994 production, this was one that focused on division and violence. By the time the 2007 production was staged, however, narratives of unity and post-sectarian identity were far more common (although not universally embraced). My readings of the two productions are built from elements including reviews, production photographs, programmes, and marketing materials. Videos have also proved useful – the Linen Hall Library holds a VHS of Gordon's performance, while BBC Northern Ireland created a documentary about the 2007 production that includes moments of Kielty's performance as well as interviews with Kielty, McElhinney, and producer (and prominent Belfast playwright) Martin Lynch. I use these elements to create as complete a picture as I can of the ways these performances addressed their specific audiences.

The works of Carlson and McConachie are useful in establishing the frames that audiences would have used to understand the performance within the larger context of life in Northern Ireland. These methodologies are intended to identify these frames, however, not to pinpoint individual audience members' feelings about the performance. As the next section explores, *A Night in November* has frequently divided audiences, eliciting both praise and criticism. Carlson and McConachie's methodologies are useful for identifying the specific contexts that produced these reactions. This specificity is essential; for example, the 1994 and 2007 productions both started in Belfast but went on to tour other parts of Ireland and the UK. These changes in venue would have significantly shaped the play's reception, and as a result I have restricted my focus to the Belfast performances. Changes in the political landscape during the tours would also have shaped audience reactions. This is perhaps most obvious in the 1994 production; its Belfast performances ended only weeks before 31 August, when the IRA announced a ceasefire. This event fundamentally changed the political situation in the state, and would have provided a new host of contexts and image schemas for audiences at later performances of the play.

The Script

A Night in November follows Kenneth McCallister, a Protestant civil servant, as he comes to realize the destructive nature of the sectarianism in which he casually participates. The play is set in 1993 and 1994, and Jones inserts her fictional character into a series of real events that rocked Northern Ireland. Kenneth's political awakening begins as he escorts his father-in-law Ernie to the World Cup qualifying match between Northern Ireland and the Republic of Ireland (the night in November of the title). The game resulted in a draw (although the Republic would go on to play in the World Cup and Northern Ireland would not), but it was overshadowed by the sectarian abuse that was hurled at the team and its supporters by Loyalist spectators. Jones has Ernie start an especially cruel chant that was actually used at the match: 'Greysteel seven, Ireland nil' (71). This refers to the massacre that took place in the town of Greysteel on 30 October 1993 where members of the Ulster Freedom Fighters (a loyalist paramilitary group) killed eight people and wounded many more in a crowded pub. Kenneth is so appalled by this behaviour that he begins to notice the subtler but still harmful sectarianism of his friends, family, and most of all himself. For example, early in the play he had used his position in the welfare office to hassle Patrick McCardle, an unemployed Catholic man. Although he knew no one would be able to see Patrick that day, Kenneth forced him to wait all day and then return the next day. Kenneth attempts to share these revelations with his wife Deborah and their friends, but they are more interested in his recent acceptance into a golf club (a sign of his middle-class upward mobility).

In Act Two, Kenneth makes a spur-of-the-moment decision to travel to New York to watch the World Cup match between the Republic of Ireland and Italy. As soon as he joins the other fans at Dublin airport, he is transformed by the sense of community he finds. He is open about his identity as a Northern Protestant, and the supporters (who are primarily Catholic and from the Republic of Ireland) continue to accept him. Realizing how little Kenneth has prepared for the trip, his fellow travellers give him a team t-shirt, suggest a place he might stay, and invite him to join them at the bar where they will watch the game. When Ireland wins, Kenneth and the ecstatic crowd spill out onto the streets of New York in a carnivalesque celebration. The euphoric tone of the play is reversed, however, as Kenneth learns of another shooting at a pub, where six Catholics were killed while watching the World Cup match. The play ends with Kenneth disavowing the killers and claiming to have finally broken with the sectarianism of his community. He states: 'I am a Protestant man, I'm an Irish man' (108).

The play also contains a significant criticism of class, and particularly the ways the middle classes have distanced themselves from the conflict in the North. Because they are not participating in the violence, Kenneth's family and friends believe they bear no responsibility for the events of the Troubles. They refuse to see the ways that the privilege they enjoy as Protestants has led them to reinforce the discrimination that was one of the key catalysts of the Troubles. Indeed, Kenneth's own petty discriminations in his role as a welfare clerk have the effect of alienating, and therefore oppressing and antagonizing, the Catholics he is supposed to serve. This focus on class was typical of Jones's work – we can trace this concern right the way back to the beginnings of Charabanc, which primarily focused on the experiences of working-class women.

The play is also significant within the context of Jones's biography. She is a Protestant and wanted the play to address the community in which she had been raised: 'I had to say things people wouldn't like. I don't want to hurt anybody, but I knew it was the right timing for me as a person who grew up in a Protestant background. It was important to me as a pacifist. I had to accept there was a lot wrong with the sectarianism I grew up with. That to be in Lord Carson's army one had to hate. Who gives you that right?' (qtd. in Barter).[1] Although not as successful as Jones's *Stones in His Pockets* (which played for three years on the London West End), *A Night in November* has enjoyed lasting popularity with audiences. Gordon reprised the role of Kenneth many times, taking the play to locations including New York and Australia. In Belfast-based productions (many of which toured elsewhere), the role has also been taken on by actors including Marty Maguire, Connor Grimes, and of course Kielty. In addition, productions have been mounted in London, Los Angeles, New York, Chicago, and Madison, Wisconsin.

The play has not been universally praised, however. In an *Irish Times* review of a 1995 performance in Dublin (still starring Gordon), Fintan O'Toole drew attention to the ways that the play depends on reductive stereotypes of Catholics and Protestants and emphasizes a false binary between the two. He opined: 'it tells a Catholic audience exactly what it wants to hear: that Northern Protestants are just like us, except that they're too tight arsed to admit it' (Insulting Both Sides). So, while the play may be flattering to the Catholics who will make up the majority of the Dublin audience, 'the flattery is really the old bigotry reversed. *A Night in November* replays bigoted images of Irish Catholic vices – shiftlessness, unpredictability, wildness – as virtues' (Insulting Both Sides). Similarly, Tom Maguire notes that Kenneth, and by extension the play, 'reverses the values ascribed to each side of [the sectarian] opposition without questioning its foundations' (*Making Theatre* 142). This is most evident in Kenneth's visit to the home of his Catholic boss, Jerry. While Kenneth's house is orderly but cold, he sees Jerry's house as disordered but happy – a place where life is allowed to happen organically. The audience is asked to view the two men's homes as representative of their larger communities, and in many ways the play reifies the sectarian binary even as it seeks to move beyond it.

At its best, the play will take the audience on an emotional journey with Kenneth, culminating in the rejection of even small acts of sectarianism. The audience may even feel a desire for a more nuanced understanding of identity which allows Irishness and Britishness to co-exist in some hybrid form (just as they did on the poster for the 2007 production). This can be read as an attempt to create what performance scholar Jill Dolan calls a 'utopian performative', which she defines as those 'moments in which audiences feel themselves allied with each other, and with a broader, more capacious sense of a public, in which social discourse articulates the possible, rather than the insurmountable obstacles to human potential' (*Utopia in Performance* 2). The appeal of such moments in the context of Northern Ireland is obvious. In a divided society anything that can, even fleetingly, bring people together should be cherished. This emphasis on Kenneth's emotional journey rather than his actions, however, prevents the play from having a more direct activist message. As Maguire notes, ending *A Night in November* with Kenneth's transformation 'switches the focus of the play from a concern with inequality and injustice to a concern with personal identity, with two effects. The first is to avoid the difficulties in proposing any resolution to the conflict more widely; the second is to endorse versions of the conflict as a matter of identity.

Individual integrity substitutes for social justice and political equality' (*Making Theatre* 141). The script, therefore, offers the potential for emotional transformation for individuals, but does not model any kind of direct or collective action that the people of Northern Ireland could take to address the complicated issues at the root of the conflict.

The Haunting of Venue and Performer

In *The Haunted Stage: The Theatre as Memory Machine*, Carlson argues that in most cultures and time periods, theatre has served as a repository for cultural memory. He suggests that this status makes audiences particularly likely to relate its elements to their previous experiences. Carlson divides the theatrical event into several component parts to examine the ways that reuse of these elements shapes audience understanding of individual performances. He writes: 'Everything in the theatre, the bodies, the materials utilized, the language, the space itself, is now and has always been haunted' (15) and this 'complex recycling of old elements, far from being a disadvantage, is an absolutely essential part of the reception process. We are able to 'read' new works […] only because we recognize within them elements that have been recycled from other structures of experience that we have experienced earlier' (4). Of the elements Carlson identifies, venue and actor are particularly useful to understanding the differences between the 1994 and 2007 productions of *A Night in November*.

The venues of the two productions were remarkably different, both in their physical structures and in their cultural significance. Even their locations within Belfast are telling. As Carlson argues: 'An audience not only goes to the theatre; it goes to the particular part of the city where the theatre is located, and the memories and associations of that part of the city help to provide a reception context for any performance seen there' (140). This is particularly true in Belfast, where the cityscape is imbued with layers of meaning clearly readable to its population. The part of West Belfast where the 1994 production was staged is one of the most iconic Catholic spaces in the city. The play was staged as part of the West Belfast Festival (also known as 'Feile an Phobail,' literally 'the people's festival'), an event designed specifically to create a positive image of the area. Founded in 1988, it hoped to counter the more prevalent images of Catholics as downtrodden victims or violent savages. The festival's overall tone is joyful; while the political position of nationalism underpins the festival, the individual acts generally do not foreground political propaganda or activism. This was certainly the case in the 1994 festival. According to journalists Suzanne Breen and

Emma O'Kelly: 'It defied categorization. No event was undersubscribed. They crowded into plays in Whiterock; they drank and danced the night away to rock, rave, and reggae in Springhill; they were enthralled by Frances Black and soprano Angela Feeney in Andersonstown; and they flocked to political debates just about everywhere' (*Irish Times* 17 August 1994). According to Breen and O'Kelly, the highlight of the festival was a comedy performance by the 'Hole in the Wall Gang' – a group of comedians who would go on to create the satirical TV show *Give My Head Peace*. Most of the Gang's jokes were directed at Sinn Féin politicians, many of whom were present in the room and apparently enjoying the performance as much as the other audience members.

In contrast, the 2007 production was staged at the Grand Opera House, which is part of the commercial (and therefore relatively non-sectarian) city centre. As a commercial venue, the Grand Opera House generally draws a more mixed audience than the West Belfast Festival. The theatre hosts a wide variety of events, from pantomimes and West End musicals to opera and new Northern Irish plays. In addition to *A Night in November*, 2007 productions included the musicals *Chicago* and *Annie*, a stage adaptation of Yann Martel's novel *The Life of Pi*, the operas *Tosca* and *La Boheme*, and Martin Lynch's *The History of the Troubles (accordin to my Da)*. These performances share an interest in entertainment and artistic excellence rather than politics or current events. Even *The History of the Troubles*, which deals with the legacies of the conflict, offers a relatively upbeat image of life in Northern Ireland. It is quick-paced and comic, and ends with the main character holding his grandchild and promising a better life in the now-peaceful state.

Those who used their knowledge of the venue to shape their expectations about *A Night in November*, then, would generally have gone in expecting to be entertained and moved, and to see a high-quality performance by Kielty. For the most part, they would not have expected to be hit with difficult questions or contentious political issues in the ways that audiences at the West Belfast Festival might have. As is generally the case with solo performances, the casting of the actor in *Night in November* has been essential to the play's success. Reviews frequently praise the performer even when they note problems with Jones's script. In his denunciation of the play's politics, O'Toole noted that the production 'has a performance of extraordinary virtuosity by Dan Gordon, full of charm and grace and passionate conviction' (Insulting Both Sides). Similarly, Imelda Foley points to the improbability of a character experiencing Kenneth's dramatic shift in values and interest over so short a period of time, and suggests that Gordon's performance created the atmosphere that allowed this suspension of disbelief: 'It was the kinesthetic presentation and superb performance by Dan Gordon as Kenneth that made *A Night in November* a theatrical experience' (51).

Carlson argues that an actor's reputation creates an 'aura of expectations' that shapes audience experiences even before the performance begins (67). A basic comparison of Gordon's and Kielty's biographies reveals many differences that would have shaped these expectations. Both were born and raised in Northern Ireland but Gordon comes from the Protestant community and Kielty comes from the Catholic community. This knowledge would have underscored audience expectations about the relationship between the actor and the Protestant character Kenneth. The press for the two productions frequently focused on this relationship. It depicted Gordon as playing someone like himself. Indeed, in an interview with *The Irish Times*, Gordon affirmed this connection, saying: 'I know only too well where the central character, Kenneth McCallister, is coming from because it's the same place I come from' (quoted in Coyle). In contrast, Kielty was depicted as playing someone quite radically different from himself. In the BBC documentary, Lynch admits to initial fears about whether audiences would accept Kielty in the role because of this disconnect between his identity and that of the character. The decision to cast a Catholic in this role, however, enacted the same kind of melding of identity promised by the hybrid British and Irish flag in the play's promotional material.

The trajectory of the men's careers has also been very different. When *A Night in November* premiered, Gordon had already made a name for himself as a stage actor. He had appeared in many plays at the Lyric Theatre (including Lynch's *Castles in the Air* in 1983) and Gary Mitchell's *Independent Voice* with Tinderbox Theatre (1993). He also already had a relationship with DubbelJoint, having appeared in their production of *The Government Inspector* in 1993. Thus, he was firmly established as a theatre actor, and one who would take roles in complicated and political plays. In contrast, Kielty had never appeared in a professional play before. Rather, he was known as a standup comic and television presenter. For this reason, as Lynch again acknowledged in the documentary, casting Kielty was a gamble on a practical level as well as an ideological one. His work on television and as a comic, however, was likely to allay some of the discomfort felt by having a

Catholic take on this role. Although Kielty's comedy often takes on political subjects and does not hide his Catholic identity, he offers little support for sectarianism or violence. Indeed in his stand-up persona Kielty regularly positions himself as a voice for the victims of violence. In addition to the content of his stand up acts and persona, the contexts in which Kielty performs would have been likely to at least partially ease the minds of those who felt he might portray his Protestant character unsympathetically. Although he first gained attention as a standup comic working throughout the island of Ireland, he truly rose to larger fame as the presenter of British reality shows like 'Fame Academy' (2002-2003) and 'Celebrity Love Island' (2005-2006). These seemingly-apolitical career choices might undermine Kielty's authority in a play that made a biting critique of the British government, but since *A Night in November* works (to the extent it does) by creating an impression of unity and good will, Kielty's persona and his public statements of empathy with Kenneth enhanced the show.

The venues and actors in these two productions drew from very different elements of audiences experiences, and would have encouraged (although not guaranteed) very different understandings of the play's importance. The context of the 1994 production suggested that it should be viewed primarily as a political play. It was staged as part of a festival with an explicit political goal – to counteract negative publicity against Catholics living in West Belfast. This context meshed well with the play's general (admittedly, highly debatable) depiction of Catholics as fundamentally happier than Protestants. Further, it was performed by an actor with a reputation for taking on roles in plays that dealt with serious political issues. The context for the 2007 production, in contrast, suggested that it should be viewed primarily as entertainment. It was staged at a commercial venue that tended to produce apolitical plays, or at least plays that took on political issues without expressing sectarian ideology. Its star was known as a comedian rather than as an actor, and his persona as a comedian and TV host working in England was also removed from the sectarian ideology at the heart of the conflict. In addition, the cross-community casting of Kielty echoed much of the rhetoric about moving on and abandoning sectarianism that, as I discuss in the next section, was prevalent in 2007.

Image Schemas and the Political Context

McConachie's work in many ways parallels Carlson's, although McConachie bases his theories on discoveries within the field of cognitive science. He particularly draws from Mark Johnson and George Lakoff's argument that humans make meaning by connecting their embodied experiences with certain 'image schemas' or 'primary metaphors' that vary between cultures and time periods. By identifying the image schemas at work in a particular historical moment as well as the specific details of a theatrical event, McConachie argues that historians can reconstruct the processes that audiences would have used to make meaning from the performances they witnessed. As his example, he demonstrates the ways the cold war schema of 'containment' would have conditioned audience experience at the 1955 New York production of *A Hatful of Rain*.[2] The 1994 and 2007 productions of *A Night in November* each took place at a time of significant political change, where these primary metaphors and schemas were highly prominent. As a result, McConachie's methodology provides a strong framework for comparing the relationships between the two productions and their larger political contexts.

A Night in November was written and premiered at a time of particular fear, turmoil, and division. This is particularly evident in the real-life reactions to the shootings that bookend the play's action. The production opened on 8 August 1994, less than a year after the Greysteel massacre and the sectarian chants at the World Cup qualifying match. The Loughinisland massacre (10 June 1994), which prompts Kenneth's final revelation and break with his own sectarianism, had happened only two months before. Although many in Northern Ireland had become at least somewhat desensitized to violence, the Greysteel and Loughinisland massacres provoked widespread outrage and pain. Newspaper articles from the time express a feeling that life in the state was finally spinning entirely out of control. A *Mail on Sunday* article argues that 'The recent, barbarous killings on the Shankill and at Greysteel have reinforced the feeling that events are passing beyond civilized control' (Collins). An article from *The Guardian* described the mood in Greysteel as one of 'dignified grief and utter despair' (Mullin, In Between are the Innocent, emphasis mine). In *The Independent*, David McKittrick argued that the Greysteel killers had 'plumbed new depths' of brutality. Following the Loughinisland massacre, a headline in *The Guardian* read 'CHEERS TURNED TO SCREAMS FOR MERCY. 'As they ran from the pub, they were laughing like hyenas', said one teenage girl, terrified of retribution.' The overarching sentiment in these articles is that the situation in Northern Ireland had now passed beyond the point where life could continue in the midst of this violence. They suggest (and sometimes explicitly claim) that the state was on the brink either of a radical turn towards peace or an all-out war.

These feelings of horror at violence and increasing sectarian division, along with the idea that something had to change provide some of McConachie's 'key image schemas' for the audience experience of the first production of *A Night in November*. Regardless of how individual audience members felt about the situation in the North or the prospects for peace, they would have (frequently unconsciously) used these prevalent narratives to understand the play. Kenneth's emotional journey in many ways mirrors these dominant narratives. At the beginning of the play, he pays little attention to sectarian conflict, but his experiences with the increasing level of prejudice and brutality will not allow him to maintain this distance. Finally, the horror of life in Northern Ireland becomes too much for him, and he breaks with his former identity. This cathartic change mirrors the rhetoric used to discuss the Greysteel and Loughinisland massacre, in which the situation in the state has become so extreme that change – either a rejection of violence and sectarianism or an entire abandonment of notions of normal society – seems inevitable. Kenneth's final decision to claim both Protestant and Irish identity would have offered one possible model for this transformation. Similarly, critics' complaints that the play reinforced stereotypes of the two communities can be linked to the growing frustration with the old models of sectarian division present at the time.

The 2007 Grand Opera House production took place nine years after the Good Friday Agreement, in vastly different political and theatrical contexts. As such the key image schemas audiences would have used to interpret it were remarkably different. Rather than violence and chaos, it was staged in a time of relative calm, and perhaps even stagnation. This production spoke to audiences conditioned to expect narratives about moving forward and discarding differences. The rhetoric of a 'shared society' – in which Northern Ireland would set aside sectarian division and truly move forward as one community – was prevalent. In March 2005, the Office of Minister and Deputy First Minister (at that time under direct rule from Britain) put forward a document titled 'A Shared Future: Policy and Strategic Framework for Good Relations in Northern Ireland.' The Secretary of State for Northern Ireland's foreword to the document emphasized this utopic vision: 'The Government's vision for the future of Northern Ireland is for a peaceful, inclusive, prosperous, stable and fair society firmly founded on the achievement of reconciliation, tolerance, and mutual trust and the protection and vindication of human rights for all' (3). Similarly, on 8 May 2007, only three months before the Grand Opera House production opened, power was once again restored to the Northern Irish Assembly. The image schemas of this moment were much more optimistic and focused on the future than those of 1994 had been.

This narrative of moving beyond a conflicted past was clear in the ways the 2007 production was framed by its creators and its critics. Most of the criticism that had attended the premiere had focused on the play's depiction of the two communities, but this topic was largely absent from discussion of the 2007 production. Those who supported the play and those who were uncomfortable with it seemed to accept the premise that it offered a reasonably accurate depiction of Northern Ireland in 1993 and 1994. They also agreed (at least in public) that these issues had been largely resolved. Both sides framed the 2007 production as a play that was essentially about historical events and problems that had once affected the state but no longer did. Their disagreement lay in whether revisiting these past events and traumas could be considered useful or dangerous. The production team, led by Martin Lynch, argued that re-examining the events of 1993 and 1994 could be healing for audience members and increase their pride in Northern Ireland's journey. As Kielty put it in the BBC documentary:

> People who saw [the play] ten years ago, who were walking back out onto the streets when this was still going on, they went home very depressed. And now they go out and they see it as an uplifting play, and you know, it is the past, and yet, they still are reminded. It's always good to be reminded of where we're coming from, so we can enjoy where we are.

This vision of the play downplayed any remaining problems with sectarianism in the state in order to emphasize narratives of progress and cooperation. To further emphasize these changes, the production's programme included an article about the ways in which football had worked to eradicate the sectarianism and racism depicted in the play.

In contrast, those who objected to the play worried that revisiting this history would needlessly open old wounds. The issue was prominent enough to become the subject of discussion on the popular BBC Radio Ulster call-in show Talkback, where host David Dunseith fielded questions about the play's relevance (including a defense of the play from Kielty). Some feared that the play's critique of Protestants but not Catholics would reinforce a narrative of the Troubles in which Catholics were the primary victims, while others simply did not want to be reminded of the past. *The Irish News'* review of the play noted: 'It has been said this play is outdated and better left on the shelf. Thank goodness it hasn't been' (Hailes). Implicit in this praise is the acknowledgement that significant opposition existed. In many ways, the resistance to the play demonstrated the anxiety that undergirded the narratives of progress and optimism. While the peace process had been largely successful, the possibility that it might collapse or that sectarianism might never be eradicated remained in the public mind. The 2007 production thus became a focal point for the question of how to remember the past while still looking optimistically to the future.

Conclusion

Politics and public life within Northern Ireland have seen massive changes in the years since *A Night in November* premiered. The play's enduring popularity provides an opportunity to examine the relationship between the theatre and the ongoing peace process within the state. Differences in the tangible elements of performance – particularly venue and actor – as well as the larger narratives of the moment mean that the same text can have vastly different significances. It will be interesting to see how producers of future Belfast productions use or struggle with these elements. A production staged in 2014, for example, would be haunted by many unionists' feelings that they had been abandoned by the state. This anger became clear with the flag protests at the end of 2012, and has not abated at the time of writing. In February 2014, a senior member of the Orange Order stated that Protestants should not study the Irish Language as it was 'part of the republican agenda' (quoted in Simpson). In light of this, Kenneth's decision to embrace Irish identity at the end of the play would be likely to be read as even more controversial. If the production team and venue were not closely linked with the Protestant community, it seems likely that many would view the production as an explicit attack on Protestant identity (as opposed to Protestant behaviour) in a way that they had not for either the 1994 or 2007 productions.

---

[1] Lord Edward Carson was the figurehead of Ulster unionism in the early twentieth century and remains an important cultural figure for unionists.

[2] Michael V. Gazzo's play *A Hatful of Rain* tells the story of a soldier returned from the Korean War where a spell in a military hospital has left him secretly addicted to morphine. It was later adapted into a film (1957) directed by Fred Zinnemann.

11 | Masculinity and the Performance of Gendered Identities in the plays of Marie Jones.

Catherine Rees

Introduction.

This chapter focuses on Marie Jones's approach to masculine identity in two plays, *Stones in His Pockets* (1999) and *A Night in November* (1994), and sets out to explore how she depicts male experience through differing theatrical forms and structures. In both cases, I seek to unpack some of the ways in which she suggests gendered identity to be unstable, fluid and performative. By using theatrical metaphor, and presenting gender as a social and political performance, Jones presents the audience with images of masculinity suffering various crises, suffering at odds with normative political and national images of male identity. In so doing, this essay argues, Jones's plays undermine myths associated with national and gender identity. In recent decades the study of masculinity has become a major area of academic inquiry, perhaps as a response to the proliferation of women's studies disciplines and debates. In the theatre, increased interest in the construction of masculine identity may be due to an assumption in earlier studies of gender whereby 'the male protagonist has been critically treated as if he were non-gendered' (McDonough 1). Exposing masculinity as a gendered category in its own terms has often resulted in masculinity being described as undergoing some form of crisis or confusion. There is powerful tension at work here, while male identity might seem to be subject to privileged norms, it could be argued that men in disadvantaged economic situations, for example, often feel marginalized and insecure. Jones's plays discussed here look at masculinity in states of anxiety as the male protagonists are undermined by strict identity politics defining what constitutes 'real' or 'secure' masculinity. As we shall see, theatrical performance has the potential to unlock some of these prejudices and problems, and explore gender identity as having more complex and multiple constructive layers.

Gender in Ireland

In order to explore masculinity in Ireland, some brief analysis of Irish female experience is useful by way of contrast. Siobhán Kilfeather's historical account of women in Ireland explains that the power of the Catholic church in the Republic of Ireland helped to define women's identity because 'the cult of Mary had a deep influence on the lives and imaginations of Catholic Irish women' (106). Kilfeather argues that the Catholic church's enthusiasm for establishing norms of Irish female experience was closely linked to desires to shore up conservative notions of national character:

> The response of the Catholic church in Ireland ... was to identify itself closely with a vision of an essential Irish character, and to demonize the attractions of liberalism or socialism as quintessentially 'foreign', where the 'foreign' was always a form of English power (106).

Importantly for this argument, women are classed as victims of a 'double colonisation' (Kilfeather 112), suffering repression from both English and masculine oppression. This argument is significant; clearly women have historically endured such domination. However, the concept of 'double colonisation' suggests another possibility – that of a repressed male identity due to analogous colonial frameworks.

In this regard, Irish men are, Máirtín Mac an Ghaill suggests, in 'a unique social location ... On the one hand, they are ascribed masculine privileges as white men. On the other hand, [they are] a subordinated masculinity' (122). Margaret Llewellyn-Jones likewise observes that masculine identity suffers from colonial dominance: 'If an effect of colonisation is the feminization of the colonised, this then poses problems for [...] masculine identity, since traditional male qualities are associated with the dominant colonisers' (93). Thus male experience also suffers a double colonial blow, feminized by colonialism and unable to save the feminized nation from attack. Recent commentators on gender studies have remarked that across the globe 'there is a recognition that men [...] are faring poorly in many different ways [and] are experiencing problems at a rate disproportionate with their numbers and with a uniqueness that seems to be a part of the lived world of men' (Kahn 165). At the heart of all this kind of analysis is the sense of real-world experiential 'crisis' of / for masculine identity.

Irish theatre has frequently taken an interrogatory approach to masculine experience, focusing not on 'the mythically heroic' but rather on men as 'weak' (Llewellyn-Jones 94). Such explorations are not new, moreover: playwrights such as J. M. Synge and Sean O'Casey have both created male characters that reject or fail to live up to heroic ideals, leading to these masculine nationalistic myths becoming available for questioning and re-examination. Tellingly, however, the playwrights exploring these ideas are often male. As a result, as Kilfeather points out, 'women writers... continue to have a very limited institutional power' (113). Marie Jones has been a notable recent exception to that rule, and it is this that makes her work so interesting in terms of the key terms driving this essay.

Researching Jones's theatrical career often starts with Charabanc Theatre Company which was founded by five female actors, including Jones, in Belfast in 1983 (Lojek 1999). Their first production, *Lay Up Your Ends* (1983), about a 1911 mill strike, focused on the lives of unemployed female linen workers, and was performed exclusively by the all-woman company. This led to what Claudia W. Harris describes as a 'stylistic technique – the women playing the male characters as they viewed them – [which] became a distinctive feature of the company' (109). What is most interesting about this device is that it leads to 'plays written, directed, and designed by women [which] would employ an eye or perspective which viewed its subject differently ... Charabanc's work with its pervasive focus – from research through writing to production – on the female perspective came close to female gaze, especially when the female actors played male characters as they saw them' (Harris, Reinventing Women 117). The end result is a complex matrix of performative layers: the women appropriated male gender roles within the performance of the play, adopting the parts for themselves, and thus, as Harris suggests, created the lens through which gender was foregrounded throughout the productions.

Jones left Charabanc in 1990 to concentrate on her own playwrighting career. Her 1995 play *Women on the Verge of HRT* returned to the discussion of femininity and of gender reversal, but *Stones in His Pockets* and *A Night in November*, the two plays which I am concerned with here, both feature an exclusively male cast with, to a lesser or greater extent, the actors taking female roles. Of course, this practice recalls traditional Elizabethan theatrical techniques, as young boys adopted the roles of female characters. It could be considered that this represents a feminization of the male, 'putting on make-up, showing off, displaying the body, pretending to be someone else, ostending emotion ... court[s] the danger of appearing to disavow codes of "masculine authenticity"' (Mangan 4). Furthermore, the men in these plays do suffer from moments of emasculation, sometimes at the hands of the very female characters the male actors are themselves performing. This destabilization of gender identity helps to deconstruct the sorts of gender myths that establish restrictive masculine roles by demonstrating that such assumptions are not natural, but rather assumed as part of a framework of cultural representation. Two of Jones's plays place masculine identity at the heart of their theatrical agenda: *A Night in November* explores masculine identity within the political context of Belfast before the Good Friday Agreement, while *Stones in His Pockets* unpacks the effect of economic deprivation on young males in Ireland's rural hinterlands. Thus this chapter explores the specifics of masculine theatrical identity in Ireland, examining the relationship between gendered cross-casting and masculine identity, power and patriarchal dominance. Driving the analysis is a concern for what has constituted the social norm of 'masculine authenticity' and a focus on how theatrical performance, through rendering it fluid and unstable, can help expose identity politics as the product of cultural representation.

In this regard, Edward Said argues that the 'job facing the cultural intellectual is [...] not to accept the politics of identity as given, but to show how all representations are constructed, for what purpose, by whom, and with what components' (*Culture and Imperialism* 380). National and gender stereotypes cause identity to be simplified and reduced to standardized images, and the question of who controls them is a political one. Given that theatre deals with representations of identity, it is well placed to interrogate these myths and expose them as something constructed and hegemonic. The nature of performance itself can be used to explore the concept of identity as having transient, unstable and flexible qualities. This concept can be applied outside the world of the theatre, as Johnston and Morrison suggest, '"Man" is best understood as a complex and strategic social performance tailored for both venue and audience' (672), implying that gender is a performative event for everyone. As Mangan points out 'the stage was always a place which disrupted and raised questions [...] about gender, power, and ideology in general, and about masculinity in particular' (5). This chapter now moves to explore and examine the presentation of masculine identity in these two plays and analyse the effect of theatrical and performative elements on the gendered identity of the characters depicted.

A Night in November (1994)

The play's structure is in the form of a single monologue; performance of the play involves one actor on stage for its entirety, narrating the events as the fictional character, Kenneth McCallister, playing the other characters and also providing an internal 'voice-over' commentary, combining psychological observations and also more traditional speech 'dialogue'. Kenneth's moment of crisis and later epiphany is performed in front of an audience, expressed literally through the relationship the actor develops with the audience through the course of the play. It is a different relationship to most plays, as in this case Kenneth does not engage with the audience via interaction with other actors, playing other characters, but instead through direct communication, telling them his thoughts and actions with no one else on stage. The structure of the monologue play therefore allows for a more direct relationship between the character and the audience, as members of the audience do not see any other fictional characters (or, at least, other fictional characters are tranquillized through the one actor on stage), but instead the actor addresses them directly – the words of the play are for their benefit only.

Tom Maguire suggests that this mode of performance involves the audience to a much greater degree, arguing that direct interaction with the audience transforms the narrative of the play from the 'there and then' of more traditional drama to the 'here and now' (*Making Theatre* 143) – that is, the events are brought alive in the moment of the performance. He also proposes that 'as monodramas, the performative mode itself points to a plastic sense of identity' (*Kicking* 79). I would add that there are also spatial elements to this manner of performance which further conspire to involve the audience in the action to a greater extent. Traditional theatre tends to stage a moment and a location for the audience to witness, for example the conventional drawing room of nineteenth-century naturalistic theatre. In these cases, action is performed in front of the audience, usually with the device of the fourth wall – an imaginary barrier between the audience and the actors, keeping them apart, and placing the viewer in a voyeuristic state, witnessing the action but not implicated or involved within it. Monologue performance radically breaks the fourth wall, as the actor addresses the audience directly. The way in which monologue theatre transforms the space of the stage then, allows the audience to play a part in the action – it forces them to consider the implications of the play in their own lives, denying them the comfortable distance conventional theatre allows. The role of the actor is of course crucial in this regard, as it is the actor, as Maguire puts it, that 'performs the transformation of the space' (Kicking 79). As the actor engages with the theatrical space around him, its meaning changes in complex ways. Given the context of this play, we could argue that this transformation also has specific geographical and political implications; the transformation from one space to another is literally the movement from one country to another. The border between Northern Ireland and the Republic, a contested and troubled line, is rendered fluid and performative, as Kenneth easily slips between the two jurisdictions. Said argues that human identity is itself similarly unfixed – it is created by unstable cultural forces and as such cannot be said to be unchanging and stable. He suggests that 'human identity is not only not natural and stable, but constructed, and occasionally even invented outright' (*Orientalism* 332). The implications of Said's comments for this play are clear. Kenneth rejects the stereotypical prejudices expressed by members of his family but experiences a moment of identity crisis as a result. When he is no longer able to assert himself through culturally acceptable means, he struggles with his national and religious identity.

> *A Night in November* explores the fragility and fracturing of identity. Kenneth uses the domestic metaphor of a fitted kitchen to describe his own religious and national identity crisis, arguing that his identity comes prefabricated in a standard format that cannot cope with any internal inconsistency that provokes chaos and mayhem (81). Such identification of role and performance recalls Judith Butler's seminal *Gender Trouble: Feminism and the Subversion of Identity* (1990), in which she argues that gender is essentially performative and that it has no 'ontological status' (185) beyond individual expressions of gender identity: 'There is no gender identity behind the expression of gender; that identity is performatively constituted by the very 'expressions' that are said to be its results' (34). Butler employs theatrical metaphor in this description, referring to 'the various acts of gender [which] create the idea of gender' (190). Thus, in place of binary essentialist categories, gender can be seen as a mask, worn and performed by individuals.

In terms of this kind of theoretical lens, it is notable that the creation of identity – national, gender or otherwise – may be described through recourse to theatrical metaphors. For example, the moment at which Kenneth's identity is transformed is marked by his changing of clothes, from nondescript suit to tricolour football strip. In changing costume, as it were, Kenneth is consciously adopting another role, much as an actor would wear different clothes to denote different characters. Maguire points out that 'in the process of costuming ... attention is drawn to the ways in which identities might be fabricated' (Kicking 77). Erving Goffman's seminal *The Presentation of Self in Everyday Life* likewise draws on performativity as a tool to explain human behaviour and interaction, explicitly framing his analysis within the term 'theatrical performance' and describing individuals as 'actors'. He identifies patterns of behaviour as a 'part or routine' and even terms those who witness these performances, family, friends, work colleagues, 'the audience'. Crucially, Goffman identifies moments in which a performer may break from consensus and challenge his own role: 'We may find that the performer may not be taken in at all by his own routine ... When the individual has no belief in his own act and no ultimate concern for the beliefs of his audience, we may call him cynical, reserving the term 'sincere' for individuals who believe in the impression fostered by their own performance' (28). This description aptly fits Kenneth, whose 'audience' demand from him the performance of specific and fixed identity markers, regardless of Kenneth's own acceptance of them. However, whilst Goffman may view this as insincere, audiences may perhaps rather interpret Kenneth's actions in the latter half of the play as his most sincere moment, and his previous adherence to his given role as the more cynical performance. Goffman identifies such crises in identity and suggests that, 'at times of crisis lines may momentarily break and members of opposing teams may momentarily forget their appropriate places with respect to one another' (199). This seems to describe perfectly Kenneth's jubilation in New York as he happily mixes with Catholics: his identity crisis and breakdown in standardized role performance leads to a temporary suspension of opposition between his Protestant identity and that of his Irish peers.

The transformation undergone in this play is made more expressive as it is narrated entirely by Kenneth, yet this implies that his identity is just another form of narrative – a narrative which competes with others in the Northern-Irish political struggle and can accommodate a spectrum of options, from redemptive transformation or a random terrorist attack. Such identity is at crisis-point throughout the play; it is partially resolved, ironically, for Kenneth in a moment in New York when he is reminded of sectarian violence by news of a shooting in Belfast. Thus, whilst the claiming of an identity free from politics and sectarianism at the end of the play is a positive experience for Kenneth it is always underpinned by the identity politics which created it. As such, his new found freedom is as much of a performance as his earlier existence, both being subject to the same rules of theatrical expression.

Jones's presentation of identity as performative, playful and ambivalent is encapsulated in the final lines of the play: 'I am a free man ... I am a Protestant Man, I'm an Irish Man' (108). What is interesting about Kenneth's assertion is that for the first time he proudly asserts a masculinized Protestant Irish identity, drawing attention to his gender identity as much as his national or religious one. Jones embraces a constructed image of gender as advocated by Butler, and so her representation of maleness is constantly underpinned by questions of politics, representation and cultural discourse. By structuring the play around a single spoken narrative the actor is able to imply this even more forcefully, as narratives are literally forming the basis of his discussion of national crisis and instability. As Eamonn Jordan argues, the structure of the play and the self consciousness of Kenneth's withdrawal from his previous existence 'lead[s] towards a mode of self expression that is made poignant, comically naïve and fundamentally performative' (52). Bringing together Butler's and Said's arguments within a theatrical context again, Gilbert and Lo use the same language to argue that monologue drama interrogates the construction of identity as 'performative in the sense that it has no ontological status apart from the various acts which point to its existence. Hence, there is no 'true' or 'authentic' self, only multiple 'selves' that come into being at the point of articulation in any one situation or event in time' (5). Furthermore, Voigts-Virchow and Schreiber argue that 'the monologue ... is an excellent means in expressing masculinity in crisis' (296) as the characters operate in a mode of confession with the audience, usually a confession of humble or dishonorable actions.[1]

The monologue form employed in this play allows Jones to offer a playful and ambiguous image of masculine identity. On the one hand, Kenneth inhabits 'a patriarchal world' (Foley 51) where he is expected to work hard, join the golf club and condemn his nagging wife for being unloving. However, as much as Kenneth lives in the privileged world of the male Protestant professional, he is alienated from his masculine identity. As Kahn argues, 'masculinity does not exist within a person, but within an interaction between a person's experience and the norms of their culture' (211). When those norms run counter to Kenneth's own values (for example at the football match) he experiences an identity crisis. At the moment where he rejoices as a celebratory 'Protestant

Irish *man*' (108), 'an apparently antithetical' (Maguire, *Making Theatre* 142) combination, he is able to happily combine his experience with his culture and environment for the first time. This celebration of identity is at the heart of the play, and of the flexible and fluid nature of monologue drama.

Stones in His Pockets

Stones in His Pockets has been a huge commercial success in both the United Kingdom and America. It initially transferred from the Edinburgh fringe to the West End (where it was very well received and popular) before moving to Broadway and tours of the States where it grossed over $5 million[2] and was nominated for three Tony Awards. The play is performed by two male actors, who ostensibly take the roles of Jake and Charlie, two men in their thirties who are employed as extras in an American film (*The Quiet Valley*) which is being shot in the local community. Much of the joy of the play, as well as its technical difficulty for actors, comes from the fact that the two actors also take on the other eleven speaking roles demanded by the script. The central conceit of the play is therefore that the extras (all locals) are elevated 'in Bakhtinian carnival style' (Llewellyn-Jones 129) to the protagonists and the American stars of the film and Dublin producers are relegated to secondary characters. The extras thus assume the narrative of the play, feeling, as they do, estranged from the stereotypical images of themselves constructed by the film-makers. As Jacqueline Bixler points out, the part of the extra is 'a marginalized, anonymous class that extends well beyond the stage to the audience and to all those who do not belong to the dominant culture' (443). The story of the play (rather than of the film which is being made) is the suicide of a local boy, Sean, who had dreamt of escaping Ireland to America but was trapped by the social and economic stagnation of rural Ireland. The last straw for Sean, the play suggests, seems to be have been the moment when the film's lead (American) actress, Caroline, has him ejected from his local pub. The two extras, Charlie and Jake, thus decide to write their own film about these events in which 'the stars become extras and the extras become the stars' (54) in order to tell the story of Sean's suicide from their point of view.

The play explores the stark economic position for young men in rural communities. Jane Kenway, Anna Kraack and Anna Hickey-Moody argue that globalization has diminished certain aspects of masculinity in rural areas, causing 'socially surplus and disposable [and] redundant' men (68). This in turn has created what they term

'Melancholic masculinity' (66) which can become 'magnified and mythologized and even more honorific than [it] once [was], a form of melancholic excess. This is evident in the hopes of quite a sizeable proportion of young adolescent males' (68-9). Such marginalization can be seen in the character of Sean as well as Jake and Charlie in *Stones in His Pockets*. Kenway, Kraack and Hickey-Moody suggest that

> When young people call an out of the way place 'dead', they mean it's a place that asphyxiates; it's a dead weight ... Young men experience this spatial paradox as although there is apparent freedom of space, there is little freedom of movement (94).

Thus, despite an apparent vastness of countryside and physical space, the economic environment creates a simultaneous lack of opportunity or excitement, and stifles the 'life' from a rural community, as seen in this play. They continue to argue that whilst young men can view their environment as 'dead' this feeling of abjection from and within their landscape is at odds with, and contradictory to, mythologized images of rural masculinity. For example, the stereotypical male is linked to 'breadwinning and mobility' (125), so limited economic opportunities serve to counter this view of dominant masculinity. Thus, if the landscapes which confront males are seen as economically 'dead' and uninspiring, narratives of male prominence in the countryside can be seen to further diminish their view of themselves as particularly masculine. The reality of rural existence is misrepresented by prevailing hegemonic ideology which suggests masculine behaviour is bound up in stereotypical images of the rural idyll. It therefore follows, as many have argued, that economic struggle equates with a perception of reduced masculinity. This is clearly evident in the play, as the American production team require the locals to be 'passive, simplified and primitivized' (Phelan, Authentic Reproductions 247), undermining their ability to express their own experiences and tell the story of their subjugated and rejected young male friend.

The film described in *Stones in His Pockets* depicts a sentimental and simplistic romance, in which Ireland figures as a poor yet tranquil and dramatic backdrop. The extras provide local 'character', and they too are represented in classically stereotypical ways – working hard on the land and uncomplainingly subject to the landowner. Clichéd images of Ireland are regularly explored by Jones, from Caroline describing the Irish as 'simple, uncomplicated, contented' (15) to the cows which are 'not Irish enough' (28), despite the fact that they are local, suggesting that 'authenticity' is something that can (indeed must) be manufactured. The image of Ireland is therefore not reflected, it is self-consciously produced, and often the constructed version is overtaken and accepted, as the politics of representation is ironically criticized by Jones. For example, when Caroline's Irish accent is criticized by the locals, Charlie remarks that there have 'been that many film stars playing Irish leads everybody thinks that's the way we talk now' (14). Indeed, the voice coach reassures Caroline by reminding her 'Ireland is only one per cent of the market' (13) so no-one will challenge her accent's authenticity. When Jake confronts Caroline with Sean's suicide, reminding her that was 'related to most of us' (39), and she fails to see her part in the tragedy, he argues, 'you come here and use us, use the place and then clear off and think about nothing you leave behind' (48).

Jones makes it clear that the villagers are reluctantly complicit in this process, dismissing the film as inauthentic yet reliant on it for the money it brings into the village. Jake says of Mickey – the oldest extra on this film who had also been an extra on *The Quiet Man* – 'Mickey has watched his whole way of life fall apart around him ... and now all it's worth is a backdrop for an American movie ... he depends on their forty quid a day and then he lives in hope for the next one' (45). Furthermore, when the producer tries to dismiss Mickey for arriving drunk to work, Mickey reminds him of his family's previous ownership of the land through patriarchal bloodlines: 'You see this ground you are standing on ... this belonged to my Grandfather, and you are telling me a Riordan to get off my land ... what is happening to the world' (54). Mickey's economic disenfranchisement is part of a wider concern Jones raises in the play with the lack of opportunity for the locals. Another young local and a friend of the dead Sean recalls how his companion had hoped for a more fortunate life away from Ireland, 'Sean always talked about getting out. He hated this place. He used to say to me, you and me, Fin, we'll escape' (37). Considering these representational dynamics, Mark Phelan argues that Hollywood appropriation of images of rural Irish identity is colonial in nature, as 'America acts both as a producer and consumer of Irishness [which] constitutes a neo-colonial relationship in a globalised context' (Authentic Reproductions 244). Indeed, the 'double colonization' highlighted in the introduction to this chapter reminds us that masculinity is particularly threatened when one dominant culture appropriates and dominates images and representations of another.

Another interesting aspect to the presentation of gender in *Stones in His Pockets* is Jones's use of the male actor to perform all the roles required by the narrative. This cross-dressing, again in the theatrical tradition of gender confusion, also emphasizes the performative aspects of gender roles, as explored by Butler above. What is interesting, beyond the transformative quality of clothing and gender mimicking, is the presentation of Caroline's character. The characterization is entirely partial as it is mediated through the characters of Jake and Charlie. Again, Caroline appears to be an unsympathetic character, and this representation of her, a female character written by a female playwright but reproduced through two male characters, is particularly interesting. Another female character, Aisling, a third assistant director, is also mocked in the narrative of the play and presented as a character the audience is encouraged to find amusing and ineffectual. Both female characters adopt traditionally patriarchal positions in the play, imposing dominant cultural hegemonies onto the mechanics of cultural representation, namely the film at the heart of the play. Against this, the male extras are effectively feminized. The roles available to them are inconsistent with hegemonic masculinity, and thus Jones presents the audience with a series of complex gender interactions, in which male actors perform as female characters, who in turn feminize the male extras by performing in more received modes of masculinity.

Laura Mulvey's influential 'Visual Pleasure and Narrative Cinema' (1975) argues that women are constantly subjected to the 'male gaze' and as such are objects of masculine representation and interpretation. Although Mulvey's essay was originally written to explore cinema, it has frequently been used to analyse other forms of media, and the performance of female identity by male performers in Jones's plays suggests its relevance to the discussion here. Mulvey argues that women's images are 'silent' and 'tied to [the position] of bearer of meaning, not maker of meaning' (834). She argues that women are oppressed by the masculine gaze of the male characters, the camera itself, and the cinema audience, through a series of stereotypical and reductive images of their sex. They exist in films (and other media) to be looked at, and this reflects inequalities in gender depiction: 'In a world ordered by sexual imbalance, pleasure in looking has been split between active/male and passive/female' (837). In Jones's plays, the female is not only gazed upon by the male character, the entire feminine identity has been constructed around masculine performance. There is no interpretation of the female characters beyond that which we see reflected by the male characters. This is an inherently troubling dynamic, particularly when we factor in Jones's position as a feminist writer. Traditionally the playing of female roles by male actors during the Renaissance era and earlier has troubled gender divisions. Perhaps

Jones's use of male actors to bring to life the characters of Caroline and Aisling is reminiscent of this tradition. Certainly, questions of representation and power are raised by the performance of gender in Jones's plays. As Michael Mangan reflects on traditional forms of Pantomime: 'Like gender ... [H]owever, the very act of representation may set in motion all kinds of questions before even a word is spoken or an action performed' (6).

Conclusion

Jones's exploration of gender in both *Stones in His Pockets* and *A Night in November* displays an ambivalent playfulness. In both plays, she confronts masculinity, and gender more generally, as a theatrical construct, an identity bound up with cultural discourse and political ideology and, as such, one which is constantly being written and rewritten, as well as performed and expressed. Harris continues her examination of the Charabanc theatrical career by arguing that the women in the early Jones plays were 'shown to be vital, active forces' with 'no hint of the misogyny found in much Irish drama' (Reinventing Women 115). However, in both *A Night in November* and *Stones in His Pockets* the construction of the theatrical event draws attention to the performance of gender through monologue form and the unusual practice of male actors playing all the roles of either gender. Thus, in these later plays, gender identity is more partial and more speculative, allowing, as we have seen, for some unflattering presentations of both genders.

In the two plays explored here, masculinity is discussed through two distinct lenses of Irish life – political sectarianism and violence and images and stereotypes of the rural idyll. Jones unpacks the representation of masculinity in the context of warfare, dismantling the hegemonic view of 'the male warrior as one of the most powerful ideals of masculinity' (Dowler 58), by showing us Kenneth at odds with the binaries that construct religious and national difference and rejecting the violent hatred he sees in the North, to embrace an identity proudly celebrating an Irish masculinity divorced from sectarian aggression. Similarly, she undermines the myth of rural masculinity as proud and independent, suggesting that 'powerlessness in relation to economic capacity ... stands at stark contrast to the spaces and practices of hegemonic rural masculinity' (Cloke 57). Both plays, however, end with a reaffirmation of the characters' masculine identity and an insistence that they define their gender in their own terms and with their own story. Any writer who considers masculinity in their work is speculating on an infinite number of masculine images, some celebratory, some troubling, some deeply problematic and traumatic. However, as this chapter has sought to discuss, the representation of masculinity can also be a performative and theatrical event, underpinned with questions of power and agency, as men suffering abjection from social and political norms attempt to take control over their own narratives.

---

[1] See also Brian Singleton's 'Am I Talking to Myself? Me, Masculinities and the Monologue in Contemporary Irish Theatre'.

[2] For more details see:
http://www.playbillvault.com/Show/Detail/8383/Stones-in-His-Pockets

12 | Paula McFetridge

Interviewed by Tom Maguire

In this interview with Tom Maguire Paula McFetridge discusses the influence of Marie Jones and the other members of Charabanc on her professional development. She recounts her experience working on Marie Jones scripts as an actor, and subsequently as a director at the Lyric Theatre (Belfast).

PMcF: I first met Marie, I think, in about 1983. I was a member of the Ulster Youth Theatre under the direction of Michael Poynor and we were building up to rehearsals for *War of the Worlds* and these five incredible women [from Charabanc] came to meet us.
TM: Did you know who they were?
PMcF: No. They had only founded the company at the start of that year. I don't know whether I had even seen them or not. But it didn't matter: they were a tour-de-force. And when I think how young they must have been – that was the other thing. To me, these amazing women arrived who sat on four tables and looked at every woman in that room, every young actress, and said that if you want to do it, you can do it. You have a responsibility as an artist, that if you decide to do it, art by its very nature is political. That doesn't mean you have to be political with a capital 'P', but you can make a difference, you can create work for yourselves and you have the perfect backdrop in which to do it. They were incredible.

Then a few years later, when I went to BIFHE to repeat my A Levels, I saw my first Charabanc shows. The first one was *Gold in the Streets*, then it was *Girls in the Big Picture* and *Girls in the Big Picture* just blew my mind ... the theatricality of it. They performed that in the old college building in Brunswick Street, in a gym. There were no big lights, there was nothing. It was my first experience of that type of theatre – being done in a non-theatre setting in a community performance venue – where quality was not tampered with. And I can remember being packed into that room watching a space we knew being transformed and there was this authenticity of voice, brilliant narrative, the performances were amazing and it just worked.

Then, in 1993-94, I was doing a lot of radio drama and appearing in plays for DubbelJoint directed by Pam Brighton, who ran the [BBC] radio department at that time. I got a phone call from Tim Loane to say they were doing a Christmas show, they had this idea for *Christmas Eve Can Kill You*. We did it as a profit-share and we all pulled together, all just mucked in. At that time Belfast was still not in great shape and the OMAC[1] was down a fairly darkly lit street and we were doing this Christmas show and we didn't know if people were going to turn up.

There were five of us in the cast and we all multi-roled. We did the OMAC, then we were invited back the following year and the OMAC gave us a little bit of money and we got paid a little bit. And that year we decided we'd take it to Hydebank [Young Offenders Centre]. It was one of the first shows that really had been taken into the prisons and Mike Moloney of the Prison Arts Foundation was very keen that projects go in ... and I remember us all sitting down and him saying that there would be a lot of noise. On we went and Richard Orr had to do one bit where he was dressed as a soldier manning a check-point and when he appeared the whole crowd were booing and hissing – the sense of old-style music hall theatre was incredible.

The following year the Arts Theatre bought it and put money into it, so we added three characters. We ran in the Arts and we were paid proper wages. Then the following year the Lyric bought it and put more money into it. The set was getting bigger each time and the cast was getting bigger, and the story was getting more complex, but the essence of it, the central narrative, remained the same. You talk to anybody who did *Christmas Eve Can Kill You* and it was Christmas for us.

In 2000/2001, for my first Christmas when I took over the Lyric, I decided to bring back *Christmas Eve Can Kill You* and we did it for two Christmases. It was the first time the Lyric had done two Christmas shows, a model I introduced at that time as I had seen it work elsewhere and I knew there was an audience who would go to the theatre at Christmas that didn't go at other times of the year.

Obviously, during that period of time I saw *A Night in November*. I remember it ... again, as its form and the casting – with Marie when the casting is right; when it's people that understand the way her scripts work ... When I was at the Lyric then with Marie I produced *Weddins, Weeins and Wakes*; I produced *The Blind Fiddler*; *Christmas Eve* ... a couple of times and then we re-did it and called it *New Year's Eve Can Kill You* in my last year there, and Karl Wallace directed that. And then we brought *Blind Fiddler* to Edinburgh.

TM: And why did you take the show to Edinburgh?

PMcF: Ian [McElhinney] and Marie really wanted to take it to Edinburgh.

TM: But for the Lyric that was a major departure?

PMcF: It was, yes. But in a way the pressure on the Lyric wasn't huge financially because they were being bought in. It was bought by the Assembly Rooms at that time. So it had a host and all that. It wasn't like we made a decision with a big show to say, 'Right. This is what we are going to do.' Also at that time *Stones in His Pockets* was being co-produced by Pat Moylan and Breda Cashe and Lane Productions. Marie and Ian had a strong relationship with the commercial-producer model, so they basically ran with it and the Lyric's involvement was to have done the original production and to have produced the book.

What I found difficult about working on Marie's work, during that period ... Going from the revival of *A Night in November* with Dan [Gordon] in the Lyric was incredible and the timing of it was key. I remember Eddie Jordan flying in by helicopter to see it and arriving in a field facing the Lyric. I mean people used to appear to see that show that we would have to fit in to get tickets. But going from that into *Weddins, Weeins and Wakes* and then *Blind Fiddler*, and *A Very Weird Manor*, I watched Marie's audiences become less loyal ... By their presence and power of footfall they showed that they expected more of her. And as disappointed as I was as the producer of those shows, I think, deep down I had a respect for the audience and I felt that it is simply not enough to produce a Marie Jones [play].

TM: But there had been a time when people were flocking in – she brought an audience – not that she could have done anything but ...?

PMcF: That's what that proved: that she couldn't do just anything. I was very glad of it in a way because I think that when Marie is at her best and when she's working with somebody [who] like Ian [McElhinney] is a great foil to her: he understands. Like, I'll be honest: I didn't like *Stones in His Pockets* and I remember sitting watching it in the [Grand] Opera House in amongst an audience that was going mad for it, just going, 'It's not for me.' I didn't get it. I didn't think it was good enough. I thought it was too sentimental and I found that, in places, the humour was cheap. Like *Christmas Eve Can Kill You*, those early shows were inspired. You had characters who had soul. You were looking at them falling apart, at the cracks that began to show in working-class love, loss, anger, frustration. There was an honesty to it that just shone through. When she gets that I don't think there's anybody better than her. There are few writers that do it. I have great respect for that. I think writing humour is completely underestimated: it's incredibly difficult. But I think that she requires really good actors and she requires a really good director and editor. Pam [Brighton] was great with her and unfortunately we all know what happened. And I think Ian is really good with her.

TM: You are talking about her ability to write working-class characters and people have commented on her ability to capture a character in speech and rhythm, though on the page that looks terrible.

PMcF: Absolutely horrific. It's so funny when you watch somebody who hasn't done Marie's work before. Marie's plays at a read-through can be toe-curling because in the room you are going to have a combination of people who have done her shows before and those who haven't. Those who have done her shows before hit the ground running, they know what they are doing and it's bang, bang, bang. Very Marie: very Marie herself as an actress. There's a rhythm to it, a speed to it: you just let it do its work and not worry about it, you'll find it in the rehearsal. And then there are those who treat it with a degree of reverence. You treat it with reverence and you're going to be swimming around there for hours. It's not going to be funny; it's not going to be sad; it's not going to work; the cadences are going to jar with you constantly. She's not that type of writer.

One of the great things about Pam [Brighton] working with her – like I can remember working on *Christmas Eve Can Kill You* and Pam would be sitting there directing something and then would yell, 'Take the fifth word out of line six. That word's one word too many.' And Pam could hear what it needed to be. I learnt a lot from Pam about working on new scripts: that one of the director's jobs is to listen for when it gets too heavy, how to maintain the lightness.

One of the remarkable things about working with her new work is what gets achieved over the rehearsal period. And Marie's very open to that. Marie loves working with actors and she loves her own plays. There's no other playwright I know – having produced her – that will sit in that auditorium for the dress rehearsal, the tech, the opening night – will come and see it, five, six or seven times and laugh at the same bits.

TM: And the complexity of the characters? You have played Northern Irish characters, including representing real people on television, and have had to avoid the stereotypes presented in the wider media. You've done an awful lot of work in Northern Ireland for Northern Irish audiences. Yet Marie's characters have been described as being stereotypical, sometimes simplistic, while you as an actor see depth there.

PMcF: There's depth, definitely depth. It's a very, very fine line. I'm not denying that Marie has written characters that are cliches and larger than life. For example, look at a play like *Weddins, Weeins and Wakes* – I saw the original production with Charabanc way back whenever at the Project Arts Centre in Dublin. And I remember thinking that it had great potential. It's all written in rhyme, accessible rhyme, and it's clever, and the rhyme exists in the vernacular. When the first full-length production was worked on at the Lyric when I was there, it was always going to be Carol [Moore] and Eleanor [Methven] who were going to play the two leads and Marie was going to be in it. In the opening scene the two characters are larger than life, yes; they're stereotypes, yes; they're cliches, yes. BUT ... within all that you are still watching two characters that you can't help but be on their side, you want them to win, want them to go on a positive journey, and whom you feel for, despite yourself. Now, it's farce, farce is not my bag. And it's got songs in it; again not overly my bag. But it was a masterclass in watching a group of performers listen to an audience. It was amazing.

You asked me about playing Marie's characters. Honestly whenever I used to play in *Christmas Eve Can Kill You*, it was a comedy, it was a farce and there were characters that were larger than life and very over the top – drunk women from West Belfast – very brash. But if I didn't nail that moment when I'm standing telling a dog that my husband has cheated on me, that I still really love him, that he's gone for a younger model and that Christmas is ruined ... Everything about that is wrong. You're not going to give your Medea, but when you nail it, if you trust her ... Being able to place ten or twelve lines in a scene, standing with a white dog who's licking my face, wearing deely-boppers on my head that have tinsel on them – it's a challenge. But when you trust it ... It just works.

But there are other characters that don't work for me. Like in *Women on the Verge of HRT* – I nearly produced it at the Lyric ... for exactly the wrong reasons ... which were that we needed a sure-fire bet and I couldn't understand why it was a sure-fire bet but I knew that people would come through the doors to see it because people loved

Marie. I remember sitting at the opening night in the Whiterock in West Belfast with a 97% female audience and just not getting it. And I think I felt disappointed because I think that Marie's a better writer than that.

TM: It's interesting that some of those plays have transferred out of Northern Ireland and have gone on to be commercial successes, including *Women on the Verge*. Yet you can't explain it?

PMcF: I don't get it, I really don't. But if somebody programs a show like that and manages audience expectations right then, fair enough.

TM: Given that you were in at the start of this latest phase in the development of contemporary Northern Irish theatre – involved in every single aspect of it – is there a legacy that comes down from Charabanc to Northern Irish theatre and Irish theatre more widely?

PMcF: Absolutely. 100% per cent. There is no doubt in my mind. Each of those women are still continuing to do that in very different ways, in their uniqueness and independence. So Marie Jones has continued to produce work, continued to act, is always very vocal about her pride in her roots in East Belfast. She has done some incredible performances on television and on stage and has continued to bring audiences to theatre. When you look at what Marie did, leading on to what Martin Lynch has done with GBL Productions, opening up the [Grand] Opera House in the summer months, with local work on the main stage, it is quite unbelievable.

For Charabanc as a company, if you look particularly at the North of Ireland and who is running the local theatre companies, they are all women: Zoe [Seaton] at Big Telly, Lisa May at Bruiser, Anne McReynolds at The MAC, Andrea Montgomery running Terra Nova, Patricia Downey running Spanner in The Works, Caitriona McLaughlin a freelance director in Derry. There are a lot of women of my generation and slightly younger who now work in theatre and whether or not we know it, hearing our own voices on stage and running theatre companies that are doing difficult work, targeting new audiences, breaking the mould, I think inevitably that has to have been the impact [of Charabanc].

There is a question of whether or not they had an impact on the South, because they focused a lot on touring in the North and bringing theatre to non-theatre venues whenever Belfast in particular was falling apart.

TM: Now there is no question that theatre is here to stay as part and parcel of the cultural and economic life of Northern Ireland.

PMcF: Yes.

TM: If you were approached to produce a new Marie Jones script, what would your expectation be? What would you expect to read?

PMcF: It would be funny. It would have soul. It would have a very small cast. I don't know why I say that, but I think it would have three maybe four people tops. It would be about here and written in a very strong vernacular ... And she'd probably only give me the first twenty-five pages! That's probably very unfair. She'd probably give me either twenty-five pages which is what happened with *A Very Weird Manor* and *Blind Fiddler* or else it would be really over-written, though she's not someone who tends to over-write. It's very much less is more which is more daunting.

TM: Would you want to direct it?

PMcF: It depends what it is. It depends on whether I'd be the right person for it ... But I think there are more plays in Marie. I mean someone who writes *A Night in November* ...

TM: You've talked about her capacity as a collaborator, but she also seems to enjoy a great deal of loyalty?

PMcF: Yes: huge. But she's also oddly private. I wouldn't say I know Marie despite the fact that I've worked with her. She has a very select inner circle and her loyalty is to Ian and her boys and her family, if you watch when her family come to see her work, her relationship to her sister and to her late mum, Sadie. Marie is very outgoing and vivacious, chats to people and is a great party host, but family comes first and foremost for her.

---

[1] A former museum building that was converted to become the Old Museum Arts Centre.

13 | 'Popular Feminisms' and the Radical Within: Menopausal Women's Desire for Visibility in Marie Jones's *Women on the Verge of HRT*

Shonagh Hill

Introduction

In a Clairol *Nice-n-Easy* hair dye advertisement aired in 2013, the narrator, Kate's husband, congratulates Kate's ability to manage 'three moves, five jobs, two newborns. It's no wonder I'm getting grey but Kate still looks like ... Kate.' What we see at work here are the ways in which ideologies of aging have infiltrated every level of popular culture. More specifically, the advert reveals how the neoliberal governance of femininity requires that the signs of female ageing be hidden away – as a result, ageing women's sexual desires and their menopausal bodies are denied a presence. Marie Jones's play *Women on the Verge of HRT*[1] is defiant in its assertion of that presence and expression of anger at the way in which society deems which bodies have worth and thus have access to cultural legibility. Indeed, Vera, one of Jones's protagonists, articulates the menopausal woman's '(f)ear of not being heard – becoming invisible' (14). This article explores how 'popular feminisms', which take up feminist ideas 'in popular forms and practices' (Hollows 193), may offer a means of working within the popular to mark the visibility of an ageing female subjectivity. Through discussion of Jones's use of popular culture and popular theatre, as well as the resultant creation of affective feminist affiliations, I wish to explore the pleasures and protest articulated through *Women on the Verge of HRT*.

The play focuses on long-time friends Vera and Anna, two of the thousands of women who, at the invitation of wholesome Irish country singer Daniel O'Donnell, travel annually to attend a tea-party in his hometown of Kincasslagh, Donegal. The occasion enables the female fans to temporarily retreat from their lives: Vera's husband has left her for a younger woman, while Anna's marriage is sexually unfulfilled. Indeed, Anna has a romantic novel beside her bed and a Daniel O'Donnell pillow on it, and we learn that her fantasies offer her vital sustenance: 'he lifts me. The songs lift me' (16). The setting of Act One, the hotel bedroom where the women are staying, draws the audience into the familiarity and openness of an old friendship. There is only one other actor on stage: a waiter called Fergal who serves the women's room-service drinks. The act explores Anna's and Vera's innermost desires and worries through the intimacy of their discussions, as well as songs and humour. Act Two shifts in location to the Donegal shoreline where Anna and Vera join Fergal to watch the dawn break. Where Act One focuses on the escapism that O'Donnell offers his fans, the second act is closely linked to the mythic realm with the vocal presence of the wailing banshee and Fergal's shape-shifting as he morphs between Vera's and Anna's husbands and their mistresses, and the women's friends. Fergal takes on the persona of O'Donnell in Act One when he performs one of his songs but in Act Two he is connected to the banshee's fairy love, the Pooka, who leaves her because she has grown old and withered: 'she just would not accept that she was no longer beautiful so when we hear her screaming it's because she knows that the Pooka is somewhere around' (34). At the end of the play Fergal disappears in a puff of smoke, as do Anna's illusions about her marriage. Thus, the illusory nature of myth and fantasy, including that which O'Donnell offers, is exposed and we are left with Anna's final words 'I'm so angry' (39), before the Finale Song. Both acts of the play are therefore defined by protest and the women's anger at becoming part of a 'big mass of middle-aged nobodies' (7), as articulated through their discussions, songs and through the banshee's wailing.

The emphasis of existing scholarship on the play tends to be on the liminal and mythic spaces of Act Two as a site of possibility, and on the resultant celebratory transformation of the two women. Maria Kurdi delineates 'the women protagonists' transformation into individuals who have their own perspective and belief in themselves' (126) and continues, '(c)reating its own imaginative space, the concluding scene of *Women on the Verge of HRT* is an expression of the Kristevan concept of *jouissance* ... Vera and Anna celebrate unrestrained female re-embodiment and resolution to reject and combat the threats of invisibility' (126). This sense of unrestraint and freedom is shared by Margaret Llewellyn-Jones: 'Transformed, as their final celebratory song/duet suggests, they will henceforth be stronger, more self-reliant and aware' (76). However, my reading of the play questions the optimistic transformation of the ending, and instead looks to the popular in the play as a source of feminist potential: that is, the use of popular theatre forms, as well as the political potential of feminism's work within popular culture.

Postfeminism, 'Popular Feminisms' and Transformation

Before addressing the presence of popular theatre forms and popular culture in Jones's play, I want to first explore the complexity of the trope of transformation as inflected by neoliberal discourse and contemporary understandings of feminisms. For the women of the play, there is no doubt that menopause, or 'the change', is a transformation which will result in their abjection from society. Older women's sexual desires are ignored and repudiated: Vera's reference to a vibrator results in Fergal turning away in embarrassment and Anna revealing that 'people' call Vera a whore (29). Furthermore, older women's unruly menopausal bodies refuse self-regulation and are medicalized and hystericized in response. Anna's husband's reaction to her hot flushes is one of awkwardness and revulsion:

> 'It's the change'. He couldn't even say the word. He might just as well as been saying leprosy the way he twisted his face and rolled his eyes. He just mimed it like I had some kind of terminal illness. No. Worse than that. Some kind of mental illness (19).

The need to maintain one's youth, of avoiding passing 'our sell-by date'(13) and being left on the 'sexual scrap-heap' (5), is fuelled by the fear, and reality in Vera's case, of being left by her husband for a younger woman. In response, Vera uses expensive anti-ageing creams and describes herself as a 'maintenance expert' (24). The discrepancy between the attempts to maintain an ideal femininity and the reality of embodiment is acknowledged by Vera's experience in the changing room of a clothes store: 'I just stood there looking in the mirror and I says; Vera you don't know what you are supposed to look like anymore' (13). The banshee of Act Two thus represents the consequences of the violent imposition of myths of an ideal youthful feminine beauty; her disembodiment echoes, furthermore, the menopausal woman's sense of dislocation and alienation, both from society and her body.

In contrast to the menopausal transformation which results in invisibility, late capitalist society places value on an idealized youthful femininity; women are urged to add value both to themselves and this ideal through consumption, as the now famous L'Oréal ads insist 'Because you're worth it.' According to the L'Oréal Paris website, the phrase was 'written in 1973 when a social revolution and a new spirit of feminism was in full swing' but the emergence of neoliberal discourse has rewritten feminist notions of freedom and worth – they are no longer optimistically transformative ideals but are intimately linked to capitalism and thereby subject to its limits. *Women on the Verge of HRT* emerges from a world in which popular culture excludes the process of ageing by deifying a cult of youth through makeover shows which 'dedicate themselves to staging rejuvenating transformations and the fantasy that ageing can be managed away' (Tasker and Negra 9). Within late capitalist society, transformation is thus an ambivalent trope: the potential for change is presented as freely chosen and the emphasis is on the individual's responsibility to self-manage and achieve success, yet many women do not have the economic power to buy transformation.

Neoliberalism thus regulates and 'transforms' women's bodies and lives, as well as shaping contemporary understandings of feminism. Postfeminism is a contested term – interpreted as alternately building on and developing, or coming after and rejecting, second-wave feminism. The former approach, sometimes labelled third-wave feminism, draws on theoretical frameworks – most obviously, post-structuralism, postmodernism and postcolonialism – in order to address the limitations of second-wave feminism. The latter media-led, backlash discourse is characterized as a form of anti-feminism which perpetuates gender inequality, and is closely connected to neoliberal discourse. In their discussion of postfeminism, Tasker and Negra note that 'much postfeminist rhetoric is of a piece with the exhortations of the 1990s 'New Economy' and the displacement of democratic imperatives by free market ones' (4). The free market values of a neoliberal economy have arguably co-opted terms such as freedom, independence and transformation; as Hollows notes, 'feminist themes can be appropriated, losing their radicalism, and becoming attached to more conservative agendas' (Hollows 198). Postfeminist discourses draw on second-wave feminist ideals but are also shaped by free market values resulting in 'the individualist, acquisitive, and transformative values of postfeminism' (Tasker and Negra 5). Postfeminism is therefore economically exclusive and its freedoms and transformative power are not available to all women.

In their discussion of feminism in popular culture, Joanne Hollows and Rachel Moseley suggest that 'powerful attachments in some feminisms to the idea that feminism can exist in an 'outside', and vanguard, position' underpins 'disagreements over the relationships between second-wave and post- and third-wave feminisms' (2). In order to negotiate these differences, commentators like Hollows and Moseley have turned to 'popular feminisms' in order to explore 'how feminist ideas are negotiated within the popular with contradictory effects' (Hollows 195). The examination of 'popular feminisms' therefore offers a way out of a simplistic either/or understanding of postfeminism. The backlash postfeminist thesis fails to understand how postfeminism has developed and responded to the demands of a different historical period evident 'in popularly available understandings of femininity and women's place' (Brunsdon, qtd in Hollows 192). Furthermore, understanding postfeminism as simply feminism co-opted by neoliberalism, asserts that second-wave feminism is the authentic form of feminism; it 'suggests that there is a better, 'unpopular' form of feminism' (Hollows 197). 'Unpopular' feminism excludes the experiences of the 'ordinary woman' through its failure to engage with feminism within popular culture. The aforementioned scholarship on Jones's play does not account for the complexity and contradictions of the notion of transformation or the potential of popular culture. An examination of the ways in which feminist ideas emerge through popular theatre forms and popular culture in *Women on the Verge of HRT*, can potentially dismantle and renew feminism. 'Popular feminisms', in other words, offer the means of avoiding the exclusivity of both postfeminism and 'unpopular' feminism, as well as articulating the discontent and pleasures of the 'ordinary woman'.

Popular Theatre's Critical Invisibility

Marie Jones's work is rooted in popular theatre; she was one of the five founding members of Charabanc Theatre Company (1983-1995), an all-woman, Belfast theatre group who drew on popular theatre traditions to bring working-class men and women into theatres (Winter 17). Charabanc's popular, political credentials were further cemented by the fact that their first play, *Lay Up Your Ends*, was directed by Pam Brighton, a director who had worked with political British theatre companies, including John McGrath's company 7:84. Stephen Lacey highlights the 'diverse and overlapping history' of popular theatre forms which can be defined by their appeal 'to the broadest possible audience within a given historical period, whether for commercial or political reasons' (125). Jones's work arguably encompasses both commercial and political definitions at different stages of her career. Jones left Charabanc in 1990 to become the writer for DubbelJoint Theatre Company, thus marking a shift from working on the radical margins with collaborative approaches which rejected hierarchies in Charabanc's early days, to working as a single, published, commercially successful author. Many of Jones's plays with DubbelJoint – *A Night in November, Women on the Verge of HRT,* and *Stones in his Pockets* – have been published and toured extensively, including runs in New York and London. However, the broad appeal of political and commercial popular theatre has not been critically reflected in Irish theatre, and feminist theatre, scholarship.

As Eugene McNulty's essay in this volume identifies, Charabanc's roots in the popular marked them out from the tradition of an Irish literary theatre. One of the founding members of *Charabanc*, Brenda Winter, notes that a *Belfast News Letter* reviewer was uncertain how to categorize *Lay Up Your Ends*:

> He was unable to fit the play into any recognizable matrix of Irish literary drama. Only the theatre cognoscenti present that night would have realised that Charabanc were engaging with methodologies from British popular, political theatre practice of the 1960s and 1970s not previously employed in this way on the stage in Northern Ireland (32).

The newspaper reviewer's hesitancy is, of course, part of a bigger picture. In his study *Joyce, O'Casey, and the Irish Popular Theater,* Stephen Watt notes the critical neglect of popular theatre; a neglect which privileges literary over commercial theatre, high over low culture, and reason over emotion: 'Because of their putative invitations to escapism, their repetitive and inartistic constructions, and their largely emotional trajectories, popular plays are thus, for many scholars, eminently forgettable' (5). Irish theatre scholarship has overlooked the importance of popular theatre to the detriment of Charabanc which has been excluded or merely mentioned in histories of Irish theatre (see: Winter 18 and Lojek 87-88). Happily, since Watt's study was published in 1991, the critical landscape of Irish theatre studies has shifted and there has been increased engagement with popular theatre. Christopher Morash's *A History of Irish Theatre, 1601-2000* (Cambridge: Cambridge U.P., 2002), for example, did much to broaden the address of Irish theatre scholarship to incorporate popular theatre before the twentieth century.

Jones's critical neglect is not solely a result of Irish theatre studies' blind-spots. In an article on American playwright Heidi Wasserstein, Jill Dolan acknowledges both her own, and feminist scholarship's, neglect of the popular – a space which she now advocates as a realm of political possibility:

> Conducting feminist practice, as third wavers advocate, from a place admittedly within capitalism (and within dominant ideology) could be advantageous, instead of holding on to what might finally be an idealist belief that feminist practice can remain outside capitalism's reach ... Perhaps it is now time to acknowledge the potential of looking inside as well, and to address feminism as a critique or value circulating within our most commercial theatres (434-435).

Wasserstein's background (upper-middle-class Manhattanite), and choice of theatrical form (realist comedy), differ from Jones's working-class background, politics and use of political popular theatre, but *Women on the Verge of HRT* entered the commercial mainstream when it transferred to the Vaudeville Theatre in London's West End in 1997.[2] Charabanc's occlusion from the canon formation of Irish theatre is perhaps partially explained by its being too firmly rooted in British political, popular theatre, but the relative neglect of Jones's later work by feminist theatre scholarship is perhaps explained by feminist attachments to a radical 'outside' resulting in Jones's work being deemed too mainstream.[3] Thus, my discussion of *Women on the Verge of HRT* necessarily addresses the ways in which Jones negotiates politically and commercially inflected definitions of popular theatre; a negotiation which underlines the importance of talking about the multiplicity of 'popular feminisms'.

I intend to shift the critical emphasis from the alternative, 'outside' spaces of Act Two and the transformative ending, by focusing on aspects of the play whose feminist potential can be better understood through the contradictions of 'popular feminisms'. Rather than suggesting that Jones's later commercially successful work assigns her to 'the ranks of the co-opted and assimilated' (Dolan 434), I intend to carry out a feminist critique from within and look, as Dolan suggests, 'at popular theatre as a vital location of pleasure, perspicacity, and political possibility' (436). I want to firstly focus on the political address of the popular theatre traditions which *Women on the Verge of HRT* draws on, before discussing the possibility of locating feminist politics within popular culture through the figure of Daniel O'Donnell, and finally, I will address the affective politics of the play as a 'good night out for girls'. Helen Lojek suggests that 'Charabanc, no doubt without fully intending to, challenged all of academia's standard hierarchical propositions, and these propositions are essentially political' (Playing Politics 88). I wish to address the extent to which Jones's later work, namely *Women on the Verge of HRT*, continues to challenge and complicate hierarchical binaries of elite/ popular culture and theatre, and 'unpopular'/ popular, or post- / feminism.

The Pleasures and Politics of Popular Theatre

In his seminal study of popular theatre, *A Good Night Out*, John McGrath identifies nine elements of working-class popular entertainment: directness, comedy, music, emotion, variety, effect, immediacy, localism (both of material and of a sense of identity with the performer) (54-59). Charabanc's work engaged with all of these elements and Jones's later work continues to be informed by them. However, where McGrath uses the term political theatre interchangeably with working-class theatre, I would argue that *Women on the Verge of HRT* draws on these elements to the political end of giving voice to those who are disempowered both by class *and* gender. Charabanc's aim of 'putting women's experiences to the fore' (qtd. in Lojek, Playing Politics 83) is shared by Jones's *Women on the Verge of HRT*. Therefore, where McGrath explicates how each of the aforementioned identifiers speak to working-class audiences, Jones deploys them to speak to female audiences, both working-class and middle-class as evidenced by the fact that *Women on the Verge of HRT* premiered at The West Belfast Festival / Feile an Phobail, then subsequently toured to commercial venues. Baz Kershaw suggests that John McGrath's understanding of the history of popular performance forms is somewhat simplistic:

> It is a mistake to suggest, for example, that forms such as pantomime and music hall once belonged to the working classes and have been appropriated subsequently by enemies of the class. Those forms almost always were part of a complex dialectic through which conflicting ideologies, conflicting interests, have been staged (154).

Through its appeal to political (working-class and feminist) and commercial definitions of popular theatre, *Women on the Verge of HRT* evidences this complex dialectic; a conflict which further resonates with the debates surrounding the contradictions of 'popular feminisms'. Both political and commercial popular theatre are defined by their breadth of appeal, and Jones's use of popular theatre forms and willingness to enter the commercial mainstream arguably marks the inclusivity of 'popular feminisms': 'The importance of some forms of 'popular feminism' such as those seen on *Oprah* is not simply about the size of their audience but the ways in which their mode of address seeks to include rather than exclude' (Hollows 202). Jones's mode of address is rooted in popular theatre traditions so I want now to address McGrath's elements as they pertain to *Women on the Verge of HRT* in order to further explore the contradictions of 'popular feminisms'.

McGrath firstly asserts the importance of directness, that 'working class audiences have minds of their own and like to hear what your mind is' (54). In *Women on the Verge of HRT*, directness is intertwined with McGrath's second element: comedy. Vera and Anna speak directly of, and to, female menopausal experience and their discussions air taboo subjects, oftentimes through the 'use of the ironic and deflationary force of humour' (McMullan 40). For the largely female audiences of the play, laughter is a result of recognition and anger:

> **VERA:** How do you prepare for being on the sexual scrap-heap? Do we all book into a sex hospice? Is there a class you can go to? Like a lie-down-and-die class? Do all us over-forties bring our sexy underwear and our face creams and throw them on a big bonfire – and some oul doll in a kimono makes us beat up a big plastic willy. Come on now, ladies – drive out those evil thoughts. Banish that nasty libido. Rid from your memory that horrible penis (5).

The allusion to bra-burning feminism reinforces 'ordinary' women's alienation from second-wave feminism's sense of celebration. The exclusivity of feminism's achievements is referenced and, in the process, the comedy acknowledges a community of 'invisible' menopausal women. Comedy is thus a means of expressing their anger at society's refusal to acknowledge them as desiring subjects, as well as uniting these 'ordinary' women. McGrath addresses middle-class audience perceptions that 'laughter makes the play less serious' (54), while also highlighting the need for critical assessment of comedy and thus acknowledgment of its sophistication and potential for anarchy. In *Women on the Verge of HRT*, comedy unleashes that which society wishes to contain: the reality of ageing women's embodied experiences, but underpinning this unruly expression are the women's very real insecurities, as well as an exposure of the need for an inclusive and accessible 'ordinary' feminism.

The central theme of *Women on the Verge of HRT*, is arguably the contradictory promise and illusion that popular culture offers and perpetuates through fantasy and myth, and this is explored through the figure of the Pooka. Fergal takes on the persona of O'Donnell in Act One and this is developed in Act Two through his shape-shifting as the Pooka; a performance which draws on a traditional element of popular theatre. McGrath notes that variety is a feature that '(m)ost of the traditional forms of working class entertainment seem to possess':

> (of being) able to switch from a singer to a comedian, to a juggler, to a band, to a chorus number, to a conjurer, to a sing-along, to bingo, to wrestling, to strip-tease, and then back again to a singer, and a comedian and a grand 'Altogether' finale, with great ease (56).

Fergal is defined by his ability to switch between roles; a character which combines entertainment, as well as critique. In Act One, Fergal sings in the style of O'Donnell about his longing for his love, the 'magic and glory' of Donegal (11-2) and his subsequent roles in Act Two serve to expose the consequences of romantic visions of woman and homeland, and their conflation. He plays a friend of Vera's and Anna's, Stella, and immediately after switches to playing Stella's husband Peter. Stella is introduced as 'someone' who calls Vera a whore and she accuses Vera of flirting with her husband at the staff Christmas dinner. Stella is convinced that Peter is having an affair and explains that he no longer writes her love poetry: 'I look at those poems now Vera and I cry because I am not like that anymore, I mean if he loved me because I was like that then, how could he love me now? ... It's not fair. Like you can't live up to nature anymore' (31). Stella's fears stem from the ageing woman's inability to embody an idealized youthful femininity, 'like the first blush of spring' (31), but her husband is equally disillusioned by romanticized notions of masculinity: 'I wanted to be the man in the Milk Tray ad' (31). These naturalized gender roles are both illusory and elusive; a description shared by Fergal's performance of O'Donnell and his shape-shifting in Act Two which result in his disappearance into a puff of smoke at the end of the play. In *Women on the Verge of HRT* Jones draws on a technique which is also utilized in *Stones in his Pockets* (1996), namely deploying theatrically playful characters to deconstruct authenticity: in his discussion of *Stones in his Pockets*, Mark Phelan notes that 'the political critique ... is corporeally embodied in meta-theatrical performance' (Performing Authentic 56). Fergal's shape-shifting persona questions the authority of his and O'Donnell's vision; a process which opens up a space for the articulation of silenced female voices and visibility for menopausal women.

Through the figure of the Pooka, Jones harnesses the techniques of popular theatre to expose the playful seductions and pleasures, as well as the limits, of popular culture, and her use of song further highlights the contradictions of working within the popular to combine pleasure and political critique. Vera's and Anna's desire to be heard and for visibility is manifested through the play's songs which are a 'vital location of pleasure, perspicacity, and political possibility' (Dolan 436). McGrath identifies the importance of both music and emotion to popular theatre, and links the two elements: 'music is enjoyable for itself, for emotional release' (55). McGrath also notes the perception that it is seen by middle-class theatre-goers 'as a threat to seriousness' (55). However, the songs in Jones's play are not simply for pleasure, they also form the backbone of the play's argument; an argument which is thus explored through affective registers to combine politics and pleasure. The emotions unleashed by the songs linger on, shaping both the characters' and audience's experiences. The songs create an affective dialogue which resonates with the concerns of the play; they are primarily concerned with articulating the women's innermost feelings and/ or exploring the elusive and illusory nature of fantasy and myth. I therefore want to briefly explore the songs of the play and their relationship to one another as they articulate the tensions within the play, thereby creating a 'communal space of profitable pleasure/ pleasurable profit' (Aston and Harris 15).

Exploration of Vera's and Anna's seemingly oppositional viewpoints shapes several of the songs in the play. Song One follows a discussion between Vera and Anna regarding Vera's desire to 'shop around' (5), a euphemism for looking for a sexual partner since her husband has left her. Anna, in her words, offers a more 'realistic' approach and asks Vera, 'I don't know why you couldn't make do' (5). The women sing alternate sections of the song to underline their divergent responses. Vera's voice of defiance, 'All I'm askin' is the right to reply / When I'm told my passion must lie down and die' (6), is contrasted with Anna's response that Vera is never satisfied: 'When she had one she didn't want at all / Now she hasn't she wants them all' (6). Seemingly, the song sets up a defiant / compliant opposition which characterizes the two women. However, Song Three, which closes Act One, is framed by Vera's opening and closing refrain: 'I want to be the one in the story / The one who has fallen in love / I want to be the one I imagine / Who makes love under the sun' (19-20). Early in the play, Vera criticized Anna's investment in the escapism of fantasy and voiced her refusal to buy into these substitutes:

ANNA: I like a good love story.
VERA: Yes and so do I. But my own. Not somebody else's. We are supposed to just be content with somebody else's excitement. Well fuck that for a game of darts (7).

Yet, Song Three somewhat surprisingly reveals Vera's investment in romantic fantasy and the act closes with an image of O'Donnell: 'For a brief moment a light on Daniel on the pillowcase – then Black-out' (20). During the interval, the audience are left pondering: is Vera as resistant as she first appears, and by implication, is Anna as compliant? The women's dialogue opens up a complex dialectic between reality / fantasy, invisibility / visibility, and compliance / defiance, and this is further explored through the figure of Daniel O'Donnell.

The figure of O'Donnell is key to several of the songs that thread through *Women on the Verge of HRT*. Song Two is performed by Fergal, in the style of Daniel O'Donnell, and presents a romantic fantasy of Donegal with the land as his love: 'Oh Donegal at each rising dawn / I will yearn for you ever more' (11). This romantic vision of the 'magic and glory' of Donegal introduces one of the key themes to which the ending will return: fantasy as something to be eternally yearned for and impossible to fulfil. Vera questions Fergal / O'Donnell's vision in Song Four which occurs close to the start of Act Two and is a dialogue between Fergal and Vera who sing alternate verses. Their discussion sets up a tension which comes to a head at the close of the play. Fergal's verses reinforce the idyllic image of 'this land of magic and wonder' from which the 'wailing old slag', the banshee, is exiled '(w)ay beyond the sea and foam' (22-23). Vera's response verses articulate both her and the banshee's desire to be heard, and thereby acknowledges the violence of idealized and naturalized myths of femininity and masculinity. However, the songs also explore the contradictions of 'popular feminisms'; of finding feminist politics within dominant ideology. Although the fantasy O'Donnell offers is questioned, it is also offered as a space in which to locate menopausal women's pleasure and anger and to counter their invisibility, as evidenced by Anna's Song Six which combines emotional release and political protest.

In contrast to Fergal's claim that the night on the beach is all about '(r)ealizing your dreams' (28), the exposure of uncomfortable truths characterizes the second act. In Song Six, 'Don't Shatter My Dreams', Anna passionately and movingly responds to Vera's dismissal of popular culture, 'that stupid oul romantic rubbish' (34); Anna argues for its sustaining qualities: 'My comfort, my warmth / My escape from the cold' (34). The repetition of the line 'Don't shatter my dreams, handle with care' highlights the fragility of these fantasies, as well as Anna's vulnerability. The song is followed by the arrival of Fergal as Anna's husband Marty and in the conversation that ensues Anna learns that Marty looks at porn magazines. Anna is outraged that Marty imagines himself taking part in his fantasies, whereas her fantasies concern other people: Anna realizes that 'you even took away my fantasy that I could be loved again that I could have somebody who will see me, love me and listen to me' (37). This serves to highlight the contradictions and vulnerability of the space offered by fantasy: it may be a space which offers the possibility of self-authorship and visibility but it is not a utopian space beyond dominant discourses of power. Anna's dreams are harshly shattered and the emotional resonances of her song linger on as the play comes to an end. Thus, Jones's songs draw on popular theatre traditions and the contradictions of 'popular feminisms' to create an affective feminist politics, rooted in pleasure, as well as profit and protest.

The Finale Song: Transformation and Celebration?

The contradictions of 'popular feminisms' can be further explored through examination of the ending of the play which, like Anna's Song Six, is hardly celebratory and therefore not simply an articulation of Vera and Anna's liberation. In an interview with Imelda Foley, Jones discusses the play's ending: 'In films it's different, the happy ending, having it all tied up. I think theatre people are much more open. In *HRT* there could have been an ending, and the audience expected that ending. When it didn't happen you could sense disappointment' (Foley 36). Foley's own reading of the play takes this lack of 'having it all tied up' into account:

> This ending is as much a mirage as the carefully constructed details that came before. The factual exposition is that Anna's life, carefully romanticized and therefore protected, has been shattered. We are encouraged simply to comply with the closure, non-feminine and didactic, to celebrate some kind of dubious victory that has hardly been demonstrated by the text (53-54).

The events that precede the Finale Song set up the ending's ambiguity. Anna seemingly consents to her invisible fate when she concurs with Fergal's acceptance of societal norms of male and female bodies:

> **VERA:** Bums. The tighter the better ... And penises.
> **ANNA:** I don't suppose it really matters what size they are.

> **FERGAL:** See? What can you do? It's basic, it's normal, it's natural.
> **ANNA:** (*resigned*) It's just natural, as Fergal says (38).

In contrast, Vera refuses to accept the naturalization of idealized myths of femininity: 'nature is destroying these women and we have to stop nature being so cruel' (38). Fergal kisses Vera in response to her outraged speech and then woos her with a love poem. Just as Vera surprised the audience at the end of Act One, she surprises us once more by responding to Fergal: 'She goes to him and kisses him. There is a puff of smoke and Fergal disappears' (39). Vera earlier mocked Anna's acceptance of romantic fantasy, yet she too is duped by its promise. However, this time the impossibility of that promise is visually exposed by Fergal's disappearance. The disclosure of his lack of substance makes a startling impact on Anna who screams 'I'm so angry' (39), echoed by the banshee's wail. In fact the women swap roles in these concluding moments: Vera is taken in by Fergal's illusions and it is Anna who loudly articulates her anger, complicating a simplistic notion of the women as either complicit or defiant.

Dawn breaks before the Finale Song begins, but whether the women are on the verge of a new age seems uncertain: the women's fantasies, both limiting and sustaining, have been shattered; and their transformation into cultural visibility is tentative. The play concludes with a protest song, 'We won't go easy; we'll go down protestin'' (39-40), thus articulating the women's desire to be heard and giving them the last word. The song also encourages the audience to join with them in their protest, 'So come on sisters' (40); an inclusivity which resonates with the potential of 'popular feminisms'. However, in contrast to this inclusivity, Foley's emphasis on the sense of 'closure, non-feminine and didactic' suggests that the ending denotes compliance with patriarchal forms. Thus, the ending intimates the contradictory effects of 'popular feminisms', evidencing both the illusion of power, as well as the co-existence of feminist potential within the limits of capitalist society. Furthermore, the ending highlights the contradictions of contemporary definitions of transformation; on the one hand it refuses second-wave feminist optimism and belief in radical change, yet it also denies the neoliberal makeover of ageing women.

The dissonance of the play's ending and its refusal of the 'feel-good factor' expected of popular theatre, the 'grand 'Altogether' finale' as McGrath terms it, expresses Vera's and Anna's anger and displeasure with society's prescription for the happiness of older women. Just as their menopausal bodies and desires are unruly and inappropriate, so too are these women's affective experiences. Both Vera's and Anna's anger regarding society's exclusion of ageing women exposes what 'happiness' conceals and thus the violence of neoliberalism. Sara Ahmed discusses the potential of those, particularly feminists, who refuse the happiness wish sanctioned by society at large, a wish which affirms appropriate affective registers. Ahmed notes that the feminist is alienated and 'out of line with an affective community … because she does not find the objects that promise happiness to be quite so promising' (34-35). The emotional trajectory of the play and its 'dubious' ending thereby registers the women's protest and places both them and the audience affectively out of line. The contradictory ending encapsulates the women's affective misalignment: on the one hand it urges holding on to 'negative' emotions (Anna's final articulation of anger and the banshee's off-stage wail), but it also acknowledges the women's expression of community and pleasure as explored through popular theatre and popular culture. Thus, the Finale Song offers a pleasurable politics through its articulation of the menopausal woman's anger and affective misalignment, as well as the possibility of affective feminist affiliations.

Popular Culture and Fantasy: 'a perfect end to a perfect day'

The contradiction of the ending resonates with 'the double-stake in popular culture, the double movement of containment and resistance, which is always inevitably inside it' (Hall 228). The Daniel O'Donnell industry is clearly collusive with capitalism, making money out of the older woman's desire for expression, but it also proves valuable for the articulation of an ageing female subjectivity and thus marks their visibility. The invisibility of older women's sexual desires results in the misreading of the appeal of Daniel O'Donnell, as Jones makes clear in an interview:

> After all, why take him seriously when the bulk of his audience is middle-aged nobodies? But I wanted to know why these thousands of women are going demented for him. The usual answer is, 'Ah, God love them, it's the son they never had, the nice clean-cut boy they'd love their daughter to marry.' But when you sit down and talk to these women, that's not it at all. The truth is they want him in their beds. And why shouldn't a woman of 60 have romantic, sexual feelings? Daniel isn't the son they never had. He's the man they never had (Dickson).

The idealized mother figure, so pervasive in Irish culture, ignores the reality of women's lives and embodied experiences. The associated mother-son relationship is augmented by O'Donnell's clean-cut, Christian image and by the fact that his tea-parties are held at his mother's home. However, for his many female fans, the importance of O'Donnell is that he helps generate their visibility through the creation of affective communities: he 'makes them *feel* good, *feel* important ... treats them like real people' (my italics, 14). O'Donnell keeps Anna going, despite her unfulfilled marriage, so when her husband mocks O'Donnell, Anna is angered by his belittling of her fantasies and dismissal of her desires: '... when you make fun of Daniel O'Donnell and all us silly women, does it not occur to you that he recognizes that we can still love, still feel, still dream? All those things that you never wanted to know about me' (37). The original production opened with a short film, 'The Daniel O'Donnell Weekend', which showed women queuing to meet O'Donnell at one of his famous tea-parties. Writing in *The Telegraph,* Charles Spencer's disparaging review of Jones's 'unashamedly populist new play' highlights the 'hilarious film that precedes the play proper' but *Women on the Verge of HRT* compels the audience to reassess their perceptions, and dismissal, of these women.

In contrast to the banshee's expression of anger and rage from the margins of society, the fantasy of O'Donnell as lover offers the possibility of visibility and sexual pleasure within dominant discourses of popular culture. Of course, escapism and fantasy have limits, as Vera notes: 'They love him because he treats them like real people – important enough to remember but how do other people treat them?' (14). The uncertainty of the ending highlights the difficulty of translating O'Donnell's acknowledgement into political efficacy and societal change. The stage directions at the opening of the play proffer 'a perfect end to a perfect day' (1) but the women's fantasies are exposed as illusion by the end of the play. However, fantasy's unleashing of menopausal pleasures and desires creates affective feminist affiliations which potentially extend to the audience of the play.

'I have had enough for one night': The audience as 'an affective solidarity'

Towards the end of Act One, a party of women in the hotel send Fergal to invite Vera and Anna to join them. Vera claims she is tired but Anna decides to go: 'I am away to this party, I am sorry, I know you're depressed; so am I many a time but I have had enough for one night' (18). The community of women at Kincasslagh create an affective affiliation united by their discontent as well as their desire to express their pleasures, and the audience are embraced in this community. In an interview with Marie Jones, Pat Moylan remarks on the dominantly female audience: 'I got great satisfaction from seeing large theatres in places like Sheffield and York filled to capacity with women. It was like going to the Chippendales – ninety per cent female' (215). The connection between the play's audience and O'Donnell's fans is further emphasized by the performance of Song Two of the play, 'Donegal'. Fergal takes on O'Donnell's persona and addresses Vera as a fan, 'Well hello there and what's your name?' (11), as he sits down on the bed and sings to her. The audience are then indulged by O'Donnell's treatment: Fergal declares 'Well ladies and gentlemen, I feel at this point I haft to come among you' (12), before entering the audience and talking to them 'just like Daniel.' Thus the audience are figured as part of the community of O'Donnell's fans; by attending *Women on the Verge of HRT* they are expressing their own sense of 'having had enough for one night'.

In *A Good Night Out for the Girls,* Elaine Aston and Geraldine Harris highlight the importance of these temporary affective communities of women: 'an affective solidarity rooted in the transformative and reparative *pleasures* of intersubjectivity; sociability and sociality' (18). Drawing on bell hooks's exploration of a feminist space of yearning, they consider the audience experience at women-centred shows, noting how 'an 'event' embracing the audience as well as the stage, came to signify something of this 'yearning': a desire for change linked to the desire for pleasure' (16). This sense of 'yearning' is thus informed by second-wave feminist anger but reshaped by contemporary 'popular feminisms' in its emphasis on pleasure and transformation *within* dominant ideology. The temporary nature of these affective identifications counters the exclusivity of neoliberalism and postfeminism, and is vital in defying attempts to render ageing women and women of limited financial means invisible. Furthermore, this expansion of feminism's address embraces the potential of popular culture and popular theatre; an embrace which enables a more complex and contradictory discussion of Jones's later, more commercial work, such as *Women on the Verge of HRT*. When transformation is no longer radical or indeed desirable, working within the limits of the mainstream offers visibility and thus may invigorate feminism. The visibility of the popular gives voice to the experience of the menopausal woman as affect alien, an experience characterized by anger which is unleashed through pleasure. Thus, 'popular feminisms' offer the means of exploring the contradictory radical within: enabling the undoing of an exclusive postfeminism and 'unpopular' feminism, whilst simultaneously revitalizing feminist politics and rage through engagement with the pleasures of the popular.

---

[1] *Women on the Verge of HRT*. By Marie Jones. Original Music by Neil Martin. Dir. Pam Brighton. Perf. Marie Jones, Eileen Pollock and Dan Gordon. The West Belfast Festival / Feile an Phobail. Aug. 1995.

[2] *Women on the Verge of HRT*. By Marie Jones. Original Music by Neil Martin. Dir. Pam Brighton. Perf. Marie Jones, Eileen Pollock and Dessie Gallagher. Design, Robert Ballagh. Lighting, Eileen O'Reilly. Vaudeville Theatre, London. 19 Feb. 1997.

[3] Melissa Sihra's seminal study *Women in Irish Drama: A Century of Authorship and Self-Representation* does not address women and popular theatre, though Sihra does note her regret that Jones was not included (12).

14 | Women's Suffrage and the Politics of Militancy in *The Milliner and The Weaver*

Dawn Fowler

Introduction

Marie Jones's *The Milliner and the Weaver* (2010) is an important dramatic intervention in the memorialization of Irish suffrage at a key moment in its history. As the opening play in the Tricycle Theatre's *Women Power and Politics* season in June that year, *The Milliner and the Weaver* offers a deceptively simple yet provocative perspective. Set in 1914, the characters Elspeth and Henrietta are the respective milliner and weaver of the title; two women from diametrically opposed economic and political backgrounds who have found allegiance in their fight for women's rights. The central principles of this complex social and political issue are dramatized during an urgent discussion in Henrietta's modest Belfast kitchen, with the narrative thrust driven by middle-class Dubliner Elspeth's aim to persuade factory worker Henrietta to continue her political campaign for female suffrage. What emerges is a short play that explores the political position of women in the run up to the third Home Rule Bill, the abysmal conditions the female labour-force faced, and the dangers posed by the increasing militancy in the campaign of the suffragettes.

What is revealed throughout Jones's play is a deft historical examination of the challenges faced by women in Ireland in the early twentieth century. Theatre critic Michael Billington wrote 'Marie Jones, with *The Milliner and the Weaver*, touchingly explores the way Belfast suffragettes in 1914 found their cause overtaken by the issue of Home Rule' (*The Guardian*, 13 June 2010). Michael Coveney described the play as 'an acid, cleverly detailed scene of feminist conflict between a suffragette and a Belfast weaver by Marie Jones' (n.p). In writing a play about the suffragettes in Ireland and the unique confrontations they faced Jones analyses how women's fight for the vote became inextricably embroiled in more dominant social and political questions. *The Milliner and the Weaver* is packed with insightful argument as we see Henrietta forced by Elspeth to make a choice between her domestic and political lives. What is dramatically revealed in the play is a subtly complex exploration of conflicting ideological standpoints as the characters agree on feminist issues but not on wider national issues. This chapter explores the analogies Jones draws between the particular political and social questions raised by this moment in history and how they set the scene for the thorough dissection of female protest and political engagement that followed in the *Women, Power and Politics* event as a whole.

The Milliner and the Weaver opens in 'a small mill house in East Belfast' (3), where Henrietta Girvan, a widow in her mid-forties lives with her six children. Outside the house there are sounds of a crowd cheering, loud voices and marching. The juxtaposition of life inside the domestic space against the major political events that were taking place on the streets of Belfast 1914 is a recurrent strategy in the play (for more on this trope see Cleary's 'Domestic Troubles' and Maguire's *Making Theatre*). We see Henrietta in her domestic duty, washing socks amongst a set of dirty boots in a hint that her unseen work inside the house enables the marching that takes place outside. Henrietta's sixteen year old son, Thomas, is a member of the Ulster Volunteers Force which at this point is large in number, armed and ready to declare war on Home Rulers. The militant drilling in the streets, heard beyond the stage space, has historical precedent and provides a sense of dramatic urgency to the scene.

An unexpected knock at the door provides a moment of tension before the entrance of Elspeth, who is 'well dressed in a beautiful expensive hat' (4). There is an instant visual class divide symbolized by the dress and behaviour of the two women. Jones creates a simple scene where the incongruity generates a ubiquitous sense of unease. Henrietta's response to Elspeth is one governed by class embarrassment but also of a natural fear that their association will be discovered as 'they have eyes in their arses in this street' (5). The claustrophobia of close communities, nosy neighbours on terraced streets and the puritanical judgement of teachers and other parents is more than an irritation as we learn that Henrietta has been playing an active role in the suffrage movement. What is more, she and her fellow workers were initially inspired by a rousing speech performed by Elspeth outside the mill where they work. Elspeth, however, has increasingly used her platform as speaker to promote Home Rule in the area and Henrietta reveals that they have subsequently lost their local support:

> Those same women are now abusing me in the street ... 'Fenian lover'. After all that hard work. They accused me of siding with them that want to destroy the Protestant people, that's all that matters now ... we have no support round here no more ... there is no point ... I wouldn't even be surprised that those same women, whose lives you think you can change, chucked the bricks that broke your office windows. (7)

In these two characters Jones has created dramatic mouthpieces for women who can find common interest and solidarity in the fight for suffrage but who express the difficulties and specific concerns that they legitimately faced.

As Jones has shown in her previous work she does not shy away from writing characters who are willing to renegotiate binary divisions. The question of women's suffrage in Ireland is certainly one of conflicting loyalties, varying interests, and particular dangers that always threatened to override the ultimate goal of winning the vote for women. Linda Connelly argues that 'it is important to acknowledge that first-wave feminism was divided (not unified) by the national question, between unionists and nationalists, and on whether the vote for women or the national cause took precedence' (62). Similarly, Pádraig Yeates states, 'In Ireland, the competing demands of nationalism and unionism complicated the situation for suffragists' (367), and indeed the 'women's question' was in many senses overridden and even obscured by the more leading question of Home Rule. Louise Ryan, drawing on Eder (1993), argues that the Irish suffrage movement represents 'a countercultural movement which engaged with and frequently criticized the dominant discourse and agenda of the Government and main social movement of that period, the Irish nationalist movement' (47). However, as Ryan continues 'in each historical period smaller, alternative, social movements have frequently been ignored or even marginalized because of the presence of larger, more dominant social movements' (52). Ryan identifies a general historical neglect of the radical position of Irish suffragettes, which has also affected the artistic and cultural representation of the women involved. Thus, Jones's intervention in the reassessment of the suffrage movement is particularly insightful in its examination of the effects of growing political consciousness on these two women. With one from a working-class loyalist Belfast setting and the other a businessman's wife from Dublin, they are at the collision point of the forces of competing nationalisms, class division and gendered politics.

Ireland and Women's Suffrage

As the Votes for Women movement gained in momentum and united women across the globe, the inciting slogan of the 1908 Irishwomen's Franchise League (IWFL) was 'Suffrage First – Before All Else' (Ward, *Suffrage First* 24), and the Irish suffrage movement certainly consisted of women who would identify as nationalist or unionist but who were prepared to override particular party loyalties in favour of women's rights. If the alliance of women over the right to vote aimed to cross political boundaries the association was not straightforward as Diane Urquhart has written:

> Relations between suffragists in the north and south of the country were cordial – suffrage speakers visited sister societies, coordinated demands to include suffrage amendments to the third Home Rule Bill of 1912-14 and, from 1913, collectively repudiated the treatment which suffrage prisoners received. However, solidarity amongst Irish suffragists, although often lauded, was always fragile. Indeed, as early as 1912, the complexity of the Irish suffrage movement was believed to be 'such a tangle that it may seem a somewhat perilous task to endeavour to unravel it' (277).

A precarious path, then, had to be forged for Irish women who wanted greater emancipation for themselves but who did not want to be seen as a traitor to their overriding political beliefs.

Another challenge for the Irish suffrage movement, as Cliona Murphy has identified, lay in the suggestion that it 'constituted little more than a shadow of the British movement, or conversely, a weak extension of the Irish Nationalist movement' (1). Indeed, as the Women's Social and Political Union (WSPU) established by the Pankhursts in 1903 became increasingly militant in its activities, the members of the IWFL were accused of colluding with the enemy to attack the cause of Irish nationalism. 'Some of the MPs', writes Murphy, 'accused the women of being anti-nationalistic and selfish. They accused them of belonging to an English movement and of being unIrish' (168). To emphasize this Elizabeth Somers (a founder member of Sinn Féin) in an article titled 'Suffrage Policy' criticized fellow Irish women who were 'following the same path as English suffragists who had a different set of conditions and a different political standard of values' (qtd. in Yeates 365).

What is clear is that a chief concern held by many suffragettes was that a lack of political power in terms of voting would lead to vulnerability in every aspect of life including the domestic and working lives of women. After a hugely controversial decision by the Irish Party to defer the question of female suffrage to three years after the Home Rule Bill was resolved, Helen Baker of the Irish Women's Suffrage Society declared to the *Irish Citizen* that this was 'sufficient provocation to make all Irishwomen drop every bit of social and church work, I think, and to become actively militant' (qtd. in Yeates 366). In addition, the Dublin lock-out of 1913 which saw a huge general strike across the labour force had made working conditions in factories a chief political priority and the suffragettes were centrally involved in supporting and providing food for the striking workers. Following the influence of prominent Irish suffragists and nationalists such as Hanna Sheehy-Skeffington (daughter of the Irish Party MP David Sheehy and founding member of The Irish Women's Workers Union) and her campaign to improve the 'appalling conditions of women workers' (Yeates, 223) in sweated labour factories, it is not outlandish that a middle-class Dublin woman such as Elspeth would have seen it as her moral duty as a suffragist to educate women working in the linen factories of the north that they deserved higher wages, safer conditions and better treatment.

In *The Milliner and the Weaver* Jones distils these historical events and indicates how the fight for the vote by Elspeth and Henrietta cannot override more dominant socio-political boundaries. One such boundary is between their views on Home Rule and their discussion of this issue is a reminder why Jones won the John Hewitt Award 'for her contributions to the cultural traditions debate' (Lojek, *Troubling Perspective* 333). Henrietta's anger at Elspeth is roused by what she sees as the contamination of the suffragette cause with national politics. She tells Elspeth in frustration, 'Oh Christ, I could scream ... you shouldn't have made that bloody speech' (9). Henrietta has found a voice and true passion with the suffragettes and joined the movement in the first place because 'I heard you speak in the park about our rights as women, not Catholic or Protestant, but all of us' (15).

Attempts to recruit working class women from factories in Belfast and Derry by holding open-air meetings was part of a sustained effort from the WSPU to diversify the membership. There was a committed campaign from 1912-14 to encourage women to take responsibility for their own lives and those of their children. While this responsibility has been imposed on Henrietta as a widow running her own home, it is clear that being encouraged to recognize her rights as a worker, even entertaining the idea of a 'strike here in a Belfast mill, could you imagine that?' (7), has generated a nascent radicalism. The vote represents a possible escape from boot scrubbing, greater economic emancipation and increased social freedom for her daughters. What we see in the case of Henrietta is an example of a bright, self-sufficient, articulate and politically autonomous woman who is swayed by the needs of her community. Her desire for a better working life for herself and an improved political future for her daughters is offset against the marching outside:

> Look ... man and boy prepared to fight and save Ulster ... save it from their own countrymen, young men, my son ... look, all fired up, proud ... and so bloody blind ... scary ... so terrible scary (8).

Elspeth, on the other hand, is spared the domestic drudgery of Henrietta's life but she also feels trapped by her circumstances and unable to voice her political beliefs in front of her businessman husband. What this effectively demonstrates is that the uneasy truce formed by the characters is conditioned not only by political questions but the stark difference in the daily realities of their lives. More than once Henrietta refers to Elspeth attempting to 'save' the local women who do not invite her intervention. In focusing on this issue, Jones dramatizes the agonizing decision individual suffragists were forced to make regarding where their political loyalties truly lay.

Both women essentially live a double life and in a neat dramatic twist that helps to explain the title of this piece they have had occasion to disguise themselves as each other when taking part in more militant activity. Along with forty other suffragettes they have disrupted a Belfast court where female prisoners were on trial by creating a commotion and throwing brandy balls at the judge. Smiling at the memory of a 'feeling like that, all us women doing something together' (10), Henrietta exclaims 'Me a weaver, dressed like a toff in your hat and coat' (10). Elspeth similarly has 'an old mill apron and a shawl' (12) to disguise herself and avoid recognition from her husband's upper-class friends. Once, when in an altercation with the police outside a Dublin hotel where Asquith was rumoured to be having dinner Elspeth reveals that her passing husband said 'right into my face ... 'You damned women are your own worst enemy, God help the poor men you are married to' (12) all the while without recognizing her.

There is a clear implication here that social and political gulfs separate these women and prevent them from becoming potential friends. Each shares a mutual admiration of the backbone and determination of the other, and indeed, Elspeth is visiting to talk Henrietta into re-joining the movement because she recognizes her talent as an influential figure. The symbolic gesture of wearing each other's clothes could seem contrived but Jones weaves a far more complex narrative into the piece as Elspeth's refusal to keep silence regarding her views on Home Rule can be read as a betrayal of Henrietta not only in a political context (Henrietta stands in very real danger by having Elspeth in her house) but also because Henrietta is now essentially forced to give up on an activity where 'I thought we could make things better' (7). What also becomes evident throughout the course of this play is the sheer difficulty for these women of finding a safe space to meet and talk in a time when the suffragettes' growing militancy cast suspicion on politically active women. Elspeth runs a hat shop in Dublin with a back-room she has named 'The War Department', the connotations of which are sharply gendered. Her husband accuses the women there of 'wittering on endlessly about peacock feathers and silk trimmings', yet Elspeth, showing the true militancy of the operation, reveals that 'we're usually planning burning down banks and post offices or kidnapping the Prime Minister' (13).

The idea of an outwardly feminine, and therefore politically innocuous, domain being re-appropriated into clandestine meeting space has historical precedent in this context and Elspeth's description of the activities that take place there acts as a reminder that the suffragette movement was a deeply political organization that was beginning to adopt increasingly militaristic methods. If the passage of time has somewhat diluted the ferocity of this struggle, as Louise Ryan states, 'that does not mean we should underestimate just how radical and earth-shattering these movements appeared when they first emerged' (55). In this sense, the subversive use of the feminine space performs a function that is both dissident and empowering. In a similar vein, Jones shows how Henrietta's home is the only place where she has autonomy and control over her own life. If the personal is political then Henrietta uses her modest home as a political weapon by offering it to Elspeth as a safe house if she should ever need it:

> If bloody Sir Edward Carson as a Member of Parliament can smuggle illegal arms, call for civil war and not get arrested, then I can break laws in his house, this is my parliament ... that way, me and him is equal. (19)

Henrietta's dominance in her home is emphasized when her sixteen year-old son Thomas returns from his march with the Ulster Volunteer

Force. His reaction to Elspeth is instantly hostile. He chastises her saying, 'you can tell your sort down in Dublin, missus, that Ulster will never be taken from us by no heathen Pope-lovers' (17). The impossibility of Henrietta's position is here made starkly clear. Henrietta's political allegiance lies with the WSPU yet, although Henrietta can clearly hold her own with her son, the truth is that by leaving the WSPU she has acquiesced to his instructions. Her language is defiant but her actions suggest otherwise: 'I can't be of much use to you any more ... upstart that he is, I have to stand by my son' (19).

Although Henrietta began campaigning for women's rights in part for the future of her daughters she is unable to voice her beliefs outside the walls of her own home, and increasingly within them. She has, in effect, been silenced:

> It's different now. I have to keep my head down and say nothin' ... understand? The women don't want to know now ... even Mrs Pankhurst, for all her great speechifying ... there's not a woman round here would listen ... not now ... you lost their trust (6).

In this sense Henrietta's future looks fairly desolate and *The Milliner and the Weaver* certainly lacks the comedic elements that have been such a feature of Jones' work previously. It is, however, encouraging to see both Elspeth and Henrietta attempt to find their own room of one's own in the reclamation of their domestic space. Perhaps, Jones suggests, it is in these hidden domestic or feminine spaces that women explored their individual worth and began the slow process of social change.

What this play reveals is a writer exposing conversations usually hidden behind closed doors, and a preoccupation with ordinary women capable of extraordinary action. The potential of Elspeth and Henrietta joining forces is emphasized when their activities in the Belfast courtroom are reported in the *New York Times*. Elspeth's exclamation 'Henrietta, we reached America' (9), deftly contrasts with a later exchange on the sinking of the *Titanic* and the devastating impact it had on Henrietta's community whose shipyard helped to build it. The two women, however, are not able to reconcile their differences and part ways: a bleak, if again, sharply historical, ending. Elspeth once again disguises herself in a shawl and leaves Henrietta her beautiful hat in fear of being recognized on the street. As Diana Crane has explored, the politics of clothing was always a major issue for the suffragettes and Elspeth's subversion of the hat shop and eventual passing on of the hat to Henrietta suggests that meeting each other has had a beneficial effect on both. The hat is an emblem that the two women were able to take a walk in each other's shoes (or hat) and learn that their common goals were not completely anomalous. This glimmer of hope is offset against the rising sound of marching outside which eventually matches the sound of Henrietta's brush on the boots, a reminder that the Ulster Volunteer Force were preparing to strike Home Rulers and also, more obliquely, that 'The immediate and absolute cessation of the suffragette campaign throughout Britain and the closure of WSPU offices in Belfast were a direct response to the outbreak of the First World War' (Urquhart 285). This image of Henrietta, alone in her house, polishing the boots of her sixteen year old son recalls a speech she makes at the beginning of this short, dense play:

> Socks and shoes ... the bane of m'life ... I dream about them ... all marchin' towards me, a big army of stinkin' socks and shoes ... all defiant buggers marchin' at me ... and just as they get this close they stop and wait ... wait for me to feel sorry for them and gather them all up and wash and clean them and make them better, but you know what I want to do ... grab them and dump the whole bloody lot in the Lagan, watch them splutterin' their way intil the Irish Sea and away for ever ... then laugh m'head off. (4)

Although the vote was granted to women over thirty in 1918, for Henrietta the inextricable pull of her community ties and care for her son do not allow her to break away from what she now sees as her domestic and cultural duty.

Impact in Context

To understand the impact of this play in its wider context it is necessary to position it alongside the other plays in the *Women, Power and Politics* programme and against the aims of the project as a whole. In June 2010 the Tricycle Theatre in Kilburn, London, premiered a series of nine short plays written by leading female playwrights under the collective title *Women, Power and Politics*. As well as Jones, the other playwrights were Rebecca Lenkiewicz, Moira Buffini, Lucy Kirkwood, Joy Wilkinson, Zinnie Harris, Bola Agbaje, Sam Holcroft and Sue Townsend, testifying to the quality of the field. To collect such a range of high-profile writers together is a radical idea in and of itself, and when split into two sections, the historical 'Then' and contemporary 'Now', the plays amounted to just over six hours of theatre when viewed as a whole. Theatre critic Dominic Cavendish, giving a synopsis of the major themes, writes:

> It's about the Suffragettes in Ireland at the time of the 1914 Home Rule Act. It's about the unspoken strains of behind-the-scenes

relations between Margaret Thatcher and the Queen. It's about Elizabeth I, her physician, John Knox, and the Earl of Essex. It's about the women of Greenham Common and their modern equivalents. It's about Margaret Beckett and whether she deserved the chance to be elected leader of the Labour Party over Tony Blair. It's about institutionalized male chauvinism at board-level, about the shallowness of student politics, about pornography and women's freedom to do as they choose, and about career politicians who put the pursuit of power before basic humanity. (*The Telegraph*, n.p.)

The plays were commissioned, states director Indhu Rubasingham, in response to a statistic showing that after the 2010 General Election women made up just 22% of MPs in the British parliament. Rubasingham writes in her introduction to the published version of *Women, Power and Politics*:

> Why is this happening and what are the obstacles that are preventing women from entering or gaining power within the political system in this country. Is it the structure of government? The media? Society? Or is it the women themselves? (vii).

These questions provided the major interrogatory topics of the plays which were also borne out in the overall set design by Rosa Maggiora, where a precariously hanging glass ceiling had been partially (but not quite fully) smashed with stones.

With its strong focus on political theatre the Tricycle seems a natural home for Jones and she had already had two plays performed there: *A Night in November* (1995, dir. Pam Brighton) and *Stones in his Pockets* (1999, dir. Ian McElhinney). Under Nicholas Kent as director, it had established itself as a vibrant venue for politically and socially engaged theatre through its tribunal and verbatim productions and large-scale performances exploring pressing controversial issues. July 2009 saw the epic *Great Game: Afghanistan* showcase eleven new plays by prominent writers that gave a thorough historical, educational, exploratory history to the war in Afghanistan, counter-balancing the dominant official and media narratives. In February 2012 *The Bomb: A Partial History* offered an exhaustive account of nuclear innovation and destruction leading to the development of the atomic bomb. The *Women, Power and Politics* project, which also included a film festival and a photography exhibit, stands alongside these fellow examples as informative, challenging events from a range of diverse and exciting voices.

As the opening play in the event, *The Milliner and the Weaver* asks how the historical depiction of Irish suffrage links to the wider political questions raised by Indhu Rubasingham about the under-representation of women in political life. Jones's play, then, works with the other plays in the programme to question and redefine key moments in women's political history. Indeed, the casting of the individual roles played a crucial part in forming contrasts and comparisons between the individual plays. Niamh Cusack who played Henrietta reappeared in the second play as an indomitable Elizabeth I in Rebecca Lenkiewicz's *The Lioness*. It seemed somehow apt to have the same woman (visually at least) who had been scrubbing boots in a kitchen now stating to her troops 'I myself will be your general, judge and rewarder ... and I ... I am not afraid of anything' (*The Lioness* 35). Stella Gonet, playing Elspeth, reappeared as a typically forceful 'T' (Margaret Thatcher) in Moira Buffini's *Handbagged* which dramatized the weekly meetings between the Prime Minister and the Queen. Although dramatizing the relationship between two high profile figures, *Handbagged*, resonated the power dynamics that can exist between two women that had been set down in *The Milliner and the Weaver* as the opening play. The casting choices provided a thread between the plays to suggest that birth and circumstances are as important as talent and passion when determining the political future of women.

The play which succinctly rounded off the 'Then' section was Lucy Kirkwood's *Bloody Wimmin* which takes place in 1984 as female protesters set up camp at Greenham Common. In a moving speech an elderly Lillian recalls her role in the protest. Her shock and the profound sense of belonging she finds as she joins forces with other women to become an unlikely anti-war protestor recall Henrietta's memory of discovering her true political passion in the Belfast courtroom. Lillian does not imagine herself and the other women around her as activists because they do not fit the stereotypical image she has of historical protesters:

> You look at Mrs Pankhurst in her lovely lopsided hat and her gorgeous skirts, little nipped-in waist, leg-of-mutton sleeves and that splendid purple sash, and then the hammer in her hand, or the policeman lifting her up, dainty boots dangling off the ground, and it just sort of takes your breath away doesn't it? It takes your breath away the dignity of it. (*Bloody Wimmin* 113)

This reference, coming at the end of the section, acted as a reminder that the seeds of protest that gave rise to Greenham Common were sown long before by the suffragettes. All of the plays in this overarching event imagined or reconfigured conversations that took place or could have taken place in various moments in history.

It is also valuable to consider the position of *The Milliner and the Weaver* against a renewed interest and resurgence of writing on suffragettes in recent years. The centenary of the death of Emily Wilding Davison in June 1913 prompted a *Suffragettes on Stage* platform event at the National Theatre in London, and the publication of a collected volume of *Suffrage Plays* (edited by Naomi Paxton, Methuen 2013). January 2015 will see the release of a blockbuster film, *Suffragette*, written by Abi Morgan, directed by Sarah Gavron and starring Meryl Streep as Emmeline Pankhurst. Perhaps the most significant and harrowing full-length reappraisal of the subject, however, is Rebecca Lenkiewicz's play *Her Naked Skin*. Lenkiewicz's play was the first original play by a living female writer to debut in the Olivier Auditorium of the National Theatre, London in July 2008 (Helen Edmundson's *Coram Boy* (2005) had been the first full-length adaptation). While 2008 seems an extraordinarily late date for female writing to achieve such a high profile debut the play itself was lauded for 'planting a defiant feminist flag on the Olivier stage' (Billington, August 2008, n.p.).

Her Naked Skin dramatizes the experience of suffragettes in London in the turbulent time immediately prior to World War I and alongside *The Milliner and the Weaver* offers a useful reconsideration of the period, especially in regards to the uneasy class divides between women involved in the struggle. Lenkiewicz recognizes the political strategizing of the Women's Suffrage Movement in Ireland as we see Prime Minister Asquith lamenting the increasing militancy of the suffragettes. He is told by the Chief Secretary for Ireland, Augustine Birrell, that 'They keep comparing their campaign to the Irish. Look where that's headed' (*Her Naked Skin* 6). Asquith's reply is indicative of the political priorities of the British government at the time: 'The Irish are the Irish. And they've been damned useful to us. What we're dealing with here is a lunatic fringe of lonely, frigid women who crave attention' (6). Here Lenkiewicz acknowledges the WSPU's support of the third Home Rule Bill and also demonstrates how the women in these organizations were not taken seriously as political activists by leading politicians.

Another cornerstone of female suffrage is how it explored and transgressed social, class and sexual normative behaviours. One major storyline in *Her Naked Skin* shows how an upper-class woman, Lady Celia Cain, is frustrated and trapped within the confines of her marriage and home and becomes attracted to machinist Eve leading to a passionate affair. The quest for suffrage in this respect allows for transcendence over pervading patriarchal structures governing female sexual conduct. Arguably the subtext of physical attraction (although not necessarily sexual) exists in *The Milliner and the Weaver*, through the mutually admiring relationship between Henrietta and Elspeth although Jones never states this outright. Although operating in a different political climate the impenetrable class divide between Celia and Eve also mirrors the power imbalance between women from different economic backgrounds. Exploitation can still exist, Lenkiewicz's play suggests, within the suffrage movement as Eve is abandoned by her lover and left to face the horrors of Holloway prison. In 'one of the most horrifying scenes on the London stage' (Billington, n.p.) Eve is held down and forcibly fed by a tube up her nose. Later she claims to Celia that she has been writing her name in blood on the walls of her prison cell. Both Jones and Lenkiewicz lean towards the view that social privilege allowed for militarism amongst the upper classes that was unavailable to ordinary working women. There is an uncomfortable assertion here that the hierarchy of the suffrage movement and its potential manipulation of working women both adopted the methods and inadvertently reflected the economic and political structures it aimed to destroy.

Conclusion

Indhu Rubasingham has written that 'theatre is reflecting, amongst other things, the immediate politics of today' (Introduction *Women Power and Politics* vi). Watching the entirety of *Women, Power and Politics* was a radical experience not only for the reason of seeing work by female writers presented together but for the vital insights it gave into neglected historical moments and the development of feminism. In 1909 George Bernard Shaw wrote of Brieux's play *La Femme Seule* (translated by Charlotte Shaw as *A Woman on her Own*) that '[women's] attempt to support themselves brings them into competition with men in the labour market, and the men thereupon deliberately drive them out of the market and force them into marriage or prostitution without any alternative at all' (qtd. in Holledge 95). A writer for *The Suffragette* took issue with this view proclaiming 'I wish some woman would write a play showing the real spirit of the Suffragette. It has never been done yet, and I do not believe a male dramatist will ever do it' (qtd. in Holledge 96). What has been imperative about the revival of interest in the suffragettes around the centenary of Davison's death is the reclamation of their important role as political activists and radical thinkers. There is much academic literature on the leaders of the suffrage movements, on the prominent public figures who supported them, and on the playwrights and actors who made women's rights their artistic aim. Yet of the women who attended meetings in secret, who lied to their husbands and workmates, who risked everything by holding clandestine meetings in their own homes little is known. The voices of Henrietta and Elspeth have previously been seriously neglected and demonstrate how Jones provides continual challenges to normative representations of women operating within specific political structures.

Marie Jones: Playography

Lay Up Your Ends (Charabanc, 1983)
Oul Delf and False Teeth (Charabanc, 1984)
Now You're Talkin' (Charabanc, 1985)
Gold in the Streets (Charabanc, 1986)
The Girls in the Big Picture (Charabanc, 1986)
Somewhere Over the Balcony (Charabanc, 1987)
Terrible Twins Crazy Christmas (Charabanc, 1988)
Under Napoleon's Nose (Replay, 1988)
Weddins, Weeins and Wakes (Charabanc, 1989)
It's a Waste of Time, Tracey (Replay, 1989)
The Blind Fiddler of Glenadaugh (Charabanc, 1990)
The Hamster Wheel (Charabanc, 1990, adapted for television 1991)
Hang all the Harpers (DubbelJoint, Marie Jones and Shane Connaughton, 1991)
The Cow, The Ship, and the Indian (Replay, 1991)
Don't Look Down (Replay, 1992)
Hiring Days (Replay, 1992)
Christmas Eve Can Kill You (DubbelJoint, 1992)
Yours Truly (Replay, 1993)
The Government Inspector (DubbelJoint, 1993)
A Night in November (DubbelJoint, 1994)
Ethel Workman Is Innocent (DubbelJoint, 1995)
Women on the Verge of HRT (DubbelJoint, 1995)
Eddie Bottom's Dream (DubbelJoint, 1996)
Stones in His Pockets (DubbelJoint, 1996; revised version, 1999)
The Wedding Community Play (with Martin Lynch, 1999)
Women on the Verge Get a Life (1999)
Court No. 2 (Tinderbox, 2000)
   Ruby (Tinderbox, 2000)

The Blind Fiddler (2004 – based on the earlier work)
A Very Weird Manor (2005)
The Chosen Room (2008, Youth Music Theatre)
Dancing Shoes: The George Best Story (2010)
Rock Doves (2010)
The Milliner and the Weaver (2010)
Fly Me To The Moon (2012)
Mistletoe and Crime (2014)

Bibliography

Ahmed, Sara. 'Creating Disturbance: Feminism, happiness and affective differences.' *Working with Affect in Feminist Readings: Disturbing Differences*. Eds Marianne Liljestrom and Susanna Paasone. Abingdon: Routledge, 2010. 31-44.

'All They See is You Clairol Nice'n'Easy Commercial.' *YouTube*. n.d. Web. 22 Aug 2013.

Aston, Elaine and Geraldine Harris. *A Good Night Out for the Girls: Popular Feminisms in Contemporary Theatre and Performance*. Basingstoke: Palgrave Macmillan, 2013.

Augé, Marc. 'Non-places.' *Architecturally Speaking: Practices of Art, Architecture and the Everyday*. Ed. Alan Read. London: Routledge, 2000. 7-12.

Barter, Pavel. 'Gossip Girls.' *The Sunday Times*. 16 June (2013) sec. Culture: 12-13

Bennett, Susan. Theatre Audiences: A Theory of Production and Reception. London: Routledge, 1997.

Billington, Michael. 'Her Naked Skin'. *The Guardian*, 2 August 2008: n.p.

---. 'Women, Power and Politics'. *The Guardian*, 13 June 2010: n.p.

Bixler, Jacqueline E. 'Performing Culture(s): Extras and the Extra-Texts in Sabina Berman's *eXtras*.' *Theatre Journal* 56 (2004): 429-44.

Block, Alice M. Letter to the author. 15 April 1997. MS.

Bort, Eberhard. 'Female Voices in Northern Irish Drama: Anne Devlin, Christina Reid, and Charabanc Theatre Company.' *'Standing in their shifts itself': Irish drama from Farquhar to Friel*. Ed. Eberhard Bort. Bremen: European Society for Irish Studies, 1993. 263-79.

---. 'Come on You Boys in Green: Irish Football, Irish Theatre and the Irish Diaspora.' *State of Play: Irish Theatre in the Nineties*. Ed. Eberhard Bort. Trier: Wissenschaftlicher Verlag Trier, 1996. 88-103.

Bourdieu, Pierre. *The Field of Cultural Production*. New York: Columbia University Press, 1993.

Breen, Suzanne and Emma O'Kelly. 'Great Craic and Absent Guests.' *The Irish Times*. 17 Aug 1994: 8.

Brennan, Tim. 'From Development to Globalization: Postcolonial Studies and Globalization Theory.' *The Cambridge Companion to Postcolonial*

Literary Studies. Ed. Neil Lazarus. Cambridge: Cambridge University Press, 2004. 120-138.

Brighton, Pam. 'Six Characters in Search of a Story', *Theatre Ireland*, No. 6 (Apr-Jun, 1984): 144-147.

Butler, Judith. *Gender Trouble: Feminism and the Subversion of Identity*. New York and London: Routledge, 1990.

Byrne, Ophelia. 'DubbelJoint Theatre Company.' *Culture Northern Ireland*, 2004. Web. 19 Sept. 2013.

Carlson, Marvin A. *The Haunted Stage: The Theatre as Memory Machine*. Ann Arbor: University of Michigan Press, 2001.

Cavendish, Dominic. 'Women, Power and Politics at the Tricycle Theatre (Review).' *The Telegraph*, 14 Jun. 2010. Web. 12 Jul.2014.

Chambers, Lilian, Ger Fitzgibbon and Eamonn Jordan eds. *Theatre Talk: Voices of Irish Theatre Practitioners*. Dublin: Carysfort Press, 2001.

Chaudhuri, Una. *Staging Place: The Geography of Modern Drama*. Ann Arbor: University of Michigan Press, 1997.

Clancy, Luke. 'Speaking for the Powerless: interview with Marie Jones.' *The Irish Times*, 20 Feb 1996.

Clark, Stuart. 'Hold the Back Page: Paul McGrath talks to Stuart Clark.' *Hot Press* 6 (1995).

Cleary, Joe. 'Domestic Troubles: Tragedy and the Northern Ireland Conflict.' *South Atlantic Quarterly* 98.3 (1999): 501-37.

Cloke, Paul. 'Masculinity and Rurality.' *Spaces of Masculinities*. Eds Bettina Von Hoven and Kathrin Hörschelmann. London and New York: Routledge, 2005. 45-62.

Cochrane, Claire. 'Playing the Community', *Irish Theatre Magazine* 2:5 (Spring 2000): 33-39.

Cockcroft, Irene and Croft Susan, eds. *Art, Theatre and Women's Suffrage*. Twickenham: Aurora Metro Publications, 2010.

Coleman, Maureen. 'Stones in His Pockets rolling on to a big screen near you', *Belfast Telegraph*. 9 Sept. 2013. Web. 18 Apr. 2014.

Collins, Patrick. 'Bordering on the Unreal', *The Mail on Sunday* 14 Nov. 1993: 86.

Connolly, Linda. The Irish Women's Movement: From Revolution to Devolution. Dublin: The Lilliput Press, 2003 .

Coveney, Michael. 'Women, Power and Politics.' *What's on Stage?* 14 June 2010: n.p.

Coyle, Jane. 'Terminator's All Greased Up. ' *Belfast Telegraph* (Sunday Life). no date. (Linen Hall Library Theatre Archives, Belfast)

---. 'Football and Fanatics. ' *The Irish Times*. 9 Nov. 1994, sec. Arts: 12.

Crane, Diana, Fashion and Its Social Agendas: Class, Gender, and Identity in Clothing. Chicago: University of Chicago Press, 2000.

Crawford, Elizabeth. The Women's Suffrage Movement in Britain and Ireland: A Regional Survey. Oxon: Routledge, 2006.

Cromer, Peter. 'Cow Trouble.' *What's On,* 9. Feb 1993.

Crown, Ryan T. '*Lay Up Your Ends* (Review).' *NI Theatre,* 22 Apr. 2013. Web. 27 Aug. 2013

Daley, Natalie. 'Story of Irish mill strike plays well in U.S. premiere.' *Gazette Times* 10 Apr. (1997).

Despard, Charlotte. 'Why I became a 'Suffragette (1907).' *The Rebels: Irish Feminists*. Ed. Marie Mulvey-Roberts. London: Routledge / Thoemmes Press, 1996.
DiCenzo, Maria R. 'Charabanc Theatre Company: Placing Women Center Stage in Northern Ireland.' *Theatre Journal* 45.2 (1993): 175-84.
Dickson, E. Jane. 'Women on the Verge of Falling in Love'. 8 Mar. 1997. *The Telegraph*. Web. 28 Aug. 2013.
Dolan, Jill. *Utopia in Performance: Finding Hope at the Theater*. Ann Arbor: University of Michigan Press, 2005.
---. 'Feminist Performance Criticism and the Popular: Reviewing Wendy Wasserstein.' *Theatre Journal* 60 (2008): 433-57. .
Donald, Ann. 'Men, Love, and Romance.' *The Herald*, 7 May 1996.
Douglas, Deborah. 'Theatre Review: *Lay Up Your Ends*.' *Culture Northern Ireland*. 18 Aug. 2009. Web. 11 Aug. 2013.
Dowler, Lorraine. 'Till death do us part: masculinity, friendship, and nationalism in Belfast, Northern Ireland.' *Environment and Planning D: Society and Space* 19 (2001): 53-71.
DubbelJoint. Play Programme for *Women on the Verge of HRT*. 1995.
Ehren, Christine. 'Playbill On-Line's Brief Encounter with Marie Jones.' *Playbill*. 20 Mar. 2001. Web. 19 Apr. 2014.
Fitzsimmons, Linda and Gardner, Viv (eds.). *New Women Plays*. London: Methuen Drama, 1991.
Foley, Imelda. The Girls in the Big Picture: Gender on the Contemporary Ulster Stage. Dublin: Bloodaxe Press, 2003.
Gale, Maggie B. and John Stokes, eds. *The Cambridge Companion to the Actress*. Cambridge: Cambridge University Press, 2007.
Galligan, Yvonne. 'Women in Northern Ireland's Politics: Feminising an 'Armed Patriarchy.' *Representing Women in Parliament: A Comparative Study*. Eds. Marian Sawer, Manon Tremblay and Linda Trimble. London: Routledge, 2006. 204-20.
Gardner, Lyn. 'The Bard of Belfast.' *The Guardian*. 11 Aug. 2004. Web. 16 Aug. 2013.
Geis, Deborah R. *Postmodern Theatric(k)s: Monologue in Contemporary American Drama*. Ann Arbor: University of Michigan Press, 1993.
Gibbons, Luke. 'Beyond the Pale: Race, Ethnicity and Irish Culture.' *Reimagining Ireland*. Ed. Andrew Higgins Wyndham. Charlottesville: University of Virginia Press, 2006. 49-68.
Gilbert, Helen and Jacqueline Lo. 'Performing hybridity in post-colonial monodrama.' *Journal of Commonwealth Literature* 32.1 (1997): 5-19.
Goffman, Erving. *The Presentation of Self in Everyday Life*. London: Penguin, 1990.
Gorman, Sophie. 'Mother of All the Behans.' *Irish Independent*, 7 July 1998.
Grant, David. 'Introduction.' *The Crack in the Emerald*. London: Nick Hern Books, 1994.
Grene, Nicholas. *The Politics of Irish Drama: Plays in Context from Boucicault to Friel*. Cambridge: Cambridge University Press, 1999.

---. 'Tom Murphy and the children of loss.' *The Cambridge Companion to Twentieth-Century Irish Drama*. Ed. Shaun Richards. Cambridge: Cambridge University Press, 2004. 204-17.

Hailes, Anne. 'In the Palm of Kielty's Hand.' *Irish News*. 11 Aug. 2007, 17.

Hall, Stuart. 'Notes on Deconstructing 'The Popular'.' *People's History and Socialist Theory*. Ed. Raphael Samuel. London: Routledge, 1981. 227-40.

Harnden, Toby. 'IRA 'Mata Hari' to play mother of Troubles victim.' *Daily Telegraph*. 22 Feb. 1999.

Harrington, John and Elizabeth Mitchell, eds. *Politics and Performance in Contemporary Northern Ireland*. Amherst: University of Massachusetts Press, 1999.

Harris, Claudia W. 'Reinventing Women: Charabanc Theatre Company.' *The State of Play: Irish Theatre in the 'Nineties*. Ed. Eberhard Bort. Trier: Wissenschaftlicher Verlag Trier, 1996. 104-23.

---. 'Review: Somewhere over the Balcony', Theatre Ireland, No. 13 (1987): 47-48.

---. 'Introduction.' *Four Plays by the Charabanc Theatre Company: Inventing Women's Work*. Ed. Claudia Harris. Gerrards Cross: Colin Smythe, 2006): ix-li.

---. ed. *Four Plays by The Charabanc Theatre Company: Inventing Women's Work*. Gerrards Cross: Colin Smythe Limited, 2006.

Hill, Ian. 'Welcome Return: Dan Gordon Stars at Lyric. ' Review of A Night in November. *Belfast News Letter* 10 Jun. 2002: 16.

---. 'Marie's Game of Two Stereotypes.' Review of A Night in November.' *Belfast News Letter* 14 Jun. 2002: 19.

---. 'Lay Up Your Ends (Review).' *British Theatre Guide*. Aug 2009. Web. 11 Aug. 2013.

Holledge, Julie. *Innocent Flowers: Women in the Edwardian Theatre*. London: Virago Press, 1981.

Hollows, Joanne. *Feminism, Femininity and Popular Culture*. Manchester: Manchester University Press, 2000.

--- and Rachel Moseley. *Feminism in Popular Culture*. Oxford: Berg, 2006.

Hurley, Joseph. 'Ordinary People, Extraordinary Times.' *Irish Echo*. 21-27 October 1998.

Irish Theatre Institute. 'DubbelJoint Theatre Company.' *PlayographyIreland*. Web. 19 Mar. 2013.

Johnston, Cathal A. B. and Todd G. Morrison. 'The Presentation of Masculinity in Everyday Life: Contextual Variations in the Masculine Behaviour of Young Irish Men.' *Sex Roles* 57 (2007): 661-674.

Johnston, Philip. *The Lost Tribe in the Mirror: Four Playwrights of Northern Ireland*. Belfast: Lagan, 2009.

Jones, Marie. *Women on the Verge of HRT*. London: Samuel French, 1999.

---. *Stones in His Pocket & A Night in November: Two Plays*. London: Nick Hern, 2000.

---. 'Marie Jones in Conversation with Pat Moylan.' *Theatre Talk: Voices of Irish Theatre Practioners*. Eds. Lilian Chambers et al. Dublin: Carysfort Press, 2001. 213-19.
---. *Somewhere Over the Balcony. Postcolonial Plays: An Anthology*. Ed. Helen Gilbert. London: Routledge, 2001. 442-69.
---. *The Blind Fiddler: A Play*. London: Samuel French, 2008.
---. 'People who could spake for you.' *Lay Up Your Ends: A Twenty-Fifth Anniversary Edition. Martin Lynch and The Charabanc Theatre Company*, ed. Richard Palmer. Belfast: Lagan, 2008.
---. *The Milliner and the Weaver. Women Power and Politics*. London: Nick Hern Books, 2010.
---. Christmas Eve Can Kill You. Theater Archive, Linen Hall Library, Belfast. Unpublished.
---. Eddie Bottom's Dream. Theatre Archive, Linen Hall Library, Belfast. Unpublished.
---. Oul Delf and False Teeth. Theatre Archive, Linen Hall Library, Belfast. Unpublished
Jones, Marie and the Company. "Now You're Talkin" *Four Plays by the Charabanc Theatre Company: Inventing Women's Work*. Ed. Claudia W. Harris. Gerrards Cross: Colin Smythe, 2006. 1-54.
Jones Marie and Martin Lynch, et al. *Convictions*. Belfast: Tinderbox Theatre Company, 2000.
Jordan, Eamonn. 'Kicking with Both Feet: Marie Jones's A Night in November.' *The Irish Review* 38 (Spring 2008): 49-60 .
Kahn, Jack S. *An Introduction to Masculinities*. Sussex: Wiley, 2009.
Fricker, Karen. 'Review: Christmas Eve Can Kill You.' *The Guardian*, 17 Dec 2002. Web. 12 Jul. 2013
Kearney, Eileen. 'Charabanc: Theatre of Social Change in Northern Ireland.' Proc. of Association for Theatre in Higher Education. Seattle, WA. 1991. Presentation. unpublished.
Kelly, Katherine E. 'Shaw on Woman Suffrage: A Minor Player on the Petticoat Platform.' *Shaw*, Vol. 14, pp.67-81.
Kelly, Ned. 'A Mother's Heart- to the heart of the conflict.' *An Phoblacht*. 18 Feb. 1999, 15.
Kenway, Jane, Anna Kraack and Anna Hickey-Moody. *Masculinity Beyond the Metropolis*. Basingstoke: Palgrave Macmillan, 2006.
Kershaw, Baz. *The Politics of Performance: Radical Theatre as Cultural Intervention*. London: Routledge, 1992.
Kiberd, Declan. *Inventing Ireland: The Literature of the Modern Nation*. London: Jonathan Cape, 1995.
Kielty, Patrick. Patrick Kielty – Live. Spirit Entertainment, 2006. DVD.
Kilfeather, Siobhán. 'Irish feminism.' *The Cambridge Companion to Modern Ireland*. Eds. Joe Cleary and Claire Connolly. Cambridge: Cambridge University Press, 2005. 96-116.
Kirkwood, Lucy. *Bloody Wimmin. Women Power and Politics*. London: Nick Hern Books, 2010.
Kurdi, Maria. 'Spatializing the Renewal of Female Subjectivity in Marie Jones's Women on the Verge of HRT .' *Echoes Down the Corridor:*

Irish Theatre – Past, present, future. Eds Patrick Lonergan and Riana O'Dwyer. Dublin: Carysfort Press, 2007. 117-28.

Kushner, Tony. *Angels in America: Millenium Approaches*. New York: Theatre Communications Group, 1993.

L'Oréal Paris. 'Because You're Worth It.' L'Oréal Paris. Web. 15 Aug. 2013.

Lacey, Stephen. *British Realist Theatre: The New Wave in its Context 1956-1965*. London: Routledge, 1995.

Lenkiewicz, Rebecca. *Her Naked Skin*. London: Faber and Faber, 2008.

--- *The Lioness. Women Power and Politics*. London: Nick Hern Books, 2010.

Llewellyn-Jones, Margaret. *Contemporary Irish Drama and Cultural Identity*. Bristol: Intellect, 2002.

Lojek, Helen. 'Playing Politics with Belfast's Charabanc Theatre Company.' *Politics and Performance in Contemporary Northern Ireland*. Eds John P. Harrington and Elizabeth J. Mitchell. Amherst: University of Massachusetts Press, 1999. 82-102.

---.'Eleanor Methven and Carol Moore [Scanlan] in Conversation with Helen Lojek.' *Theatre Talk: Voices of Irish Theatre and Practitioners*. Eds Lilian Chambers, Ger FitzGibbon, and Eamonn Jordan. Dublin: Carysfort, 2001. 342-54.

---.'Troubling Perspective: Northern Ireland, the 'Troubles' and Drama.' *A Companion to Modern British and Irish Drama 1880-2005*. Ed. Mary Luckhurst. Oxford: Blackwell, 2006. 329-40.

Lonergan, Patrick. 'Marie Jones.' *Irish Women Writers: An A-to-Z Guide*. Ed. Alexander G. Gonzalez. Westport, CT: Greenwood Press, 2006. 164-8.

---. *Theatre and Globalization: Irish Drama in the Celtic Tiger Era*. New York: Palgrave Macmillan, 2009.

Love, Walter. 'Marie Jones, Actress and Playwright.' *Ulster Tatler* Oct. 2000: 23-24.

Lynch, Martin, 'Why This Play?' *Lay Up Your Ends: A Twenty-Fifth Anniversary Edition. Martin Lynch and The Charabanc Theatre Company*; ed. Richard Palmer. Belfast: Lagan. 2008.

Lynch, Martin, and The Charabanc Theatre Company. *Lay Up Your Ends: A Twenty-Fifth Anniversary Edition*. Ed. Richard Palmer. Belfast: Lagan. 2008.

Lynch, Martin, Conor Grimes, and Alan McKee. *The History of the Troubles (Accordin' to My Da)*. Belfast: Lagan Press, 2005.

Mac an Ghaill, Máirtín. 'Irish Masculinities and Sexualities in England.' *Sexualising the Social: Power and the Organisation of Sexuality*. Eds Lisa Adkins and Vicki Merchant. Basingstoke: Macmillan, 1996. 122-44.

MacDabhaid, Padraig. 'Arts Council Censorship.' *An Phoblacht*, July 29, 1999, 17.

Maguire, Tom. 'Kicking With Another Foot: Contesting memories in Marie Jones's *A Night in November* and Dermot Bolger's *In High Germany*.' *Performance Research* 5.3 (2000): 76-81.

---. 'Binlids at The Boundaries of Being: A West Belfast community stages an authentic self.' *Kunapipi* 22.2 (2000): 106-17
---. 'Marie Jones.' *Dictionary of Literary Biography*, Vol. 233: *British And Irish Dramatists Since World War II*. Ed. John Bull. Detroit: Bruccoli Clark Layman, 2000. 182-7.
---. *Making Theatre in Northern Ireland: Through and Beyond the Troubles*. Exeter: University of Exeter Press, 2006.
---. "You're Only Putting It On': Dressing Up, Identity and Subversion in Northern Irish Drama.' *Postcolonial Text* 3.3 (2007): 1-14. Web. 3 Jul. 2014.
Mangan, Michael. *Staging Masculinities: History, Gender, Performance*. Basingstoke: Palgrave Macmillan, 2003.
Martin, Carol. 'Charabanc Theatre Company: 'Quare' Women 'Sleggin' and 'Greggin' the standards of Northern Ireland by 'Tappin' the People.' *The Drama Review: TDR*, 31. 2 (Summer, 1987): 88-99.
McConachie, Bruce. 'Doing Things with Image Schemas: The Cognitive Turn in Theatre Studies and the Problem of Experience for Historians.' *Theatre Journal* 53.4 (Dec. 2001): 569-594.
McDonagh, Martin. *The Beauty Queen of Leenane*. London: Faber and Faber, 1999.
McDonough, Carla J. *Staging Masculinity: Male Identity in Contemporary American Drama*. Jefferson and London: McFarland, 1997.
McGrath, John. *A Good Night Out. Popular Theatre: Audience, Class and Form*. London: Nick Hern, 1996.
McKinnie, Michael. 'The state of this place: Convictions, the courthouse, and the geography of performance in Belfast (Tinderbox-Theatre-Company).' *Modern Drama* 46.4 (2003): 580-97.
McKittrick, David. 'Gunmen are Savage, Sinful, Wicked, Depraved.' *The Independent*. 1 Nov. 1993, 1.
McMillan, Joyce. 'A Night to Remember. ' (Linen Hall Library Theatre Archives, Belfast)
McMillen, Robert. 'Anti-RUC play has funding removed.' *Irish News*, 23 Jan. 23, 1999, 14.
McMullan, Anna. 'Gender, Authorship and Performance in Selected Plays by Contemporary Irish Women Playwrights.' *Theatre Stuff: Critical Essays on Contemporary Irish Theatre*. Ed. Eamonn Jordan. Dublin: Carysfort Press, 2000. 34-46.
Moore, Brian. DubbelJoint Play Program for Black Taxis. 2003.
Moore, Carol. 'Impulse to Imagination.' *Lay Up Your Ends: A Twenty-Fifth Anniversary Edition. Martin Lynch and The Charabanc Theatre Company*; ed. Richard Palmer. Belfast: Lagan. 2008.
Moore, Paul, 'Stap Fightin' – Accents of Violence in the Works of James Young.' *Performing Violence in Contemporary Ireland*. Ed. Lisa Fitzpatrick. Dublin: Carysfort, 2009. 265-279.
Moriarty, Gerri. 'The Wedding Community Play Project: A Cross-community Production in Northern Ireland.' *Theatre and Empowerment: Community Drama on the World Stage*. Eds

Richard Boon and Jane Plastow. Cambridge: Cambridge University Press, 2004. 13-32.

Moroney, Mic. 'Just as a Play.' *The Irish Times*. 29 July 1999.

Mullin, John. 'Cheers Turned to Screams for Mercy.' *The Guardian*. 20 June 1994, 2.

---. 'In Between are the Innocent. At Times You Can't Go On.' *The Guardian*. 1 Nov. 1993, 1.

Mulvey, Laura. 'Visual Pleasure and Narrative Cinema', (1975), *Film Theory and Criticism: Introductory Readings*. Eds. Leo Braudy and Marshall Cohen. New York: Oxford University Press, 1999. 833-44.

Murphy, Cliona. *The Women's Suffrage Movement and Irish Society in the early Twentieth Century*. Hertfordshire: Harvester Wheatsheaf, 1989.

Murray, Christopher. *Twentieth-century Irish Drama: Mirror up to Nature*. Manchester: Manchester University Press, 1997.

A Night in November. Writ. Marie Jones. Dir Pam Brighton. Perf. Dan Gordon. DubbelJoint Media Productions, 1996. VHS.

O'Broin, Eoin. 'A Clear Case of Political Censorship.' *Fortnight Magazine*, Sept. 1999, 22.

-----. 'A Community's Starring Role.' *An Phoblacht*, 7 Aug. 1997, 15.

O'Doherty, Malachi. 'Double Trouble.' *Fortnight Magazine*, Sept. 1999, 21-22.

-----. 'Play-acting of the wrong kind for an audience in west Belfast.' *Belfast Telegraph*, 3 Aug. 1999, 10.

OFMDFM. 'A Shared Future: Policy and Strategic Framework for Good Relations.' *Office of the First Minister and Deputy First Minister,* 2005. Web. 3 Aug. 2012.

O'Kane, Pat. 'More Kicks Than Micks.' *The Irish Times* 13 Nov. 1993: Weekend.

O'Leary, Deirdre. 'Staging the City: Site Specific Theatre in Contemporary Belfast.' *Modern Mask: A Journal of the Arts* 1.1 (2006). Web. 21 Apr. 2013.

---. 'No Go/New Show: Staging Belfast in The Wedding Community Play and Convictions.' *Foilsiu: An Interdisciplinary Journal of Irish Studies* 6:1 (Spring 2008): 57-78.

O'Toole, Fintan. 'Light Heart, Heavy Heart.' *The Irish Times* 20 Sept. 1994: 10.

---. 'Insulting Both Sides.' *Irish Times* 5 Dec. 1995, sec. Second Opinion, 12.

---. 'Review of *A Night in November.*' *Critical Moments: Fintan O'Toole on Modern Irish Theatre*. Eds. Julia Furay and Redmond O'Hanlon. Dublin: Carysfort Press, 2003: 157-129.

Owicki, Eleanor. 'Rattle Away at Your Bin: Women, Community, and Bin Lids in Northern Irish Drama.' *Theatre Symposium* 18 (2010): 56-66.

'Patrick Kielty and A Night in November'. BBC Northern Ireland. 29 Sept 2008. Television.

Paxton, Naomi, ed. *The Methuen Drama Book of Suffrage Plays*. London: Methuen Drama, 2013.

Phelan, Mark. 'The Fantasy of post-nationalism in Northern theatre: *Caught Red Handed* transplanting the planter.' *Australasian Drama Studies* Special Issue, 43 (Oct 2003): 89-107.

---. "Authentic Reproductions': Staging the 'Wild West in Modern Irish Drama.' *Theatre Journal* 61 (2009): 235-48.

---.'Performing 'Authentic' Ireland: (Dis)Connecting the Cultural Politics of the Irish Revival and the Celtic Tiger on the Irish Stage.' *The Dreaming Body: Contemporary Irish Theatre*. Eds Melissa Sihra and Paul Murphy. Gerrards Cross: Colin Smythe, 2009. 55-69.

Pilkington, Lionel. *Theatre and Ireland*. Basingstoke: Palgrave Macmillian, 2010.

Privas, Virginie. 'Monological Drama to Reshape the Northern Irish Identity: *A Night in November* by Marie Jones.' *Estudios Irlandeses* 5 (2010): 68-80.

Rianda, Leonora. '*Lay Up Your Ends* Packed With Music, Universal Issue.' *The Daily Barometer*. 11 Apr. 1997.

Richtarik, Marilynn J. *Acting Between the Lines: the Field Day Theatre Company and Irish cultural politics*. Oxford: Clarendon Press, 1994.

Roche, Anthony. *Contemporary Irish Drama*. 2nd ed. New York: Palgrave Macmillan, 2009.

Ryan, Louise. 'An analysis of the Irish suffrage movement using new social movement theory.' *Social Movements and Ireland*. Eds Linda Connelly and Niamh Hourigan. Manchester: Manchester University Press, 2006..

Said, Edward. W. *Orientalism*. New York: Vintage, 1979.

---. Culture and Imperialism. London: Vintage, 1994.

Seabrook, John. Nobrow: *The Culture of Marketing, the Marketing of Culture*. New York: Vintage Books, 2001.

Sihra, Melissa, ed. *Women in Irish Drama: A Century of Authorship and Self-Representation*. Basingstoke: Palgrave Macmillan, 2007.

Simpson, Mark. 'Orangeman Says Protestants Should Not Learn Irish Language.' *BBC News*. 1 Feb. 2014. Web. 20 March 2014.

Singleton, Brian. 'Am I Talking to Myself? Men, Masculinities and the Monologue in Contemporary Irish Theatre.' *Monologues: Theatre, Performance, Subjectivity*. Ed. Claire Wallace. Prague: Litteraria Pragensia, 2006. 260-277. .

Smyth, Damian. 'Shots in the Arts.' *Fortnight Magazine*. Nov. 1999, 22.

Spencer, Charles. 'Menopausal Women Behaving Badly.' *The Telegraph*, 8 Mar. 1997. Web. 28 Aug 2013.

Tasker, Yvonne and Diana Negra. *Interrogating Postfeminism: Gender and the Politics of Popular Culture*. Durham: Duke University Press, 2007.

Theatre Company, *Lay Up Your Ends: A 25th Anniversary Edition* (Belfast: Lagan Press, 2008).

Tricycle Theatre. *Women, Power and Politics Now*. London: Nick Hern Books, 2010.

Trotter, Mary. *Modern Irish Theatre*. Cambridge: Polity Press, 2008.

Urban, Eva. *Community Politics and the Peace Process in Contemporary Northern Irish Drama*. New York: Peter Lang, 2011.

Urquhart, Diane. "An articulate and definite cry for political freedom': the Ulster suffrage movement.' *Women's History Review* 11:2 (2002): 273-292.

Voigts-Virchow, Eckart and Mark Schreiber. 'Will the 'Wordy Body' Please Stand Up? The Crisis of Male Impersonation in Monological Drama – Beckett, McPherson, Eno', *Monologues: Theatre, Performance, Subjectivity*. Ed. Clare Wallace. Prague: Litteraria Pragensia, 2006. 278-96.

Ward, Margaret and Marie-Thérèse McGivern. 'Images of Women in Northern Ireland.' *The Crane Bag* 4.1 (1980): 66-72.

Ward, Margaret. "Suffrage First, Above All Else!' An Account of the Irish Suffrage Movement.' *Feminist Review*, No.10 (Spring, 1982): 21-36.

Waters, Maureen.*The Comic Irishman*. Albany, NY: SUNY Press, 1984.

Watt, Stephen. *Joyce, O'Casey, and the Irish Popular Theater*. New York: Syracuse University Press, 1991.

BBC NI. 'Wedding Drama.' *BBC Eyewitness*. Web. 5 May 2013.

White, Victoria. 'Cathleen ni Houlihan Is Not a Playwright.' *Theatre Ireland* 30 (1993): 26-29.

Winter, Brenda. 'Introduction. 'That's Not Theatre, Love!' The *Lay Up Your Ends* Experience.' *Lay Up Your Ends: A Twenty-Fifth Anniversary Edition*. Martin Lynch and The Charabanc Theatre Company; ed. Richard Palmer. Belfast: Lagan, 2008. 17-39.

Yeates, Pádraig. *Lockout: Dublin 1913*. Dublin: Gill and Macmillan Ltd, 2001.

Yeats, W. B, *Cathleen ní Houlihan* (1901), *The Major Works*. Ed. Edward Larrissy. Oxford: Oxford University Press, 1997.

Notes on Contributors

Fiona Coffey holds a PhD from Tufts University, an MPhil from Trinity College, Dublin and a BA from Stanford University. Her research focuses on women in Irish theatre and Northern Irish theatre and film. Her manuscript *Sectarian Warfare, Gender, and Performance: Women on the Northern Irish Stage, 1921-2010* is the first social history of women on the Northern Irish stage, placing women's contributions within the dual contexts of Irish theatre history and the Northern Irish conflict.

Dawn Fowler is a Senior Lecturer in Drama at the University of the West of England where she leads the modules The Radical Self and Theatre and War. She has published chapters on the treatment of war in plays by Charles Wood and David Greig, radical Bristolian drama and the participation of women in political movements.

David Grant, currently a Senior Lecturer in Drama at Queen's University Belfast, has had a distinguished career as a theatre professional. He worked for the Belfast Festival, directed the Dublin Theatre Festival and was an editor of *Theatre Ireland*. His experience includes a number of significant professional directing credits, including a time as Artistic Director of the Lyric, Belfast and a range of applied drama projects. He has also served on the boards of Replay, Tinderbox, Youth Action and the Ulster Association for Youth Drama.

Charlotte J. Headrick is a professor of Theatre Arts at Oregon State University. A past president of the American Conference for Irish Studies, West, she has directed numerous premieres and productions of Irish Plays all over the United States. Widely published in the field of Irish drama, she is a former Moore Visiting Fellow at National University of Ireland, Galway and a co-editor of *Irish Women Dramatists 1908-2001* (2014, Syracuse University Press). She is a recipient of the Kennedy Center/American College Theater Festival Medallion for service to that organization and is an Elizabeth P. Ritchie Distinguished Professor at Oregon State.

Shonagh Hill completed her PhD at Queen's University Belfast, and has published articles on women in Irish theatre in *Theatre Research International* and *Etudes Irlandaises*, as well as contributing to the edited collection *Staging Thought: Essays on Irish Theatre, Scholarship and Practice* (Bern: Peter Lang, 2012). Her current research focuses on neoliberalism, feminism and affect. She is a member of the International Federation for Theatre Research's Feminist Working Group.

Wei H. Kao received his doctorate from the University of Kent and now lectures at National Taiwan University. His articles on Irish writers and culture have appeared in *Journal of Beckett Studies*, *English Studies in Africa*, *Journal of War and Culture Studies*, *Irish Women at War* (2010), among others. His monograph, *The Formation of an Irish Literary Canon in the Mid-Twentieth Century* (2007) was published by ibidem-Verlag.

Tim Loane is a writer, director and actor in film, television, theatre and radio. After graduating from Queens University Belfast, with a degree in Psychology, he co-founded Tinderbox Theatre Company in 1988, that would go on to become Northern Ireland's leading independent company dedicated to developing and producing new writing, of which he was joint Artistic Director until 1996. His stage plays include the political satires *Caught Red Handed* (Tinderbox, Belfast) which won the Irish Times Best New Play Award and the Stewart Parker Award (2002) and *To Be Sure* (Lyric Theatre, Belfast) in 2007. He wrote and directed *The Civilisation Game*, a satire on suburban shenanigans in 2012 (Lyric Theatre). As well as appearing alongside Marie Jones on screen, Tim was in the original production of her adaptation of *The Government Inspector* for DubbelJoint and was producer for the first staging of *Christmas Eve Can Kill You* at the Old Museum Arts Centre.

Tom Maguire is a Senior Lecturer in Theatre Studies at the University of Ulster. He teaches and researches in areas of contemporary British and Irish theatre practice and in heritage studies, as well as making performance work. His *Making Theatre in Northern Ireland: through and beyond the Troubles* has become a landmark in Irish theatre studies and he published *Performing Story on the Contemporary Stage* in 2015. He co-edited with Karian Schuitema *Theatre for Young*

Audiences: a critical handbook (2012) and has contributed essays to a range of international journals and edited collections.

Eugene McNulty is a Senior Lecturer in the English Department of St Patrick's College (Dublin City University). His main research interests focus on Irish theatre history and the politicality of cultural production. He is the author of *The Ulster Literary Theatre and the Northern Revival* (2008) and the co-editor of *Crime Cultures: Figuring Criminality in Fiction and Film* (2010); *Patrick Pearse: Collected Plays* (2013); and *Hearing Heaney* (2015). His current project is an exploration of the relationship between Irish drama and the law.

Paula McFetridge is the Artistic Director of Kabosh Theatre Company. Having been involved in performance through youth theatre and circus in Belfast while at school, she progressed to Dartington College of Arts. She interrupted her degree studies to join Tinderbox Theatre Company as an actor; performed with Charabanc in Sue Glover's *Bondagers* and Tom McLaughlin's *Frontline Café*; and appeared in productions at the Abbey and with DubbelJoint in Marie Jones's adaptation of *The Government Inspector*. She was the Production Manager on *The Wedding Community Play*, served as Artistic Director for Tinderbox's *Convictions* in Crumlin Road Courthouse and, in 2001, exchanged the role of Education Officer at Belfast's Lyric Theatre for that of Artistic Director. At The Lyric, she revived *Christmas Eve Can Kill You* (and later, *New Year's Eve Can Kill You*) and produced *Weddins, Weeins and Wakes* and *The Blind Fiddler*. The last Marie Jones piece she produced for The Lyric was *A Very Weird Manor*. She went on to take over as Artistic Director of Kabosh, developing the company's reputation for innovative site-specific performances.

Deirdre O'Leary is Associate Professor of English at Manhattan College. She has published articles and reviews on Irish and American theater and performance in *American Writers Supplement, British Writers Supplement, Irish Journal of Gothic and Horror Studies, Irish Studies Review, Theatre Journal, Theatre Survey, e-Celtoi, New England Theatre Journal* and the *Eugene O'Neill Review*.

Eleanor Owicki is a lecturer in the Department of Performance Studies at Texas A&M University. Her research focuses on performance in contemporary Northern Ireland, with particular attention to the legacies of the Troubles and the experiences of ethnic and sexual minorities. She received her PhD from the University of Texas at Austin

Department of Theatre and Dance's Performance as Public Practice Program in 2013.

Catherine Rees is Lecturer in Drama at Loughborough University. She specializes mainly in contemporary Irish theatre, and particularly the plays of Martin McDonagh and Marie Jones. She is also involved in research into wider areas of Irish Studies, including interdisciplinary connections with film, literature and cultural studies. Her theoretical interests lie primarily in nationalism, gender, trauma studies and political theatre and performance.

Brenda Winter-Palmer joined the staff in Drama Studies at Queen's University Belfast in 2009 after a thirty-year career as an actress, writer and director in professional theatre, film and television. In 1983 she was one of the founders of Charabanc, the Irish women's theatre company. In 1988 she established Replay, Northern Ireland's longest established educational theatre company, and was its first Artistic Director for a period of seven years. Between 1998 and 2004 she was Creative Director of The Mixed Peppers Training Project in Theatre Arts for Young People with Motor Disabilities. Since coming to Queen's she has been engaged in a practice as research process which involves the translation of archival material and oral histories into performance. Her research activities have resulted in two new plays *Just Shiels* (2008) and *The Medal in the Drawer* (2014).

Index

A

America, 7, 10-11, 18, 73, 76, 81-82, 109, 149, 151, 188, 202
Andrews Lane Theatre, 113
Arts Council of Northern Ireland, vi, ix, 8, 23-24, 75, 117, 126, 202
Arts Theatre, Belfast, 35-36, 42, 47, 55, 65-69, 124, 156

B

BBC, 5, 47, 77, 101, 105, 129, 135, 139, 156, 204-206
Belfast Agreement, see Good Friday Agreement, 115-16, 118
Big Telly Theatre Company, 1, 49, 68, 89, 104, 120, 160
Bort, Eberhard, 74, 97, 197, 200
Brenda Winter, vii, ix, 2, 6-7, 23, 29, 32, 47, 51-52, 55, 65, 168, 210
Brighton, Pam, 4-5, 8-9, 19, 31, 34, 37, 56, 66-67, 69, 107, 108, 110, 115, 118-20, 125, 128, 156, 158, 167, 180, 190, 198, 204

C

Campbell, Brian
Des, 69, 118
Voyage of No Return, 121
Campbell, Brian and McKeown, Lawrence
Laughter of Our Children, The, 118
Carlson, Marvin, 128-29, 133, 135-36, 198
Carr, Marina, 117
Celtic Tiger, 14, 74, 202, 205
Charabanc Theatre Company, *passim*
Girls in the Big Picture, The, 36, 41-44, 155, 195, 199
Gold on the Streets, 36
Now You're Talkin', 39, 92-95, 98, 195, 201
Oul Delf and False Teeth, 36-39, 44, 69, 195, 201
Somewhere Over the Balcony, 44-46, 55, 59, 63, 70, 92, 95-99, 124, 195, 201
Terrible Twins Crazy Christmas, 47, 195

The Girls in the Big Picture, 36, 41, 43-44, 195, 199
Chaudhuri, Una, 76, 198
collaboration, 5, 32, 120
Connaughton, Shane, 8, 108, 117, 119, 195
Convictions, 16, 49, 79-80, 89, 201-204, 209
Crimea Square, 3

D

Devlin, Anne
  Ourselves Alone, 2
diaspora, 74, 81, 82, 197
DiCenzo, Maria R., 28, 45, 48, 104, 199
Dolan, Jill, 132, 169
DubbelJoint Productions, vii, 4-5, 8-9, 12-13, 19, 59, 92, 107-21, 125, 128, 135, 156, 168, 195, 198-200, 203-204, 208-209

E

Eagleton, Terry
  White, the Gold and the Gangrene, The, *108*
Egan, Jo, 3, 86, 101
Elliot, Pearse
  Mother's Heart, A, 117

F

Féile an Phobail, 8-9, 108, 111, 114
feminism, 20, 30, 146, 165-71, 179, 183, 193, 197-201, 208
Field Day Theatre Company, 23, 27-28, 67, 107, 109, 120, 123-24, 205
Foley, Imelda, 8, 134, 175
Forced Upon Us, 116-17

G

gender, 17, 28-31, 34, 40, 44, 83, 87, 95, 141-48, 151-53, 166, 170, 172, 198-99, 203, 205, 207, 210
globalization, 18, 62, 76, 149, 197, 202
Good Friday Agreement, 19, 87, 89, 105, 138, 144
Gordon, Dan, 5, 9, 19, 61, 81, 114, 124-25, 128, 134, 180, 200, 204
Grand Opera House, Belfast, 3, 19, 55, 61, 111, 127-28, 134, 138
Grant, David, vii, ix, 2, 4, 6, 23, 36, 48, 52, 59, 60, 207
Group Theatre, Belfast, 3, 16

H

Harris, Claudia, 27, 29, 32, 34, 36, 45, 51, 54, 56, 59, 64, 200
Hill, Conleth, 5
Hinds, Andy, 23, 31, 65, 67, 105

J

Jones, Marie, *passim*
  Blind Fiddler of Glenaduach, The, 8, 47
  Blind Fiddler, The, 5, 8, 16, 59, 92, 97-99, 105, 157, 195-96, 201, 209
  Chosen Room, The, 17, 196
  Christmas Eve Can Kill You, 5, 8, 77, 80, 84, 108, 119, 125-26, 156-59, 195, 201, 208-209
  Courtroom No. 2, Convictions, 16, 49, 79-80, 89, 201, 203-204, 209
  Dancing Shoes: The George Best Story, 17, 196
  Eddie Bottom's Dream, 13, 78, 84, 119, 195, 201

Ethel Workman Is Innocent, 12, 195
Fly Me to The Moon, 5
Government Inspector, The, 9, 59, 108, 111, 114, 118-19, 125-26, 135, 195, 208-209
Hamster Wheel, The, 5, 18, 47, 59-60, 63, 195
Hang All the Harpers, 8, 108
It's a Waste of Time, Tracy, 77, 195
Milliner and the Weaver, The, 17, 89, 181, 182, 185, 188, 190, 192, 193, 196, 201
Night in November, A, viii, 5, 9-12, 19, 48, 56, 59-60, 63, 80-88, 92, 99, 101, 104, 114, 118-19, 126-46, 153, 156-57, 161, 168, 190, 195, 200-205
Rock Doves, 17, 196
Ruby:the life of Ruby Murray, 16
Stones in His Pockets, 1, 5, 13-14, 16, 44, 48, 59-63, 77, 80, 82, 114, 119-20, 131, 141, 143, 149-53, 157, 195, 198
The Cow, the Ship, and the Indian, 7
Under Napoleon's Nose, 7, 70, 195
Very Weird Manor, A, 17, 126, 157, 161, 196, 209
Weddins, Weans and Wakes, 5, 47, 70, 157, 159, 195, 209
Women on the Verge of HRT, 8, 12-13, 20, 48, 59-60, 111-13, 119, 143, 159, 163-72, 174, 178-80, 195, 199-201
Women on the Verge...Get a Life!, 121
Yours Truly, 7, 195

Jones, Marie and Lynch, Martin
Wedding Community Play, The, 15, 86, 89, 92, 101-105, 195, 203-204, 209
Jordan, Eamonn, ix, 81, 104, 148, 198, 202-203

K

Kielty, Patrick, 19, 61, 114, 127, 129, 131, 134-36, 139, 200-201, 204
Kushner, Tony
Angels in America, 76, 202

L

Lambert, Mark, 5, 8, 107, 120
Lane Productions, 157
legal case, 5
Loane, Tim, viii, ix, 5-6, 8, 123, 126, 156, 208
Lojek, Helen, 28, 34, 56, 92, 95, 104, 143, 168, 170, 185, 202
Lynch, Martin, 15-16, 31, 33, 35, 48, 54-55, 66, 67, 75, 86, 101, 114, 124, 129, 134, 139, 160, 195, 201-203, 206
Lyric Theatre, Belfast, 29, 31-32, 61, 66, 88, 108, 119, 135, 155, 208-209

M

Maguire, Tom, v, vi, vii, 1, 9, 23, 89, 121-23, 132, 145, 155, 208
Mahon, Derek
High Time, 109
masculinity, 8, 19, 104, 141-42, 144, 148-53, 172, 174, 198-203
McAuley, Maureen, 2, 29
McConachie, Bruce, 128-29, 136, 138, 203
McCready, Sam, 23

McElhinney, Ian, 3-4, 55, 61-62, 127, 129, 157, 190
McFetridge, Paula, viii, ix, 1, 4-8, 155, 209
McGrath, John, 16, 18, 25-26, 31, 67, 71, 81, 167, 170-76, 198, 203
  Good Night Out, A, 16, 18, 71, 170, 179, 197, 203
McGuinness, Frank, 76, 104, 117
McKeown, Laurence and Campbell, Brian
  In a Cold House, 121
Methven, Eleanor, 2, 4, 24, 29-30, 39, 45, 51, 56, 96, 123, 159, 202
Metropolitan Arts Centre (The MAC), Belfast, 2, 88, 160
Mitchell, Gary
  Remnants of Fear, 121
monologue form, 105, 148, 153
Monstrous Regiment, see Pam Brighton, 31, 34, 69
Moore, Brian
  Ballad of Malachy Mulligan, The, 121
  Black Taxi, 108, 121, 203
  Session, The, 121
Moore, Carol, see Carol Scanlon, 31, 36, 56, 58, 96, 202
Morash, Christopher, 168
Murphy, Brenda
  Working Class Heroes, 121

O

Old Museum Arts Centre (OMAC), 108, 156, 161, 208
O'Toole, Fintan, 61, 80, 132, 204

P

Parker, Stewart, 89, 104, 124, 208
Paulin, Tom
  Riot Act, The, 109
Phelan, Mark, 14, 74-75, 82, 151, 172
Playzone, 23, 31, 65, 67, 105
Pollack, Eileen, 107
popular culture, 5, 18, 20, 73-74, 86, 88, 163-79
popular theatre, 18, 21, 26, 48, 63, 163-80
popular theatre, 18, 21, 26, 48, 63, 163-80

R

Reid, Christina
  Tea in a China Cup, 2
Replay Productions, 6
Richtarik, Marilynn, 28, 205
Robinson, Mary, 74
Rubin, Leon, 23, 68

S

Scanlon, Carol, 2
see also McGrath, John, 16, 18, 25-26, 31, 67, 167, 170
Shankill Road, 3, 42, 47
Sheridan, Peter, 70, 117
Sihra, Melissa, 180, 205
stereotypes, 92, 96, 110, 112, 132, 138, 144, 153, 159

T

Tinderbox, 15-16, 49, 68, 75, 89, 104, 124-25, 135, 195, 201, 203, 207-209
touring, 5, 13, 23, 34, 49, 59, 65, 69, 88, 105, 107-108, 111, 114, 119-20, 125, 160
Tricycle Theatre, London, 17, 20, 59, 61, 111, 119, 181, 189, 198, 205

W

Watt, Stephen, 168
West Belfast Festival, see Féile an Phobail, 5, 8-9, 61, 109, 125, 133-34, 170, 180

Winter, Brenda, vii, ix, 2, 6-7, 23, 29, 32, 47, 51-52, 55, 65, 168, 210

Y

Young Lyric, 4
Young, James, 3, 6, 203

Carysfort Press was formed in the summer of 1998. It receives annual funding from the Arts Council.

The directors believe that drama is playing an ever-increasing role in today's society and that enjoyment of the theatre, both professional and amateur, currently plays a central part in Irish culture.

The Press aims to produce high quality publications which, though written and/or edited by academics, will be made accessible to a general readership. The organisation would also like to provide a forum for critical thinking in the Arts in Ireland, again keeping the needs and interests of the general public in view.

The company publishes contemporary Irish writing for and about the theatre.

Editorial and publishing inquiries to:
Carysfort Press Ltd.,
58 Woodfield,
Scholarstown Road,
Rathfarnham,
Dublin 16,
Republic of Ireland.

T (353 1) 493 7383
F (353 1) 406 9815
E: info@carysfortpress.com
www.carysfortpress.com

HOW TO ORDER

TRADE ORDERS DIRECTLY TO:
Irish Book Distribution
Unit 12, North Park, North Road,
Finglas, Dublin 11.

T: (353 1) 8239580
F: (353 1) 8239599
E: mary@argosybooks.ie
www.argosybooks.ie

INDIVIDUAL ORDERS DIRECTLY TO:
eprint Ltd.
35 Coolmine Industrial Estate,
Blanchardstown, Dublin 15.
T: (353 1) 827 8860
F: (353 1) 827 8804 Order online @
E: books@eprint.ie
www.eprint.ie

FOR SALES IN NORTH AMERICA AND CANADA:
Dufour Editions Inc.,
124 Byers Road,
PO Box 7,
Chester Springs,
PA 19425,
USA

T: 1-610-458-5005
F: 1-610-458-7103

Blue Raincoat Theatre Company

By Rhona Trench

Since its foundation in 1991, Blue Raincoat Theatre Company is Ireland's only full-time venue-based professional theatre ensemble and has become renowned for its movement, visual and aural proficiencies and precision. This book explores those signatures from a number of vantage points, conveying the complex challenges faced by Blue Raincoat as they respond to changing aesthetic and economic circumstances. Particular consideration is given to set, costume, sound and lighting design.

ISBN: 978-1-909325-67-8 €20 (Paperback)

Across the Boundaries: Talking about Thomas Kilroy

Edited by: Guy Woodward

Thomas Kilroy's long and distinguished career is celebrated in this volume by new essays, panel discussions and an interview, reconsidering the work of one of Ireland's most intellectually ambitious and technically imaginative playwrights. Contributors are drawn from both the academic and theatrical spheres, and include Nicholas Grene, Wayne Jordan, Patrick Mason, Christopher Murray and Lynne Parker.
ISBN :978-1-909325-51-7 €15.00 (Paperback)

Tradition and Craft in Piano-Paying,
by Tilly Fleischmann

Edited by Ruth Fleischmann and John Buckley
DVD Musical examples: Gabriela Mayer

This is a document of considerable historical importance, offering an authoritative account of Liszt's teaching methods as imparted by two of his former students to whom he was particularly close. It contains much valuable information of a kind that is unavailable elsewhere. It records a direct and authentic oral tradition of continental European pianism going back to the nineteenth century.
ISBN: 978-1-909325-524 €30 (Paperback)

Wexfour: John Banville, Eoin Colfer, Billy Roche, Colm Toibin

Edited by Ben Barnes
A dedication of four short plays by Wexford writers to celebrate the 40th Anniversary of Wexford Arts Centre.

ISBN: 978-1-909325-548 €10

For the Sake of Sanity: Doing things with humour in Irish performance

Edited by Eric Weitz

Humour claims no ideological affiliation – its workings merit inspection in any and every individual case, in light of the who, what, where and when of a joke, including the manner of performance, the socio-cultural context, the dynamic amongst participants, and who knows how many other factors particular to the instance. There as many insights to be gained from the deployment of humour in performance as people to think about it – so herein lie a healthy handful of responses from a variety of perspectives.

For the Sake of Sanity: *Doing things with humour in Irish performance* assembles a range of essays from practitioners, academics, and journalists, all of whom address the attempt to make an audience laugh in various Irish contexts over the past century. With a general emphasis on theatre, the collection also includes essays on film, television and stand-up comedy for those insights into practice, society and culture revealed uniquely through instances of humour in performance.

ISBN: 978-1-909-325-56-2 €20

Stanislavski in Ireland: Focus at Fifty

Edited by Brian McAvera and Steven Dedalus Burch

Stanislavski in Ireland: Focus at Fifty is an insight into Ireland's only arthouse theatre from the people who were there. Through interviews, articles, short memoirs and photographs, the book tracks the theatre from its inception, detailing the period under its founder Deirdre O'Connell and then the period following Joe Devlin's arrival as its new artistic director. Many of Ireland's leading theatre and film artists trained and worked at Focus, including Gabriel Byrne, Joan Bergin, Olwen Fouèrè, Brendan Coyle, Rebecca Schull, Johnny Murphy, Sean Campion, Tom Hickey and Mary Elizabeth and Declan Burke-Kennedy. The book comes complete with a chronological list of productions.

ISBN: 978-1-909325-43-2 €20

Breaking Boundaries. An Anthology of Original Plays from the Focus Theatre

Edited by Steven Dedalus Burch

Almost from the beginning, since 1970, new plays became part of the Focus's repertory. Of the seven plays in this anthology, all exhibit a range in styles from Lewis Carroll's fantastical world (*Alice in Wonderland* by Mary Elizabeth Burke-Kennedy), to a couple on the brink of a philandering weekend disaster (*The Day of the Mayfly* by Declan Burke-Kennedy), to a one-man show about Jonathan Swift (*Talking Through His Hat* by Michael Harding), an examination of two shoplifting thieves and the would-be writer who gets in their way (*Pinching For My Soul* by Elizabeth Moynihan), a battle royal between two sides of a world-famous painter (*Francis and Frances* by Brian McAvera), the reactions of multiple New Yorkers to that moment in September, 2011 (*New York Monologues* by Mike Poblete), to the final days of an iconic movie star (*Hollywood Valhalla* by Aidan Harney).

ISBN: 978-1-909325-42-5 €20

The Art Of Billy Roche: Wexford As The World

Edited by Kevin Kerrane

Billy Roche – musician, actor, novelist, dramatist, screenwriter – is one of Ireland's
most versatile talents. This anthology, the first comprehensive survey of Roche's work,
focuses on his portrayal of one Irish town as a microcosm of human life itself, elemental
and timeless. Among the contributors are fellow artists (Colm Tóibín, Conor McPherson, Belinda McKeon), theatre professionals (Benedict Nightingale, Dominic Dromgoole, Ingrid Craigie), and scholars on both sides of the Atlantic.

ISBN: 978-1-904505-60-0 €20

The Theatre of Conor McPherson: 'Right beside the Beyond'

Edited by Lilian Chambers and Eamonn Jordan

Multiple productions and the international successes of plays like *The Weir* have led to Conor McPherson being regarded by many as one of the finest writers of his generation. McPherson has also been hugely prolific as a theatre director, as a screenwriter and film director, garnering many awards in these different roles. In this collection of essays, commentators from around the world address the substantial range of McPherson's output to date in theatre and film, a body of work written primarily during and in the aftermath of Ireland's Celtic Tiger period. These critics approach the work in challenging and dynamic ways, considering the crucial issues of morality, the rupturing of the real, storytelling, and the significance of space, violence and gender. Explicit considerations are given to comedy and humour, and to theatrical form, especially that of the monologue and to the ways that the otherworldly, the unconscious and supernatural are accommodated dramaturgically, with frequent emphasis placed on the specific aspects of performance in both theatre and film.

ISBN: 978 1 904505 61 7 €20

The Story of Barabbas, The Company

Carmen Szabo

Acclaimed by audiences and critics alike for their highly innovative, adventurous and entertaining theatre, Barabbas The Company have created playful, intelligent and dynamic productions for over 17 years. Breaking the mould of Irish theatrical tradition and moving away from a text dominated theatre, Barabbas The Company's productions have established an instantly recognizable performance style influenced by the theatre of clown, circus, mime, puppetry, object manipulation and commedia dell'arte. This is the story of a unique company within the framework of Irish theatre, discussing the influences that shape their performances and establish their position within the history and development of contemporary Irish theatre. This book addresses the overwhelming necessity to reconsider Irish theatre history and to explore, in a language accessible to a wide range of readers, the issues of physicality and movement based theatre in Ireland.

ISBN: 978-1-904505-59-4 €25

Irish Drama: Local and Global Perspectives

Edited by Nicholas Grene and Patrick Lonergan

Since the late 1970s there has been a marked internationalization of Irish drama, with individual plays, playwrights, and theatrical companies establishing newly global reputations. This book reflects upon these developments, drawing together leading scholars and playwrights to consider the consequences that arise when Irish theatre travels abroad.

Contributors: Chris Morash, Martine Pelletier, José Lanters, Richard Cave, James Moran, Werner Huber, Rhona Trench, Christopher Murray, Ursula Rani Sarma, Jesse Weaver, Enda Walsh, Elizabeth Kuti

ISBN: 978-1-904505-63-1 €20

What Shakespeare Stole From Rome

Edited by Brian Arkins

What Shakespeare Stole From Rome analyses the multiple ways Shakespeare used material from Roman history and Latin poetry in his plays and poems. From the history of the Roman Republic to the tragedies of Seneca; from the Comedies of Platus to Ovid's poetry; this enlightening book examines the important influence of Rome and Greece on Shakespeare's work.

ISBN: 978-1-904505-58-7 €20

Polite Forms

Harry White

Polite Forms is a sequence of poems that meditates on family life, remembering and reimagining scenes from childhood and adolescence through the formal composure of the sonnet, so that the uniformity of this framing device promotes a tension. Throughout the collection there is a constant preoccupation with the difference between actual remembrance and the illumination or meaning which poetry can afford. Some of the poems 'rewind the tapes of childhood' across two or three generations, and all of them are akin to pictures at an exhibition which survey individual impressions of childhood and parenthood in a thematically continuous series of portraits drawn from life. This is his first collection of poetry.

Harry White is Professor of Music at University College Dublin.

ISBN: 978-1-904505-55-6 €10

Ibsen and Chekhov on the Irish Stage

Edited by Ros Dixon and Irina Ruppo Malone

Ibsen and Chekhov on the Irish Stage presents articles on the theories of translation and adaptation, new insights on the work of Brian Friel, Frank McGuinness, Thomas Kilroy, and Tom Murphy, historical analyses of theatrical productions during the Irish Revival, interviews with contemporary theatre directors, and a round-table discussion with the playwrights, Michael West and Thomas Kilroy.

Ibsen and Chekhov on the Irish Stage challenges the notion that a country's dramatic tradition develops in cultural isolation. It uncovers connections between past productions of plays by Ibsen and Chekhov and contemporary literary adaptations of their works by Irish playwrights, demonstrating the significance of international influence for the formation of national canon.

ISBN: 978-1-904505-57-0 €20

Tom Swift Selected Plays

With an introduction by Peter Crawley.

The inaugural production of Performance Corporation in 2002 matched Voltaire's withering assault against the doctrine of optimism with a playful aesthetic and endlessly inventive stagecraft.

Each play in this collection was originally staged by the Performance Corporation and though Swift has explored different avenues ever since, such playfulness is a constant. The writing is precise, but leaves room for the discoveries of rehearsals, the flesh of the theatre. All plays are blueprints for performance, but several of these scripts – many of which are site-specific and all of them slyly topical – are documents for something unrepeatable.

ISBN: 978-1-904505-56-3   €20

Synge and His Influences: Centenary Essays from the Synge Summer School

Edited by Patrick Lonergan

The year 2009 was the centenary of the death of John Millington Synge, one of the world's great dramatists. To mark the occasion, this book gathers essays by leading scholars of Irish drama, aiming to explore the writers and movements that shaped Synge, and to consider his enduring legacies. Essays discuss Synge's work in its Irish, European and world contexts – showing his engagement not just with the Irish literary revival but with European politics and culture too. The book also explores Synge's influence on later writers: Irish dramatists such as Brian Friel, Tom Murphy and Marina Carr, as well as international writers like Mustapha Matura and Erisa Kironde. It also considers Synge's place in Ireland today, revealing how *The Playboy of the Western World* has helped to shape Ireland's responses to globalisation and multiculturalism, in celebrated productions by the Abbey Theatre, Druid Theatre, and Pan Pan Theatre Company.

Contributors include Ann Saddlemyer, Ben Levitas, Mary Burke, Paige Reynolds, Eilís Ní Dhuibhne, Mark Phelan, Shaun Richards, Ondřej Pilný, Richard Pine, Alexandra Poulain, Emilie Pine, Melissa Sihra, Sara Keating, Bisi Adigun, Adrian Frazier and Anthony Roche.

ISBN: 978-1-904505-50-1   €20.00

Constellations - The Life and Music of John Buckley

Benjamin Dwyer

Benjamin Dwyer provides a long overdue assessment of one of Ireland's most prolific composers of the last decades. He looks at John Buckley's music in the context of his biography and Irish cultural life. This is no hagiography but a critical assessment of Buckley's work, his roots and aesthetics. While looking closely at several of Buckley's compositions, the book is written in a comprehensible style that makes it easily accessible to anybody interested in Irish musical and cultural history.   *Wolfgang Marx*

As well as providing a very readable and comprehensive study of the life and music of John Buckley, Constellations also offers an up-to-date and informative catalogue of compositions, a complete discography, translations of set texts and the full libretto of his chamber opera, making this book an essential guide for both students and professional scholars alike.

ISBN: 978-1-904505-52-5   €20.00

'Because We Are Poor': Irish Theatre in the 1990s

Victor Merriman

"Victor Merriman's work on Irish theatre is in the vanguard of a whole new paradigm in Irish theatre scholarship, one that is not content to contemplate monuments of past or present achievement, but for which the theatre is a lens that makes visible the hidden malaises in Irish society. That he has been able to do so by focusing on a period when so much else in Irish culture conspired to hide those problems is only testimony to the considerable power of his critical scrutiny." Chris Morash, NUI Maynooth.

ISBN: 978-1-904505-51-8   €20.00

Buffoonery and Easy Sentiment':
Popular Irish Plays in the Decade Prior to the Opening of The Abbey Theatre

Christopher Fitz-Simon

In this fascinating reappraisal of the non-literary drama of the late 19th - early 20th century, Christopher Fitz-Simon discloses a unique world of plays, players and producers in metropolitan theatres in Ireland and other countries where Ireland was viewed as a source of extraordinary topics at once contemporary and comfortably remote: revolution, eviction, famine, agrarian agitation, political assassination.

The form was the fashionable one of melodrama, yet Irish melodrama was of a particular kind replete with hidden messages, and the language was far more allusive, colourful and entertaining than that of its English equivalent.

ISBN: 978-1-9045505-49-5   €20.00

The Theatre of Tom Mac Intyre: 'Strays from the ether'

Eds. Bernadette Sweeney and Marie Kelly

This long overdue anthology captures the soul of Mac Intyre's dramatic canon – its ethereal qualities, its extraordinary diversity, its emphasis on the poetic and on performance – in an extensive range of visual, journalistic and scholarly contributions from writers, theatre practitioners.

ISBN 978-1-904505-46-4 €25

Irish Appropriation Of Greek Tragedy

Brian Arkins

This book presents an analysis of more than 30 plays written by Irish dramatists and poets that are based on the tragedies of Sophocles, Euripides and Aeschylus. These plays proceed from the time of Yeats and Synge through MacNeice and the Longfords on to many of today's leading writers.

ISBN 978-1-904505-47-1 €20

Alive in Time: The Enduring Drama of Tom Murphy

Ed. Christopher Murray

Almost 50 years after he first hit the headlines as Ireland's most challenging playwright, the 'angry young man' of those times Tom Murphy still commands his place at the pinnacle of Irish theatre. Here 17 new essays by prominent critics and academics, with an introduction by Christopher Murray, survey Murphy's dramatic oeuvre in a concerted attempt to define his greatness and enduring appeal, making this book a significant study of a unique genius.

ISBN 978-1-904505-45-7 €25

Performing Violence in Contemporary Ireland

Edited by Lisa Fitzpatrick

This interdisciplinary collection of fifteen new essays by scholars of theatre, Irish studies, music, design and politics explores aspects of the performance of violence in contemporary Ireland. With chapters on the work of playwrights Martin McDonagh, Martin Lynch, Conor McPherson and Gary Mitchell, on Republican commemorations and the 90th anniversary ceremonies for the Battle of the Somme and the Easter Rising, this book aims to contribute to the ongoing international debate on the performance of violence in contemporary societies.

ISBN 978-1-904505-44-0 €20

Deviant Acts: Essays on Queer Performance

Ed. David Cregan

This book contains an exciting collection of essays focusing on a variety of alternative performances happening in contemporary Ireland. While it highlights the particular representations of gay and lesbian identity it also brings to light how diversity has always been a part of Irish culture and is, in fact, shaping what it means to be Irish today.

ISBN 978-1-904505-42-6 €20

Plays and Controversies: Abbey Theatre Diaries 2000-2005

Ben Barnes

In diaries covering the period of his artistic directorship of the Abbey, Ben Barnes offers a frank, honest, and probing account of a much commented upon and controversial period in the history of the national theatre. These diaries also provide fascinating personal insights into the day-to-day pressures, joys, and frustrations of running one of Ireland's most iconic institutions.

ISBN: 978-1-904505-38-9   €25

Interactions: Dublin Theatre Festival 1957-2007. Irish Theatrical Diaspora Series: 3

Eds. Nicholas Grene and Patrick Lonergan with Lilian Chambers

For over 50 years the Dublin Theatre Festival has been one of Ireland's most important cultural events, bringing countless new Irish plays to the world stage, while introducing Irish audiences to the most important international theatre companies and artists. Interactions explores and celebrates the achievements of the renowned Festival since 1957 and includes specially commissioned memoirs from past organizers, offering a unique perspective on the controversies and successes that have marked the event's history. An especially valuable feature of the volume, also, is a complete listing of the shows that have appeared at the Festival from 1957 to 2008.

ISBN: 978-1-904505-36-5   €20

Synge: A Celebration

Edited by Colm Tóibín

A collection of essays by some of Ireland's most creative writers on the work of John Millington Synge, featuring Sebastian Barry, Marina Carr, Anthony Cronin, Roddy Doyle, Anne Enright, Hugo Hamilton, Joseph O'Connor, Mary O'Malley, Fintan O'Toole, Colm Toibin, Vincent Woods.

ISBN 978-1-904505-14-3   €15

www.ingramcontent.com/pod-product-compliance
Lightning Source LLC
Chambersburg PA
CBHW070312230426
43663CB00011B/2106